About the Editors

Michigan native Peter Hanson studied film at New York University and journalism at the University at Albany–SUNY. He is the author of *Dalton Trumbo, Hollywood Rebel* (a finalist for the Theatre Library Association Award), and *The Cinema of Generation X*. He directed the documentary feature *Every Pixel Tells a Story* and the award-winning short *Stagehand*, and cowrote the narrative feature *The Last Round*. His articles have appeared in *Script* and *Written By*, and he moderates a screenwriting-themed film series sponsored by Final Draft, Inc. His Web site is www.GrandRiverFilms.com.

Paul Robert Herman graduated from the University of North Carolina at Charlotte with a degree in psychology. He earned his teaching credentials from the University of Colorado at Boulder, specializing in creative writing and film. After moving to Hollywood, he completed UCLA's Professional Program in Screenwriting. He worked for several years as an assistant producer for an entertainment company in Pacific Palisades before branching off on his own. He has written, directed, and produced short films through his multimedia company, Jade Tiger Productions (www.JadeTiger.com).

In 2009, Hanson and Herman premiered the companion film *Tales from the Script* at the Palm Springs International Film Festival; *Variety*'s Todd McCarthy called the feature-length documentary "a lively collection of war stories." The movie is set for release in 2010. Visit the film's Web site at www.TalesfromtheScript.com.

Tales from the Script

Also by Peter Hanson

The Cinema of Generation X

Dalton Trumbo, Hollywood Rebel

Tales from the Script

50 Hollywood Screenwriters Share Their Stories

Edited by
Peter Hanson and Paul Robert Herman

With Photographs by Peter Hanson

itbooks

AN IMPRINT OF HARPERCOLLINS PUBLISHERS

HarperCollins books may be purchased for educational, business, or sales promotional use. For information, please write: Special Markets Department, HarperCollins Publishers, 10 East 53rd Street, New York, NY 10022.

FIRST EDITION

Designed by Ashley Halsey

Library of Congress Cataloging-in-Publication data is available upon request.

ISBN 978-0-06-185592-4

10 11 12 13 14   OV/RRD   10 9 8 7 6 5 4 3 2

Contents

Introduction

For several months in late 2007 and early 2008, screenwriters took to the streets in an aggressive labor action that caught the world's attention by cutting a TV season in half and stalling the production of numerous major films. The issue was nominally the monetization of new-media exhibition, but the underlying tensions were more troubling. "The writer in Hollywood is truly an abused entity," notes Bruce Joel Rubin, an Academy Award winner for the screenplay of *Ghost*. "It is really cruel on some levels that writers have so little participation in the work they create."

Yet in the midst of the strike, the film industry gave birth to that rarest of creatures: the celebrity screenwriter. The stunning success of *Juno* scribe Diablo Cody reminded everyone why screenwriters struck in the first place: Great movies begin with great ideas. In rare instances, someone like Cody gets to take the whole ride, sharing in the production and release of the film she wrote. More often, however, writers get left behind while actors, directors, and producers divide the limelight and the profits. That inequity motivates every writers' strike: Those who plant the seeds watch others reap the harvest.

Nonetheless, the dream of writing the next Great American Screenplay has never been more popular. A cottage industry of books, magazines, and seminars encourages the aspirants who hope to turn their story ideas into three-picture deals, hit movies, and

Introduction

Academy Awards. For some, the dream reflects a noble desire to connect with the human community through storytelling. But for others, the dream is dangerous, because it is not grounded in a realistic understanding of the obstacles involved.

This book is intended for both types of dreamers.

If you want to write screenplays for the sheer love of movies, then the following chapters will give you all the inspiration you can handle. You will meet screenwriters like Justin Zackham, who surmounted a creative dry spell by writing the deeply personal script for *The Bucket List,* which enticed Morgan Freeman and Jack Nicholson to play the leading roles. Zackham's dream came true because he went after it on his own terms.

However, if you believe you can game the system by cynically assembling bits of other movies into a script that Hollywood can't resist, prepare to receive the most important education of your life. So few scripts actually become movies that if the only satisfaction you can derive from writing a screenplay is cashing the checks when it becomes a box-office smash, then you will quickly learn what it means to be unsatisfied.

No false promises are made that if you read these pages, you will learn the formula for writing a million-dollar screenplay; in fact, the dirty little secret of screenwriting books is that anyone who promises such formulas is lying. There is no one-size-fits-all advice for screenwriters, and that's why this book exists. Rather than simply detailing *how* people write movies, this book is an investigation into *why* people write movies.

If you finish this book bursting with enthusiasm to create your next script, then you have learned that you possess the stamina to pursue your dream despite the hardships you will face. And if you finish this book determined to steer clear of the minefields that endanger Hollywood screenwriters, then you have acquired a deeper admiration for the brave souls who step into the breach.

Tales from the Script lets screenwriters at every conceivable stage of their careers explain how they broke into Hollywood, how they turned early success into sustained employment, and how they endure the vicissitudes of a bruising professional environment without losing the creative spark that got them through the door in the first place. The goal of this book is to create the ultimate screenwriting panel discussion, in which newcomers and veterans can respond to and expand on one another's insights, thereby painting the most complete portrait possible of what it really means to be a Hollywood screenwriter.

At first glance, the portrait these individuals paint may seem ugly. Most scripts don't sell. The majority of scripts that sell don't get made. And many scripts that get made are changed so extensively that by the time the movie is released, the original writer has to seek legal recourse to ensure that his or her name appears onscreen. On top of that, films that actually cross the finish line often turn out badly, because so many compromises have been made that the underlying concept has gotten buried in lousy ideas.

But on closer inspection, the portrait reveals a kind of savage beauty. Battle-scarred veterans still love what they do. Years after the initial sting of rejection, Frank Darabont can laugh about the fact that the Indiana Jones movie he spent a year writing was discarded. Now that time has passed since the movie flopped, William Goldman can compartmentalize the failure of his passion project, *Year of the Comet*, because he realizes it was the wrong movie at the wrong time. These are two of the most celebrated writers ever to pen screenplays, and they recovered from heartbreaking disappointments. That takes courage.

And more, it takes love. Love of story. Love of screenwriting. Love of movies. Because if you love something deeply enough, nothing can discourage you from trying to make that something part of your life.

This project was born during Paul Robert Herman's course work in UCLA's Professional Program in Screenwriting, when he conceived the idea of a nonfiction book about the rejection screenwriters face. Concurrently, Peter Hanson was in the midst of writing his first produced narrative feature, the latest project in an expansive career that has included books, films, and years in the trenches of regional journalism. When the two crossed paths, they joined forces to tackle the rejection project.

Over the course of three years, something broader took shape. This book and the documentary feature film of the same name offer a comprehensive look at the lives of screenwriters. The value of this book to beginning screenwriters, and even established professionals, is evident on every page; the appeal for movie buffs who relish behind-the-scenes anecdotes is equally significant.

Whatever your reason for picking up *Tales from the Script*, you're in for an experience as entertaining as it is enlightening. Screenwriters endure an infinite number of psychic body blows throughout their careers, but they still find the strength to conjure narratives that enthrall the entire world. The stories behind Hollywood's storytellers are as absurd, funny, shocking, and touching as any of the movies they've ever written.

Tales from the Script

The Adventure
Begins

The means by which enterprising individuals claw and scratch—or sometimes merely stumble—into the world of screenwriting are myriad. Many gain a foothold in other aspects of professional writing, or in different parts of the entertainment industry, before deciding to craft narratives for feature films. Others commence their professional lives without any plans to enter show business. Richard Rush wanted to be an astronaut. Antwone Fisher served eleven years in the U.S. Navy. Ari B. Rubin fancied a career in politics, though being the son of Oscar-winning screenwriter Bruce Joel Rubin made him a prime candidate for entering the family trade.

The reasons why people pursue screenwriting are equally varied. John Carpenter learned that writing scripts could advance his directing career. Naomi Foner seized movies as a platform for conveying political messages. Mike Binder simply wanted to broaden his reach as an entertainer, following years in the smoky nightclubs of the stand-up comedy circuit. Every intrepid soul who aspires to write movies embarks on a unique path for a unique reason. The commonality that joins them is the power of the form they employ.

To the untrained eye, a screenplay is a perplexing document. Presented in a rigid format of page-wide screen directions and thin strips of dialogue, feature-film scripts are littered with numbers and abbreviations and jargon that make them virtually incomprehensible to those not involved with film production. A screenplay is not a genuine literary document, for the author's ultimate goal is not seeing readers engage the words as they're written; the author's ultimate goal is seeing the words transformed into moving pictures. And yet a screenplay is very much a genuine literary document, for it represents a writer's expression of a narrative.

That dichotomy underlies much of the screenwriting experience. Accordingly, it seems fitting to precede a discussion of how screenwriters began their professional lives with remarks that attempt to explain exactly what these artists spend their professional lives doing.

Words and Pictures

STEVEN E. de SOUZA: Alfred Hitchcock said it best. He said, "A lot of writers think they're filling a page with words, but they're filling a screen with images."

WILLIAM GOLDMAN: Screenplays are structure, and that's all they are. The quality of writing—which is crucial in almost every other form of literature—is not what makes a screenplay work. Structure isn't anything else but telling the story, starting as late as possible, starting each scene as late as possible. You don't wanna begin with "Once upon a time," because the audience gets antsy.

RON SHELTON: Screenwriting is rigorously disciplined, in the sense that movies are two hours long, give or take. Well, that's like telling the painter how big your canvas is every time. But in that two hours, you can tell a wonderful little story or you can tell a huge, gigantic epic.

MARK D. ROSENTHAL: The word *screenwriting* is a kenning, which means it's a composite of two nouns. This is my literary background. Everybody stays focused on the *screen* part, because it's Hollywood and it's fun and it's money and it's fame. The *writing* part, no one talks about.

The most difficult thing a screenwriter does, which is the most difficult thing in moviemaking, is to make a precise, detailed decision. It's easy to say, "Let's have an exciting chase along the beach here, where he finds out that his partner is gonna betray him." The person who says that thinks, "Oh, I'm a genius. I just came up with a scene." That's not hard. Anybody can do that after a while of watching movies.

The precise second-to-second detail of that scene—what each character is doing, feeling, and saying—is really hard, because it forces the mind to get as particular as mathematics. It's the only reason moviemakers use screenwriters. Otherwise, why pay us this money? It's too hard to try to come up with all those details while you're making the movie. You have to have them laid out first.

DOUG ATCHISON: Screenwriting is a very difficult thing to master. It requires both halves of your brain. You need that artistic, impulsive, creative aspect—and you also need that objective part as well, because a screenplay is precise. It's not like a novel. You write it over a long period of time, but you experience it in a finite period of time. And you have to find within that very precise structure ways to access very imprecise feelings and emotions and motivations.

JOE FORTE: A novelist can go inside the brain of a character and tell you what they're thinking. *The Great Gatsby* is a great novel, but it's never worked as a movie because the escalation and the forward movement of the novel is the narrator changing and perceiving the characters differently. You can't do that in a screenplay. You have very few tools, and you have to learn how to use those tools well.

JOHN D. BRANCATO: A screenplay is a blueprint. It's not that much fun to read. I'm not worried about the fact that it's not in itself valuable. It's okay to be a means of bringing something alive onscreen. I mean, the more I think back on some images that were just crazy crap in my own head, and are now up there in films that I've written—that's pretty amazing. It's like having some projector from your brain.

FRANK DARABONT: Done well, screenwriting is real writing. Yes, there is hack work, but the same is true of novels. There's a lot of crap on the bookshelves, and very few novels that will transport you and uplift you or illuminate some truth of the human condition. The notion that somehow writing novels is real writing and writing screenplays isn't is horseshit—usually shoveled by somebody who couldn't write a movie that would move people if you held a gun to their head and said, "Show me what great screenwriting is."

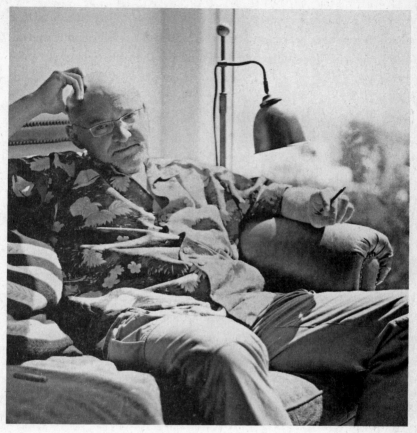

Frank Darabont

GERALD DiPEGO: If you go to a store and buy a play by Tennessee Williams or someone, you can come home and read it and have a real experience with it. You haven't seen the play, but you've read it. Well, the same thing should be true of a good screenplay. You bring it home, sit in your chair, and you should have an experience with it, because the writer has created a play.

JOSH FRIEDMAN: A screenplay is a piece of writing, and the best of them are great pieces of writing. But they will be interpreted, and if you're a good screenwriter, you take that into account.

The Path to Hollywood

PAUL MAZURSKY: I started as an actor. I was in Stanley Kubrick's first picture, *Fear and Desire.* I was in *Blackboard Jungle.* Then I moved out to California. I was in the Second City comedy revue. That led to me writing for Danny Kaye's television show for four years. That was the first steady job I'd had in show business. While working for Danny Kaye, I wrote the pilot for *The Monkees* with Larry Tucker, and wrote a script with Larry called *H-Bomb Beach Party,* which was optioned but never made. Came close. *The Danny Kaye Show* ended, we got an office on Sunset Boulevard, and Larry and I wrote *I Love You, Alice B. Toklas!* My agent got it to Peter Sellers, who read it and said he wanted to do it. That was an amazing foot in the door of writing for movies.

RICHARD RUSH: I was at UCLA as an astronomy and physics major, hoping to be the first man on the moon. After the first year, I realized the math was killing me, so I switched my major to theater, and it was the first semester of the movie department at UCLA. It was fortuitous in that sense. The idea was to become a director, and writing was the intrinsic part of it. That's how I started.

LARRY COHEN: I started writing movies when I was a kid. I was probably only nine years old. I was writing my own comic books, and they were basically storyboards for movies. I didn't deal with superheroes; I dealt more with dramatic stories. I was doing the same thing then that I'm doing now, to tell you the truth. When I sit down at the table and start writing, I feel like I'm back in my room as a kid.

WILLIAM GOLDMAN: I had written a novel called *No Way to Treat a Lady,* which was very short. So to make it longer, I made a lot of chapters—there were, like, sixty chapters in a 150-page book. Some chapters were one word long, some chapters were all of a sentence. The actor Cliff Robertson got ahold of it and thought I had written a screen treatment. He asked me to do a movie for him, which I did, and then he fired me from it immediately and won the Oscar for it. So he was not dumb. But it was all by mistake.

DAVID S. WARD: At UCLA, the films I was making just got longer and longer, and as the films got longer, the scripts got longer. My thesis film was supposed to be a thirty-, thirty-five-minute film. It felt like a feature idea, so I just let it go to feature length and actually wound up writing my first feature script. It was a film called *Steelyard Blues,* which I was fortunate enough to get made a year after I graduated from UCLA.

PAUL SCHRADER: I was a protégé of Pauline Kael, and I thought I would become a film critic. I had gone to UCLA, but I had gotten an MA in film studies, not an MFA in filmmaking. I also did coverage for Columbia Pictures. Coverage is just writing a synopsis of a book or a screenplay. I'd gotten fired because I was too snide in my coverage, but I knew what scripts were, so that really helped. And then, you know, I hit a rough patch in my life, and I had to turn to fiction—to fantasy—to sort of exorcise these things that were eating me up. Out of that came *Taxi Driver*, and then I went on and wrote other scripts.

JOHN CARPENTER: I made a movie in the seventies called *Dark Star*, which I hoped would get me directing jobs. It didn't get me any directing jobs. It did get me an agent, who told me the way to get into the movie business is to write your way in. So I just started writing screenplays—outlines, treatments, screenplays.

STEVEN E. de SOUZA: Well, if you dispense with about seven or eight years of freelance writing, and working in local television, and collecting maybe 150 rejection slips from magazines—if you skip all that, I'm an overnight success, in that within five days of arriving in Hollywood, I had an overall deal as a writer at Universal Pictures.

When I decided I had to get out of local television, I said, "I'll give myself three months to be successful in Hollywood." I knew enough to bring writing samples that were screenplays. I came out to California, and I had an aunt and uncle out here with a sofa bed. My aunt's best friend was Merv Griffin's secretary, but she says, "Well, gee, all we do here at Merv Griffin Productions is the game shows. We have the talk show, but Merv just makes up whatever he says. Wait a minute—there was a lawyer who worked for Merv, and I heard he became an agent."

I get to that guy when he's literally moving into his desk at an agency. He said, "Do you have writing samples that are screenplays?" I said, "Yes, I do." Forty-eight hours later, he called me up and said, "I love your stuff. If you don't mind, I'm gonna give your scripts to another client of mine." This is, like, the fourth day I'm in Los Angeles.

He calls back and says, "Go see these guys Harve Bennett and Allan Balter. They're producers at Universal." I go there, and I'm in this meeting, and they're talking about my stuff, and it's very encouraging. Then they say, "Go see Claire. She'll give you your parking information." So I go, "Uh, well, I've got my thing right here—you can stamp me here." And they go, "Ha, ha, ha." I didn't realize that I'd already been hired. Monday morning, I go to work on *The Six Million Dollar Man*.

Steven E. de Souza

RON SHELTON: I came from a family of storytellers—you know, people who stood around the kitchen and took two hours to tell the story of a five-minute trip to the grocery store. I grew up not being able to go to movies—kind of the rigorous Baptist background: no movies, no alcohol, no cards. So, of course, I became a heavily drinking film director.

When I played baseball, I went to movies every day. My film

school education was going to the theater every day at one o'clock for year after year. I just started writing out of the blue. I just started writing some not very good screenplays, but I was smart enough to throw 'em away when I was done. And over a several-year period of writing and throwing away and writing and throwing away, I started to figure out what this screenwriting thing was all about.

NAOMI FONER: I was a producer in public television. I worked for years at the Children's Television Workshop—I was part of the team that developed *The Electric Company.* As a producer, I worked with a bunch of different screenwriters, and the whole time I thought, "Well, I'd like to write," but I was afraid I would fail.

A friend of mine who was running a program on PBS, which was like the precursor of *American Playhouse,* offered me the opportunity to actually write one. I was pregnant with my daughter, and I was thinking about how my life was gonna change, and I decided I would try. I wrote it, and they produced it, and all of a sudden I had an agent and I was a writer.

I got into screenwriting out of an interest in politics. I had this underlying agitprop idea, which is that you reach more people with an idea that's buried in storytelling—if you made people feel something, maybe they'd think about it. I thought we lived in a country where a lot of things needed changing.

ROBERT MARK KAMEN: I had just finished my PhD in American studies. I spent a year doing fieldwork in Afghanistan, and it really affected me on a core level. I came back and wrote a novel about it. A cousin of mine knew a film director. The director read the novel and gave me three screenplays to read, so I figured out the form and turned the novel into a screenplay. Through the same director, I met Richard Dreyfuss, who had just won the Oscar for *The Goodbye Girl*. He could get anything done, and what he wanted done was my screenplay. It didn't matter that the lead character was twenty-one and Richard was thirty-two. He got Warner Bros. to buy the screenplay for $135,000. I was making $6,200 a year as a lecturer at the time, so I never bothered to go to my next lecture class.

NORA EPHRON: At a certain point in my career as a journalist, I was approached by a couple of producers who offered me money to write screenplays. The money was modest by today's standards, but it was way more than I earned as a journalist, and it was something new, something different. So I tried it, and then other people offered me work. I had small children, and it made more sense to stay home and not run around reporting on stories. Then I was divorced with small children, and I needed the money. Finally, one of my scripts was made into a movie, and the director was kind enough to let me be involved in the process. It was way more interesting than journalism.

MARK D. ROSENTHAL: I was finishing a doctorate in Chaucer, but I knew I wanted to be around the movies. I finished school in Northern California, checked out of my apartment, packed my records in the car, and drove to L.A. I had heard that you could get paid for reading scripts, and I called up a new studio called Orion. Luckily, it was lunchtime, and the secretarial staff was gone—because if I had called and said, "I'm interested in a reader job," they would have said, "We'll put your name on the list." The story editor picked up, and she laughed out loud when I told her I just finished a doctorate in Chaucer. She said, "You sound really unusual. Come on in."

She gave me a stack of scripts, and I proceeded to evaluate them like I was doing a paper for my doctorate—you know, I was using Latinisms and talking about the character development. I gave my evaluations back to her, and she said, "What, are you crazy? Just tell me if they're gonna make money or not." She gave me a second chance, and within about six months, I became an official reader at Orion. After that, it dawned on me that I could write as poorly as the people whose scripts I was reading.

JOHN D. BRANCATO: I tried to be a cartoonist. That didn't go well. The first job I got out of college was in journalism, writing for a newspaper in Long Island. Then I came to California, just because I wanted to get three thousand miles away from my family, and I wound up taking a job with Larry Flynt at *Hustler*. Interesting job. Luckily, it didn't last all that long. While I was there, I was approached to collaborate on a screenplay for a horror film. I hadn't ever intended to write screenplays. I read as many as I could, and I thought, "This is a form I can handle." It wasn't writer-ly with a capital *W*. It was more a matter of visual imagery. I could think like a cartoonist. I felt like, "Oh, this is what I should do with the rest of my life."

MIKE BINDER: I did quite a few years as a stand-up comic, and a bunch of things went wrong. I was cast as part of *Saturday Night Live* and then fired. I did pilots. I thought, "I gotta learn how to make the pie instead of being served a piece of the pie." The people that I really admired were Woody Allen and Mel Brooks and Albert Brooks. So I just started studying screenwriting, studying movies, and I said, "Okay, that's what I wanna do."

JANE ANDERSON: I started out as an actor, and I found that writing was so much more appropriate to my metabolism. As an actor, I could never cry on cue. I didn't have the emotional dexterity that really good actors have. I also was limited by my physicality, because back then I looked about sixteen even when I was hitting thirty. I could never play really interesting roles, and I started to discover that as a writer, I could be anything. I could be male or female, I could be of any class, any ethnicity.

I got a small role on *The Facts of Life*. They had just fired a bunch of writers, and they were looking for new writers—women in particular. I don't know where I got the nerve, but I said to the producers, "I wanna work on your show as a writer." They said, "Give us a spec script." I wrote a spec script, gave it to them, and they hired me.

FRANK DARABONT: Even when I was in junior high school, I was writing screenplays. You know, I'd write a *Star Trek* episode even though *Star Trek* was no longer on the air. Once I graduated high school, I started applying enormous amounts of time to getting a screenwriting career going. That became a very, very focused effort in my early twenties, during which time I was set dressing, which is nailing sets together, bringing the furniture in, putting the stuff on the walls that the director has chosen. I was not making much money doing it, but it kept the rent paid, and when the job was over, I would have enough saved up to sit at home for a month and just write. I treated writing like a full-time job. I would sit at home until the bank account bottomed out, and then I'd call my friend Greg, who was an art director—and these days, my production designer—and I'd say, "Get me on the next gig, dude!"

Nine years after graduating high school, I started making a living as a screenwriter, and I haven't looked back—but that nine years involved a lot of sittin' in the chair and trying to figure out how to become a professional-level screen storyteller.

BILLY RAY: When I got out of college, I was a gofer for two TV-movie producers named Jim Green and Alan Epstein. I would read everything that came into the office and write at night. I decided to write a novel, and that took about a year. I couldn't get the novel published, and then I wrote another one. That took another year, and I couldn't get that published either. Then I wrote my first script, which took quite a while—couldn't get that sold. And then I rewrote it and finally got it sold, I think for $5,000. It wasn't enough even to quit, but it was enough to make me feel like I was a writer. Then I sold my first pitch, and that was enough money that I could quit my job and actually just write full-time.

GUINEVERE TURNER: I just wanted to make a movie about lesbians, so my girlfriend and I decided we were going to make a movie about lesbians. We wrote a script, which was *Go Fish*. It was far more widely successful than we had ever anticipated, and hence life went into screenwriting.

JOE STILLMAN: I got an opportunity to write copy for a movie trailer company because I had been a messenger for a trailer cutter. That led to me becoming a freelance copywriter in movie advertising, and that eventually led to me writing promos for Nickelodeon and other cable networks. During this very long period, I was also writing screenplays, imagining that each one I finished would be the one that would get me the call from Steven Spielberg and change my life into something golden and wonderful. Of course, that didn't happen. Writing promos for Nickelodeon eventually led to writing shows for Nickelodeon and working on *Beavis and Butt-Head*. That got Mike Judge to decide to give me a shot at the *Beavis and Butt-Head* movie.

JOHN AUGUST: I grew up in Boulder, Colorado, not really knowing much about the film industry or even knowing that there was a job like screenwriting. I was always a writer, but it wasn't until some time in high school that I first realized that there was actually a script behind a movie that you saw. I went through school, and it wasn't until about midway through getting my journalism degree that I realized I actually wanted to do movies. I applied to a summer film program at Stanford—very hands on, cutting 16 mm. I loved that. I applied to the USC film school, and I ended up coming out here.

JUSTIN ZACKHAM: I went to the University of Vermont and managed to fail out twice my first year, which is a feat. When they told me they weren't going to have me back the second time, I went and worked on a three-hundred-foot-tall ship based in Grenada, in the Caribbean. I was the only white member of an all-black crew (this screenplay's written, of course), and they beat the crap out of me, threw me overboard in the middle of the ocean. Twice. One guy tried to stab me. I made it through the whole thing, and I was planning on living down there. You're in the Caribbean, on a ship, hot chicks, swap out every week—not too shabby.

I broke my leg at sea one day—got hit by this metal pipe that shattered my ankle. We had just left port, so I was at sea for a week and they had no good drugs. My job was to wake up in the morning, go sit at the bar, drink as much as I possibly could all day long to numb the pain. I was really entertaining that week.

I had to come back to the States to have my ankle operated on. While I was recovering, my dad had an angioplasty. This was back when there was only one guy in the country doing it, in San Francisco. I went out there with him, and I could only visit him for an hour in the evening. I was twenty-one years old in San Francisco, by myself, straight. There was very little to do.

I just started seeing movies. I remember the first day I saw *The Godfather: Part III*, *Goodfellas*, and a Zhang Yimou film called *Ju Dou*, which is still one of my favorite movies. I just did it because I was bored, and I started seeing the craft behind this stuff. I went to a bookstore and I bought this little book called *Feature Filmmaking at Used-Car Prices*, and that was it. From that point on, I bored everyone to tears talking about film.

ANTWONE FISHER: I used to be homeless when I was a teenager, because I didn't have any family. I had heard no all my life, and that I would never be able to accomplish this or that. After being in the navy for eleven years, there were a lot of things that I accomplished that previously I thought I could not.

I was a security guard on the Sony Pictures Entertainment lot. I was using Sony Pictures as a way station before I found a better job. I found my family and I wanted to go and meet them, but I hadn't been at the job long enough to acquire any leave. So I told my boss why I wanted to go, and once I told him a little bit of my story, he said, "Go ahead." When I came back, a lot of people wanted to hear my story, and they said that it would make for a good movie.

I insisted on writing it. Being in the navy made me understand that if I put effort toward something, at least I could find out whether I could do it or not. I owed it to myself to try. I got myself some legal pads and I wrote it out by hand. The funny thing is that at that time, all the guards at Sony had been to film school. I was the only one who didn't have any aspirations toward filmmaking.

Antwone Fisher

ARI B. RUBIN: I wrote my first mini-screenplay when I was thirteen, and my first full screenplay when I was fifteen. I always had in the back of my mind that I would do it on the side—it was a hobby. I went to NYU, dropped out after a year and a half, and ended up going to a liberal arts program at Wesleyan. I was pursuing politics, very much going in that direction. I came out to L.A., still kind of writing on the side, and then the Iraq war happened.

That prompted me, in a very short period of time—about eleven days—to write a script about a secretary of state who realizes that his government is pursuing a war for reasons other than they were ostensibly proclaiming. I was applying to law school at that point, and I got so invested in writing the screenplay that I literally missed the day that I was supposed to take the LSATs.

That script sold about three weeks later, and that was that.

The Courage of the Young

LARRY COHEN: You don't need much confidence when you're a kid, because you have nothing to lose. It's not like you have any kind of established position to maintain; you're nobody. I never assumed there would be any obstacles whatsoever when I started out. I knew it was inevitable I would succeed, because I couldn't do anything else. When you have no other talents but one, you must succeed at that one talent.

JOHN CARPENTER: Anyone who writes or directs or acts or does anything creative—you're completely naïve. You don't know what to expect, and I think that's probably best. Because if you knew what was gonna come, you wouldn't do it.

DAVID HAYTER: I was as naïve as Han Solo heading into the asteroid field when C–3PO starts telling him what the odds of survival are, and he says, "Never tell me the odds." It wasn't that I didn't understand that those were the odds. I just felt that I could overcome them. You come to town and you don't really know how the town works, and you don't even really know what you're doing, in a sense. All you have is your belief in yourself and your energy and your enthusiasm.

NORA EPHRON: I knew when I was very young that in addition to my parents' success as screenwriters, they had lots of disappointments—plays that were never produced, movies that had flopped. In fact, when I was about ten or eleven, I read one of their unproduced plays and was so outraged it had never appeared on Broadway that I sent it to a famous Broadway producer. My parents were beyond embarrassed.

But they were contract writers at Fox, and what they wrote was almost always produced, immediately. When I started as a screenwriter and wrote six or seven scripts that weren't made, I couldn't help thinking about how much easier it had been in my parents' day to get a movie made. And, of course, I thought, "I will never get a movie made, ever."

MICK GARRIS: The first screenplay you write is rarely going to be sold and made into a movie, but it might be a good sample to get you hired to write something else. I probably wrote a dozen scripts before I ever got paid to do one.

STEPHEN SUSCO: I've had three movies made to date: *The Grudge* in 2004, *The Grudge 2* in 2006, and *Red* in 2008. That's three scripts. I've written thirty-eight screenplays. *The Grudge* was my first film. It was my twenty-fifth screenplay.

ARI B. RUBIN: Because I had watched my father go through it, I think I was actually better suited to deal with a lot of the challenges than many of the people who come out here. On the upside, I had my father to watch. On the downside, my father was not the best model. He made a lot of mistakes, and I emulated a lot of those mistakes in the early part of my career. So on a scale of one to ten, I would say I was probably a five in terms of naïveté. But I definitely knew it was going to be hard.

BRUCE JOEL RUBIN: I wrote a movie called *Quasar*, with my friend David Beinstock, and somehow we got Ingo Preminger—right when he was producing the movie *M*A*S*H*—to love the script. I was in my twenties, and I thought, "It's happening just like I dreamt it." And then, for reasons that are hard to explain—the Hollywood reasons—the movie didn't get made, and that was that. The door just shut.

It took me years to write another movie, and that became *Brainstorm*, which took almost ten years to get made. I thought, "I've arrived, I'm a Hollywood person." The film didn't make money, and nobody would take my phone calls.

I was still living in the Midwest, and I thought, "My God, what does it take to arrive in Hollywood?" I was sending scripts off, and nothing was coming back. My wife looked at me, and she knew how hungry I was for this. She went to the head of the department where she was teaching in Illinois, and she said, "We're moving to California." She had all this faith that it was going to work. I had nothing but fear.

I was in my forties. We had two kids and enough money to live in L.A. for maybe a couple of months. We just took off. And the career started to happen. A seed falls in the right soil, and it grows.

Without my knowing it, a script that I had written called *Jacob's Ladder* had been in an article about the best unproduced screenplays in Hollywood. Because of that article, people all over town had read it. I arrived in Hollywood as a known entity, which was shocking. I would go into meetings, and they would say, "You wrote *Jacob's Ladder*? We love *Jacob's Ladder*."

You can't cut yourself out of the game. If you really want this, fight for it. That's a dangerous thing to say to some people, because it doesn't always work, obviously.

It's huge, taking a leap of faith. I have done it about four times in my life, where I've given up things and just said, "Go, see what happens." It has worked every time. If you believe in yourself that much, that alone generates things. But if you have a leap of faith that is underpowered—where you're questioning it as you leap—you don't get to the other side. You can't leap without complete and absolute willingness to die for what you want.

Bruce Joel Rubin

ADAM RIFKIN: You're a boxer. Your job is to get punched in the face and to keep swinging. It's easy for anybody to say, "I wrote five scripts. None of them sold. I gave it my best shot. I'm moving back to Chicago." You can't do that. If you want a career in Hollywood, you can't fail. You can quit, which most people do when they don't achieve success as quickly as they'd like, but you can't fail. There are as many opportunities as you can create for yourself. You can write a script a day, every day, for your whole life, if you're that motivated.

JOSE RIVERA: I do some teaching every once in a while, and I always tell my students, "Don't have a backup plan." As a younger person, I intentionally never developed another skill that I could fall back on, because I didn't want to fall back on anything. I said, "I've gotta succeed at this, if it takes thirty years." Luckily, it happened sooner than that. But I was prepared from a young age to stick with it for the long haul.

MIKE BINDER: I painted myself in a corner. There was nothin' else that I was gonna do in my life. I had no other skill set. I started very young. It was my dream, and I proclaimed it, and I went after it. I jumped in the water. I don't know what I would have done if I had failed. I was poor for many, many years, and I got used to that.

JAMES L. WHITE: The long drought till you get to be a real screenwriter—the years of not having money, and people going, "So you're a writer, and what else do you do? How do you pay your bills?" That's a reality. I think you need to be prepared for that.

KRISS TURNER: If you have children, or you've got this over-head that you've gotta handle, then that limits you. But if you're twenty, then that's not a big deal 'cause you're crashin' with your friends and eatin' Top Ramen. But you've got to make some financial choices. Can you sacrifice a lifestyle for the dream?

JOSH FRIEDMAN: I remember some quote I saw about being a professional gambler: "It's a hard way to make an easy living." I think screenwriting is kinda the same thing. It's a lot of fun, and it's the hardest thing you'll ever do.

RICHARD RUSH: There is a natural, physical resistance in the universe toward finishing "it," whatever "it" happens to be. It's always a mountain slightly higher than you could have imagined, and it takes a little more strength than you thought you possibly had. But the trick is finishing "it" no matter what they're throwing at you.

PAUL SCHRADER: Occasionally people ask me about whether they should get involved in screenwriting or filmmaking. I usually say, "If you can find any happiness or satisfaction in another field of endeavor, you should do so, because the real reason to get involved in the arts is because you have no choice—you have issues that you need to address through fantasy and fiction." That said, there is also a very commercial incentive for being in the arts, but I've never really given that too much thought, because that was never my intent. I got involved as a form of self-therapy, and I stay in it that way.

DANIEL PYNE: You don't wanna take this up as an avocation unless it's something that you would do for free. There are so many variables, not just skill and talent and perseverance. There's also luck. In the book *Fever Pitch*, Nick Hornby talks about how in English football, there are no undiscovered strikers—there are no great defenders who no one knows about—whereas there are probably great writers who never get movies made. I know people who have worked really hard at it, who are good writers, who haven't been that successful. That's the luck factor.

Peter Hyams

PETER HYAMS: I began writing at a very young and precocious age, including a lot of bullshit lowercase poetry. You know, "i seek/ in my life/frailty," that kinda thing, which at the High School of Music & Art could get you laid. My aspirations were to be a documentary filmmaker, because I thought that was the best combination of writing and imagery and relevance.

I was with CBS for seven years, and made a lot of documentary stuff. I ultimately found myself more interested in writing a sentence that I thought was effective or clever than something that was giving information. So I decided I wanted to go into feature film.

I was twenty-six, and I had two kids. I came home and said to my wife, "I quit my job and I'm gonna make feature films." My wife, who was a history teacher, said, "Are we gonna struggle?" I said, "I would expect so." She said, "Okay. I'll make up a struggling list."

I shouldn't be given credit for being bold. I was stupid. I had no idea how difficult it was. I thought all you had to do was write a script, and somebody would buy it.

I wrote a script, and Paramount bought it.

It got sent to the right people, because somebody I knew since I was a kid wound up in charge of Paramount. So when I wrote it, he said, "Send it to me." I sent it to him, and he said, "I wanna make it."

I am a complete anomaly. I didn't have years of sending stuff out and having it all come back from studios or agents. It's just stupid, blind luck.

The Educator's Perspective: Kris Young

Kris Young

*The personal interaction inherent to the collegiate experience
helps many beginning screenwriters discover whether they're truly
suited to a career in show business, and Kris Young has seen that
experience from several different perspectives. As an undergrad-
uate film student at USC, he learned from noted instructor Irwin
R. Blacker. Then he worked as a screenwriter for several years
before earning his MFA at UCLA, where he studied with screen-*

writing guru Lew Hunter. Today, Young teaches at UCLA, and he co-chairs the Writers Guild of America's Asian-American Writers Committee.

Lessons in Learning

Now that I'm a teacher, I realize everybody comes to film school because they have a big dream of going through school, learning how to write a great screenplay, selling the big script, and launching their career.

I wanted to be a *Playboy* photographer. My parents said, "It's better to go to college—why don't you go to film school, because that's kinda like photography, isn't it?" That's how I wound up in film school. At USC, I made a film called *Blazing Fists,* a martial-arts comedy. It was the most popular film of the whole season, but the teachers hated it because it was this fusion of Bruce Lee and *Blazing Saddles.* The teachers would not allow me to go on as a director. That's when I started thinking about going into writing.

Irwin Blacker was great. Up until I had his class, I think the longest paper I'd ever written was five to ten pages. And then he stood up there and said, "You must write a fifty-page treatment." I said, "There's no way." And then I just did it, because you were forced to—he was kind of a scary older guy in a suit—and he gave me an A-plus. I had no idea that was gonna happen, and then I realized: Maybe I can be a writer.

I was a working professional when I went to UCLA, so I'd kinda been through it all when I went to school the second time. Lew Hunter was my main mentor. Lew expects your highest work. He's very firm with "You're gonna have a script done in nine weeks," and you just do it. I think in his class, a lot of people would say that they did some of their best work.

With every teacher I've had, I just said, "I'm gonna do everything they tell me to do." So no matter who they were, I walked out of their class with a finished screenplay. By experience, you find out which teachers you like better. I just took them almost randomly, and then the ones that worked, I took again—like Lew, who I took many times.

The goal of the undergrad program is essentially to give students enough training to continue until they either quit or succeed. In the undergrad program, a lot of them are total beginners, where they've not even written a screenplay before. The difference in the master's program is the people are usually more mature, or they came out of undergrad programs, so they've written more scripts. They're the cream of the crop from everywhere else. But the goal is the same—to equip people to become professionals.

A master's might give you a leg up on some people, in the sense that maybe people will look at that and go, "If he went through the UCLA MFA screenwriting program, he's probably not an idiot." But ultimately, you're judged by your work.

Put Up or Shut Up

You can watch a film just for fun, and then you can watch it again and start breaking it down with the timer on your DVD player to see what kind of things happen at certain times and to look for patterns. You can get a simple book, like one of those Syd Field books, and see if things are actually falling on these different structural places. But it's a dangerous thing too, because I find that a lot of people wrote great screenplays without having to know all these structural paradigms, so you want to balance that with still enjoying film and writing from your heart.

I have my students read a screenplay a week—hopefully great ones. And I think that's where you learn. There's rhythm; there's the way things look on a page. Not just formatting, but things that can't really be explained in a book. So many people seem to need focus and discipline. The "voice" part of screenwriting can't be taught, but I think school can shave maybe a couple of years off somebody's eventual career—the typical mistakes that you'd have to learn by the school of hard knocks.

There's something they talk about in the orientation for screenwriting school, and I think it's very important. You will find out in a year or two if it's for you or not—I guess in the same way that Michael Jordan played baseball versus basketball. You know—no harm, no foul. At least you can move on with your life. But if you find out that something is ignited in you, and it's a passion that cannot ever be quenched, then that's a great thing.

I think a lot of people hold on to this dream, even if they're never gonna write a script, because it's a great dream to hold on to—that someday you might write an Academy Award–winning screenplay. Going to film school, it's a put up or shut up kind of a deal.

Teaching newcomers to screenwriting, I try not to dwell too much on the negative aspects. I guess it's like telling new soldiers, "You're all gonna get killed." It's a lesson you learn for yourself when you've been in it long enough. So many people drop out after a few classes. Most people never finish a screenplay. So I don't like to tell them horror stories up front.

I impress on my students to finish in the time allotted. There are a lot of perfectionists out there who kinda circle around and research and read books and study—and they never really finish screenplays. What I took away from my teachers was they made me finish scripts.

Kung Fu Screenwriting

You need to learn that it's more about the journey than the destination. This is something that I teach in my lecture "Kung Fu Screenwriting," which is based on some Bruce Lee philosophy—there's a difference between doing and being. When you venture forth to *do* screenwriting, like many people do, then the moment you stop, you're not a screenwriter. But if you move toward the idea of *being* a writer, then it never leaves you. And I think that's a higher thing to aspire to—to *be* a writer. You keep writing not necessarily to sell a script or to get a movie made, but because that is who you are.

I look for people who are already self-motivated. People who already have a high level of interest in the subject—they're really not gonna do anything else. They're writing before school begins, they're gonna keep writing when school stops. It's not something they do, but it's something they are.

Be a writer as opposed to someone who *does* writing.

I had never really applied for a job as a screenwriting teacher. I knew a teacher here. She had to go on vacation, and she said, "You wanna sub for me for a semester?" I was very fearful. I had thought about teaching in the sense that if I ever did it at UCLA, I'd wanna come in with an Academy Award, or some big film that could front for me, because I was very insecure about it: Why would they listen to me?

I really enjoy teaching. It's something that I'm passionate about, and it's something that comes naturally. It's kinda like I don't have to do it—I just am that, you know? I have a lot of fun with it. I mean, the hardest part is reading all those scripts, though. I've gotta admit that.

Some of my students are just starting to get some recognition. I feel an extreme sense of pride in the people I've helped—I don't even wanna say *taught*. I tell students I'm more of a personal trainer. I'm just telling them, "Do more of this, do more of that." You know, "Gimme ten more."

2

Breaking In

Maddening as it may sound, there is no surefire means of becoming accredited as a screenwriter. A first-time scribe has as strong a chance of getting in the door as someone with a master's in screenwriting, because good fortune is as important as discipline, personality, and professionalism. Ironically, the sheer number of people trying to enter the field creates the biggest obstacle of all: Barricades have been built around Hollywood to block the barrage of amateur screenplays.

As a result, the early years of most screenwriting careers are filled with disappointments. Conventional wisdom suggests that it takes a decade to launch a career in show business, but screenwriters face a unique handicap. Emerging directors have short films to show for their efforts, and struggling actors can tout appearances in commercials and plays. Writers merely have unproduced scripts, no matter their level of artistic achievement. Everything changes the minute a writer makes his or her first sale, but until then he or she is merely one of the great horde trying to storm the gates.

Against this bleak backdrop, miracles somehow occur. Mick Garris was on food stamps when his deliverance arrived in the form of a job offer from Steven Spielberg, whom he had interviewed for television.

David Hayter covertly rewrote the special-effects extravaganza his friend Bryan Singer was directing, a fact both hid from the studio as long as they could. Allison Anders and Andrew W. Marlowe raised their profiles by winning important contests. The lesson from all such stories is that writers have to put themselves on the map—short of those born into show-business families, few receive easy entrée into the world of screenwriting.

There is one more daunting reality that aspiring writers need to embrace in the early days of their careers, because this fact will underscore every phase of their Hollywood journeys: In the movie business, writers are disposable. As Bruce Joel Rubin notes, screenwriters occupy the lowest stature among the major players behind films. Actors, directors, and producers all control the fates of screenwriters, often capriciously and sometimes maliciously.

Strap yourselves in, because the roller coaster is about to hit the first big drop.

The Totem Pole

BRUCE JOEL RUBIN: In Hollywood, you're dealing with a power structure where the writer is really at the bottom of the totem pole. Actually, I think that the writer isn't even at the bottom of the totem pole—they're at the part that they stick in the ground, and then there's the totem pole.

MICHAEL WOLK: A writer is kind of a pawn in the game, really. People describe screenwriting as the only literary form that is read by five people. When you're in production, there are a few more people who read the script, although I'm not sure many of them read it all the way through, even the actors. It's important to realize that a Hollywood movie is a collaboration that requires that your vision be compromised.

JOHN CARPENTER: The Writers Guild is a wild place, because there are so many members of the guild, and so few of them ever get work. A lot of guys get used and abused. A lot of guys come up with ideas, but they can't pull 'em off, so they're rewritten and they're dumped. It's a rough game. It's a real rough game.

FRANK DARABONT: If your colleagues have respect for you and recognize your value, then you're gonna be treated great. And if they don't, you're gonna be treated like shit. I've been treated both ways. We all have. I am somewhat of the Zen opinion that you endure the one and appreciate the other. The potential for the crap that a screenwriter has to endure never goes away. No matter what your level is, no matter what your reputation is, no matter what your credibility is, no matter what the work is that you've done, the potential for being treated as an afterthought—if you're a screen-writer—is always present.

NORA EPHRON: Movies are not necessarily about individual voices. There are all sorts of movies, like Woody Allen's, that you could characterize that way, and there are also all sorts of movies that aren't. But it's rare that the individual voice is the writer's voice—it's much more often the director's.

ADAM RIFKIN: It's the director's movie. That's the hierarchy of moviemaking. The director is the creative boss. Essentially the director's job is to take a script and interpret it the way they see fit. If you're a purist and you don't want your words touched, you should either be a playwright or an author. Because if you're gonna be a screenwriter and expect that your words are gonna be treated like gold, that's just not reality.

JANE ANDERSON: A play script stays whole throughout the process. A film script is deconstructed and melted down and shattered into a million pieces, then put back together again. The effect of a movie is as dependent on the cameraman, the sound man, the editor, and the director as it is on the writing.

PETER HYAMS: Screenwriters do not have the same contract that the playwrights' guild has in New York, thank God, because the process is different. When you write something, you're sitting in front of a keyboard and a screen. But on the set, sometimes there's not enough money to do what you wrote. Sometimes there aren't enough days in the schedule to do what you wanted. A movie is a year preparing and a year recovering from approximately two to three months of production. It's like training for the Olympics, and then it's a sprint. You don't have the luxury that a playwright has of sitting in the back row, with the cigarette dangling from your mouth, and watching and watching and watching, and then changing something.

MICHAEL JANUARY: There's often nothing as useless on a movie set as a writer. He's that guy standing in the back by the craft service table, looking very pained. People go, "Who is that guy? He keeps hanging around."

I had a film shot in Vancouver. I paid my way to go up there. I'm wandering around the set, looking at things, and the production designer comes running up to me and says, "You're the writer?"

And I go, "Yes." He says, "Which lamp do you like better?" I go, "Well, that's really the director's decision." He says, "Well, yeah, but he's kind of busy. Can you tell me which one you like?" I go, "I like that one." He says, "Oh, thank you," and he runs off.

The writer's contribution to the filmmaking process was the choice of lamps on the set.

Michael January

No Means No, and So Does Everything Else

WILLIAM GOLDMAN: If you wanna write movies, you can't stop after you get pissed on and rejected, 'cause you're gonna get pissed on and rejected. Nobody wants your stuff. Once you become somebody, they'll read it—but nobody wants to give anybody their first shot.

PETER HYAMS: A man much smarter than I once described this venture as a horse race without a finish line. Just because you wanna do it doesn't mean you're gonna get to do it. However, if you are really talented, you are so separated from the overwhelming majority of the people who are trying to do it that I think you'll get noticed. It may take a few times. Rejection is as much a part of this as physical fitness is part of being a marine. If you're not prepared to do a lot of push-ups, don't enlist in the Marines. If you're not prepared to be rejected, don't try to write films.

RON SHELTON: Maybe my background as an athlete helped prepare me for this, because sports are all about dealing with losing. You get knocked down, you get up again. Any career that sustains itself is about getting up again.

MIKE BINDER: You have to learn how to take no for an answer. You also have to learn how to ask. Asking is so important. Asking people to read your script, asking people for advice, asking people to help you get it made. And with asking comes hearing no. You can't say, "Well, I asked and everyone said no," then close up shop and head home.

Next to the work ethic of writing and writing and writing, the muscle that needs to be developed the most is the ability to handle rejection. There are so many reasons why someone says no to something. Someone could read a great script in a bad mood, then not wanna finish it. Someone could say, "I read something just like it and my boss didn't like it, so I don't wanna pass this up the ladder." It could be as simple as you get a reader who hates cars, and you're submitting a movie about cars.

Success in this business distills down to a bone-marrow belief in yourself and what you're doing. If you take rejection as a chance to strengthen the belief in yourself, it can actually be seen as a positive thing. Listen, I've always thought I was better than everyone else thought I was. At the same time, I've always thought I was worse. It's the two evils, you know? Grandiosity and self-loathing go hand in hand.

I went though a long period where a lot of the guys I started with had gone on to become incredibly successful, and I'd say, "Maybe I just don't have the talent they do, or the luck they do." It was a matter of really listening to that voice in my head that said, "I'm on the right path, but the right people haven't figured it out yet."

MICK GARRIS: The needs of the buyer are not often the needs of the seller. Almost every writer I know, their best work has never been produced, if even bought. The more personal a script, often the better the script—but the less likely it is to be produced, particularly today. The studios like the lowest common denominator and the projects that require the least thought. They're looking for something like something that was successful before.

NAOMI FONER: A lot of it is corporate. Nobody is out there to hurt you, although it hurts. So if you can be pretty clear about it not being personal, I think you can get through a lot more of it.

JOE FORTE: I try to view the business from a point of view of empowerment, versus victimization. Every script is an opportunity to get better at something, especially early in your career, when that learning curve is really going at a sharp angle up. If you look at experiences as opportunities to get information about what your voice is and what you're good at and what you're not good at, it makes the rejection or the disappointment something you can use.

There's a phrase you hear in Hollywood: "It's a movie." I didn't really understand that phrase when I first came into the business. It's code for, "This script encompasses everything we need it to be: It can attract an actor, it can attract a director, it can be marketed. It's complete." A lot of times, a writer will write a great first act, but not a good second or third act—or the characters will be great, but there's no plot. Those kinds of things make it easier for somebody to say no.

DENNIS PALUMBO: They're not in trouble if they say no. Nothing bad can happen to them, and they won't lose any money. The moment they say yes, their troubles begin. If you're an agent, you now have a new client for whom you have to get work. If you're a studio executive, you have to sell this idea to all of your compatriots. If you're a producer, you have to go get some studio interested in actually making this movie. If you say no, you can just go to lunch.

LINDA VOORHEES: Many people in the industry don't have an intellectual reason why they're rejecting a script. It's actually a visceral reason, and they don't have the ability to articulate why it doesn't work for them, so they'll say anything. "The ending doesn't work." "It's too linear." "It's too episodic." "You need more character in your characters."

People reject you nicely. They don't tell you it's a piece of shit. They will nice you to death, but the niceness is actually, I think, more brutal, because you'll then chase it: "She said I just have to change the ending." "She said I just need a subplot." "She said if I just changed the beginning . . ." Those are all lies. It was just to get you to go away.

Linda Voorhees

MICHAEL JANUARY: There are different kinds of rejections. There are soft passes and hard passes and cold passes and helpful passes and encouraging passes. I mean, the cold pass is, "It's not right for us, thank you very much," which tells you absolutely nothing. There is the hard pass, which is, "This is crap, don't call us again!" There is the warm pass, which is, "We enjoyed this, but it's just not right for what we're doing at our company." And sometimes that includes, "Please let us know what you're doing next." There's the encouraging pass, which is, "If you made some changes, we might be willing to look at it again." Then there's the annoying pass, which is, "We like this a lot, but we have something similar in development."

DAVID S. WARD: The harshest pass is somebody not ever responding. You sent 'em a script and never heard from 'em. They didn't even have the decency to call back and say, "I don't get it," or "I'm not interested." You feel like you sent the script out and it just kept on going, never to come back again.

ADAM RIFKIN: Is there anything a writer can do to make a script rejection-proof? Yes. One hundred percent guaranteed. If your best friend is Tom Cruise and he attaches himself to star in that script, your script is rejection-proof. You win! So I recommend that to everybody.

RON SHELTON: There's no such thing as a rejection-proof script, and there shouldn't be. If you're trying so hard to connect every dot and hit every target commercially and dramatically, you're probably gonna hit every cliché in the world, because studios don't want things that are original. They want formulas. And then if you try to write a formula, they may say, "We've got nine of those in the pipeline already." I think that the goal is to start by writing something really, really good, and really, really compelling, and hoping that it has a place in the marketplace, rather than aiming at the marketplace. If you just aim for the marketplace, the marketplace might have changed by the time you get there.

MARK FERGUS: If you believe in your script utterly and it gets rejected a hundred times, in a way you're just waiting for that right opportunity—you know this is gonna be the bull's eye for the right person. And how many times have we heard that story? "I sent it out a million times, great people rejected it, and then one guy stumbled on it and said, 'This is exactly what I've been looking for,'" and it went on to become some great film. That happens all the time.

JUSTIN ZACKHAM: If you finish a screenplay and you don't think it's the greatest thing since sliced bread, you're not finished. The first script I went out with was this action comedy called *Choco Canyon*. I remember finishing this thing, and I thought, "I'm so made. It's gonna be so easy from this point on." And it just got crushed by everyone. Some people liked it and I got a few meetings out of it, but there was mostly, "Yeah, the writing's just not good." I was shattered, 'cause I thought it was the greatest thing since sliced bread. Sliced bread's impressive.

You go through that, and it's terrible, and you're wracked with self-doubt, and you think, "Everyone's saying it's terrible and I think it's great—either they're stupid, all five thousand of them, or I'm stupid."

What happens is you start to grow calluses. You get rejected with the second script. It sucks, and it takes you a while to recover. Then you get rejected again, and again, and again. Gradually it gets to the point where you have to decide: Have you made it as good as it can possibly be? Have you thrown everything you have into this thing?

BRUCE JOEL RUBIN: The greatest hope for anybody who's writing a screenplay is that they're writing. The mere fact that you're writing is hope. It's alive on the page. It may not be a good screenplay—it may be the worst thing you've ever written—but you're putting it out there. You're juicing the machine. This is really essential.

A writer writes. Does a writer write good things? Sometimes. Does a writer write bad things? Sometimes. But if you keep writing, the balance will work out. You write enough bad things—and believe me, I've done it—the good things start to come. Don't be afraid of rewriting. Don't be afraid of reimagining your own material. When fourteen people tell you they don't like this character, believe them—something is not right with that character. Go back and fix it. You can always make it better.

LINDA VOORHEES: You have a feeling when you begin that you'll reach a threshold and the concept of rejection just won't be part of your writer's life, because you will have proven yourself—you'll have a certain résumé, you'll have a certain number of contacts that have the ability to say, "You've got a green light." None of that is true. That's the lie we tell ourselves out of naïveté. It just gets to a different level of rejection as you work your way up. You're rejected by a higher class of producer, a higher class of development executive, or a higher class of director, but the rejection is still there. That constancy is the part that I think none of us figures on.

PAUL SCHRADER: There are a great many scripts, and only a certain number of movies gets made. You just do the math. It's like if you're an actor. You go out for fifty jobs, and if you're lucky, maybe you'll get one of them. The math is against you, and the rejection is part of what you do, so you keep doing it. It only takes one buyer, and sometimes it takes years to find that buyer. When you're starting out, you're sort of curious about why they passed, but you never get the right answer anyway, so you just learn to say, "Okay, so they passed. Next?"

One Is the Loneliest Number

LARRY COHEN: Many writers are depressed, because they don't like the isolation of sitting down by themselves and writing a script. Some people have to be prodded into doing it—they find writing to be a painful experience. They're looking at those blank pages, and it depresses them to know that "Oh, I've gotta come up with something."

ANDREW W. MARLOWE: It's easy to become disconnected from life. You sit in the writing chair, you deal with your imagination, and you're not among people.

GUINEVERE TURNER: I find it incredibly difficult to write solely by myself. I'm always asking friends to come over, and I'm like, "Can you read this? What do you think? Let's talk about it." I'm a compulsively social person, so the fact that I'm a writer by profession sort of bums me out sometimes. I'm so fortunate to have had Rose Troche on *Go Fish* and Mary Harron on two movies. I want a screenwriting posse. I want a team called the "Guinevere Turner Team."

RONALD SHUSETT: I started as a producer, not a writer. I always had the strength of story structure, but the first three years that I tried to write scripts, they were awful. And so I would go around to all the colleges and put up a notice: "Budding young producer has a couple of great story ideas. If you like my ideas, we can collaborate. If you're weak on structure but you're good with character and dialogue that moves the plot, I'd like to share my ideas with you."

Tons of people expressed interest, because they were all struggling like me, and I developed a couple of very good scripts because I had an eye for knowing a good writer. Even though I could get jobs by myself and keep all the money, I realized ultimately the scripts would only be half as good. So I carefully selected writers who excelled at character—my main weakness as a writer. I'd rather have my name as cowriter of a brilliant script than sole writer of good script.

STEVE KOREN: I was a struggling actor. Then I started trying some stand-up comedy, and that led to becoming a comedy writer. I got a job as a tour guide at NBC, and began handing jokes to Dennis Miller in the hallway. That eventually led to a receptionist job, a researcher job, and then a writing job on *Saturday Night Live*. A couple of characters I worked on got some attention for movies, so I wrote *A Night at the Roxbury* with Will Ferrell and Chris Kattan, and *Superstar* with Molly Shannon. Then I proceeded to partner up with Mark on some of the bigger, more expensive productions.

MARK O'KEEFE: I started out writing in television, kinda like Steve. I wrote for Letterman. That was my first real paying job. And then I wrote for some sitcoms, like *NewsRadio*. But actually, Steve taught me everything I knew about writing movies. I had never written a movie before.

STEVE KOREN: I'll tell you where having a partner hurts you. When you get paid, you have to split the money.

MARK O'KEEFE: Yes, this is an issue.

STEVE KOREN: We haven't been able to get over this. We've argued. . . .

JOHN D. BRANCATO: I met my writing partner, Michael Ferris, many years ago. We were friends in college, and we had a very similar record collection, and we liked the same movies. We just had really sympathetic instincts, while also having very different outlooks on life in general. But we pretty much agreed on the way things oughta be. I worked with somebody else very early in my career—actually, we were hired to do the first draft of the movie *Spider-Man*, back in 1985. Mike and I started working together around 1986, 1987—and it just felt really easy. It's a great thing to have somebody with you in the process. You're not up against it alone. You can at least laugh about it when things go wrong. When you're alone, it's a little bit more depressing. It's easier to spiral down into a hole.

ZAK PENN: My writing partnerships have each been unique in their own way. But I think having a writing partner is a great idea for a struggling young writer, because it does the most important thing: It forces you to write. And by the way, if you have a writing partnership where you don't feel forced to write, you should probably get out of it. But for me, having someone else in the room to answer to made me do my work.

I have written with a lot of different types of people. My first writing partner was Adam Leff. I was writing partners with Mike White, who's been very successful. I was writing partners with Toby Emmerich, who's now president of New Line Cinema. I was writing partners with Simon Kinberg for *X-Men: The Last Stand*. Since my first writing partnership, I've never had a problem with any of my writing partners. But my first one, it got a little ugly for a while because we didn't really expect the success that we were gonna get.

MARK FERGUS: I met my writing partner, Hawk Ostby, at Showtime. Both of us worked the kind of jobs that allowed us to write six, seven hours a day. I was in accounting; he was in film traffic or whatever. Somebody introduced us, and we started talking. I never would've pegged us for a good collaboration, and I was never looking for a partner. It was just a complete happy accident, and we've been doing it now twelve years.

We don't like to sit in the same room. He lives in Vermont. I live in Los Angeles. That's part of our longevity, I think, as a writing team. We don't get in each other's faces. He's got a normal life, like a house full of kids, and has a really quiet existence. I live in this nutty place, and I have dogs and a wife, but I don't have a structured life like he has. Somehow, the combination works. He's able to get something great done over there, I do my thing, and together, we manage to get the work done.

It's chaos, but I really wouldn't wanna work any other way.

MARK D. ROSENTHAL: When you have a partner, you're sharing your foxhole while they're lobbing hand grenades at you. You turn in a draft they didn't like, or they fired you off something, or they gave you a note that is just ludicrous—at least you can console each other. A partner is a great psychic balm. It's not just the craft that is helped—it's the hurt and the self-doubt.

Self-doubt is really the great enemy of an artist. You know: "Am I good enough?" "Am I as good as that guy?" My partner and I talk about this. We always wanted to put out a mock issue of *Variety* that's called *Anxiety*. And the front page is: "You Don't Get the Three-Picture Deal," "That Guy You Hate Is Nominated for an Academy Award," "Everybody but You Just Got a Production Bonus." That's how it plays in your mind. So when you have a partner, you can at least vent with someone. It helps.

Getting in the Game

WILLIAM GOLDMAN: The greatest movie of all time, as everybody knows, is *Gunga Din*, which I have seen sixteen times. I saw it first, I think, when I was eight. It really is about stupid courage, and I didn't know that I was moved by stupid courage until I began my career. Look, if you wanna go to law school and be a lawyer, or go to business school and work on Wall Street, you can do that. No one's gonna stop you. They're looking for bright young people. The thing about writing is it's such a crapshoot, and there's no logic to it.

I wrote my first novel when I was twenty-four. It came out when I was twenty-five. And the reason it came out was I had been in the army with a guy who had met an agent, a wonderful man named Joe McKrindle. Joe was very, very, very rich, and he went to law school, and then he went to work in publishing because he wanted to deal with writers. He discovered that as an editor, he was dealing only with agents, and he hated that, so he became an agent so he could deal with writers. He went around the country to all these schools, and he picked up Philip Roth—he picked up an amazing number of writers who eventually became famous.

I sent him my novel, and I said, "I met so-and-so who had met you." Joe read it and he knew somebody from when he had been an editor at Knopf, and they published it. Well, that's a fluke. I mean, all of those things had to happen for any of that to happen. If that book had not been published, I never would have written a second book, because I had not shown any signs of talent.

LARRY COHEN: I wanted to write movies, so I used to haunt the various sets where they shot in New York City—whether it was

North by Northwest, where I followed Hitchcock around from one location to another, or the live television programs that were on in those days, where I used to sneak into the studios at NBC and watch them rehearse. That's what I did every weekend, and I kinda learned by watching.

I started off beating the bushes in New York City, asking people if they needed a script. I remember one gentleman said, "Well, why don't you go write a script?" I said, "Fine," and I was back on the following Monday, which was three days later. He said, "You have further questions?" I said, "No, here's the script. I wrote it. Can I call you next week?" He said, "No, if you can write it over the weekend, I can read it tonight. Call me tomorrow."

So he was impressed. I kept going back to that same company, which was Talent Associates in New York, and barraging them with material. Finally they started giving me things to do, but they didn't pay me. I figured if I did enough things for free, eventually they'd be so embarrassed by their situation that they would give me a job, which they did. They broke down and paid me $1,500 to write a script for a live television show, and I was in business.

RON SHELTON: I had a couple scripts out there that people liked but were deemed uncommercial, and I was hired to do a rewrite on a movie called *The Pursuit of D.B. Cooper*. It was already shot and unreleasable, and they wanted to reshoot some things. That's how I got to go to a movie set, write for actors on the fly—and in two weeks on a movie set, I felt like I'd been to five years of film school.

I then was hired by Ed Pressman, the producer, to be his story editor. This was in 1980. He optioned a script of mine and he didn't have any money to pay me, so he offered me a job. I had to read twenty scripts a week and report on them—and at night I was writing my own. If you read twenty scripts a week, you really quickly learn what a good screenplay is and how it's put together. You learn that after page ten, you can quit reading—if it's no good on page ten, it isn't gonna get better. You learn that page one matters. It was a real crash course in how to write a screenplay.

STEPHEN SUSCO: I showed up at USC very starry-eyed. You know, there was the Steven Spielberg Scoring Stage and there was the George Lucas building . . . I had no idea what I was doing. I had just driven out from Indiana. So that day, I went up to the internship board and I saw that there was a company at Warner Bros. called Spring Creek Productions. I called them up the very next day. Then on, like, my third day in Los Angeles, I was drivin' onto the Warner Bros. lot, and it was the coolest feeling. I was like, "There's the water tower!" I'll never forget that day.

They ended up hiring me as their intern. *Hiring* is a loose term, because I didn't get paid, but my job was to alphabetize the script library. I would go in two days a week and alphabetize a roomful of screenplays. I got to read a lot of 'em, and I got to listen to phone calls happening around me. I started to get a sense of the mechanics of the business, which was really critical. My second semester, I upgraded my internship to Silver Pictures, which is Joel Silver's company. You know, *Die Hard, Lethal Weapon*—all the movies I loved that brought me out to Hollywood.

I had written a couple of scripts with a friend of mine at USC, just for shits and giggles, and one of them ended up with a manager who read it and liked it. I didn't know that he was sending it out.

Well, one day I was at the internship, and Damon Lee, who I think was the vice president at the time, just screamed: "Susco, get in my office!" I didn't know what I had done. I went scrambling in there, and dropped the toast I'd been making for somebody. He held up the script and he went, "Is this you? I didn't know you wanted to be a writer." It turned out the script had been sent to Silver Pictures, unbeknownst to me, and the guys really liked it. They were really nice. They gave me an hour of their time, and talked about the career of screenwriting.

Stephen Susco

ALLISON ANDERS: In 1986, I was leaving college and I was a single mom, so anything with dollar signs on it, I applied. I entered three screenwriting contests. The first one was the Nissan Focus Awards, which no longer exists. I failed miserably, apparently, because they sent me a rejection notice with a list of screenwriting books I might wanna read. I submitted to the Samuel Goldwyn Writing Awards and to the brand-new contest that year, the Nicholl

Fellowship. I won both. I won the top prize in the Goldwyn, and I won one of five Nicholl Fellowships. The Goldwyn had been around a long time, so there were journalists and agents waiting around to hear who won. The Nicholl Fellowship was new, so there wasn't so much attention around that, but it was quite a juicy prize. At that time, it was $20,000. Everybody wanted to read my script.

ANDREW W. MARLOWE: Coming out of USC, I had written a small coming-of-age screenplay about an imaginative thirteen-year-old boy who sees his ideal summer take a turn for the worse when his financially strapped parents are forced to sell the beloved summer cottage. Certainly not the big action-adventure stuff that I'm known for. It was sweet story in the vein of *Stand by Me,* and I was fortunate enough to have it get noticed by the Nicholl committee.

Winning a Nicholl Fellowship is a really heady thing for somebody who's trying to break into the industry, because one day you're stuffing foreclosure notices into envelopes at your temp job—and wondering how you're going to get your cavity filled, because you don't have money for it—and the next day you're in the halls of the Academy of Motion Picture Arts and Sciences with some of the greats that you've admired all your life. They have this celebratory dinner for you, and it's really remarkable. It's as if you've won the Academy Award, and you haven't really started your career yet. You know, people like Robert Wise and Eva Marie Saint and Hal Kanter and Jack Lemmon—and they're honoring you? It's very *Twilight Zone.*

Probably the best thing that happened is that one of the women who won that year met me and we hit it off. She's now my wife. As my stepdaughter was fond of saying when she was young, "Mommy won Andrew in a contest."

ARI B. RUBIN: My father has been a great teacher in my writing, and he was the axis point for me getting to my agency, and hence to the rest of this business.

In terms of getting that initial access, if you don't have a father in the business, you find someone else in the business. Nepotism is not a plus in this industry. I think it's a necessity. If not through family, then through friends—I don't know how people get in if not through personal relationships. It sounds like a barrier that's too hard to cross, but really, it's not. You come out here, and at least you meet someone who can pass your script along to an agent. There's no direct route. There's no company you can drop an application at, and suddenly become a screenwriter.

Even though I was given almost immediate access to an industry that most people fight for years to get into, there was definitely an earning process of some sort that came afterward. I had to learn how to function in this business, and I had to build all of those relationships that I hadn't built initially.

JOSE RIVERA: Luck is part of everything you do, and you try to make your own luck by being smart about the kind of connections that you make. I would say the luckiest day of my life was meeting Walter Salles when he was looking for a writer to adapt *The Motorcycle Diaries*. I had been working since 1992 on screenplays, and never had one made, so I always felt like a beginner. But after *The Motorcycle Diaries*, things turned around completely. Up until I started working with Walter, I'd always felt that writing screenplays was something you do just to earn some money, but you never actually see your movie made. And then when he said, "We're actually gonna make it," I was shocked.

David Hayter

DAVID HAYTER: I came to Los Angeles when I was twenty, with the intention of being an actor for my career, and that went along haltingly for six or seven years. I did a couple of movies and some TV, but I wasn't really satisfied. And then I produced a small feature in '97, a little quarter-million-dollar art-house film with Bryan Singer called *Burn*. At the end of that, I had accomplished something major, but I was now a broke independent producer, and I needed a job. Bryan was kind enough to give me a job answering the phones on his next production, which was *X-Men*.

I did that for about three weeks, and the whole time, Bryan was complaining about the script and saying, "I hate this. This isn't working. This is gonna ruin my career." Having been a fan of the X-Men from the time I was twelve years old, I knew the characters very well. So one day I just said, "Look, why don't you have a scene where Wolverine and Cyclops run into each other on the mansion grounds? Wolverine says this, Cyclops says this, and that'll tie up what you've already done and set you up for what you wanna do down the road." He said, "Yeah, go write that scene for me."

I had written probably eight or nine short films and a couple of screenplays, but I had done it primarily to make myself a better actor—to understand the mechanics of film better. It's like they say: Good luck is when opportunity meets preparation.

Bryan put the scene in the movie, and he asked me to start coming to story meetings and take notes—and not tell the studio what I was doing. I would work on the script all night after everyone else had gone home. Through a long, strange series of events, the studio eventually found out. They ratified my deal, and I ended up getting sole credit when the movie came out. So I was extremely fortunate with my first writing job.

MICK GARRIS: I had done journalism in the days of the underground newspapers—Cameron Crowe and I both wrote about music for the *San Diego Door* at the same time. I'd always been interested in screenwriting. I interviewed Steven Spielberg, along with several other people, on the old Z Channel, which was a pay-TV channel here in Los Angeles, and he gave me my first opportunity. His company liked a spec script I'd done, so they called me up and said, "We'd like you to write for this new show called *Amazing Stories*." I found out later I was the first one asked to write one of the scripts, all of which were based on stories that Spielberg had written. I was on food stamps at the time, and this was a tremendous opportunity. I wrote it in three days, based on Steven's story, and they asked me to do another one right away. Before I was halfway through it, they called and asked me to go on staff as the story editor. So I went from food stamps and good wishes to working for Steven Spielberg.

The Contest Administrator's Perspective: Greg Beal

Greg Beal

Presented by the Academy of Motion Picture Arts and Sciences, the Nicholl Fellowships provide a substantial cash prize, the imprimatur of the organization behind the Oscars, and interest from representatives and producers throughout Hollywood. Only a few dozen people have become fellows since the program launched in 1986, so the club is quite exclusive. In an average year, as many as six thousand scripts are submitted to the contest. A team of about fifty freelance readers reviews the submissions and assigns each script a number grade. Roughly 5 percent of the submitted screenplays advance to the quarterfinal stage. Eventually, ten scripts are selected as finalists. Then a committee comprising about one dozen industry professionals reads the *finalist screenplays, and debates their merits at a spirited annual meeting, before selecting up to five winning scripts, the authors of which receive fellowships. Since 1989, the program's coordinator has been Greg Beal, himself a onetime wannabe screenwriter.*

The Power of Story

I coach the readers. I give them instructions that say, "What we're interested in are good writers, good stories, good story-telling—the best scripts, whatever that means." It's a little bit amorphous, but the best scripts, no matter what the budget is. If you think this is a huge studio movie—or bigger than any studio movie and nobody can make it because the budget is so big—I don't care. Is it a good script? Or if it's some nihilistic, dark, deadly, morbid, ghoulish script—nobody's ever gonna make this unless some writer goes off and makes it independently, and then it's gonna have no audience—I don't care.

I have a little note in the guidelines that I hand out to the readers that says, "If there's something that strikes you as really unusual but you don't think it's very good, let me know." Several readers avail themselves of that particular note, and come in saying, "I gave this a low score, but there's something here—maybe somebody else will like it better." Especially early in the submission process, when there are very few scripts here, comparatively speaking, it's easy to be lenient, to go below the mark. The mark is sixty—that's what gets a script a reread. Occasionally scripts will get saved by a second reader.

The vast majority of scripts that make it into the quarterfinals or beyond are technically pretty good. But an extreme example is certainly Mike Rich's *Finding Forrester.* It was extremely rough. It was submitted in ten-point type, dialogue and description justified the same way. The story was so powerful that it captured readers.

You pick up a script and you start reading it, and you know right away: This person's a writer. That's the first thing that I notice. This person knows what they're doing in terms of language, both in description and in dialogue. The second thing that I notice is whether the person's a screenwriter or not. Do they know how to put words to the proper service so that they're not overwriting? Do they know how to be concise in their description, how to move the story forward?

After that, there's something about the script that's intriguing: These characters are doing something that's interesting to me—it's a story that I can't stop reading. You just want to keep turning the pages. You think, "I'm in the hands of a storyteller." It's that same kind of wonder when you started out reading kids' books when you were little. You want to know how it ends. It's good enough to keep me going.

With bad scripts, reading becomes a chore. I know ten, twenty, thirty pages in that this isn't gonna get better—it's gonna be at this level, and that level's not high.

During the finals, we've got the committee around a big table. We pick the order out of a hat so that the ten finalists end up on a sheet in a random order. We talk about each of those scripts in turn, and let all of the committee members speak about each script. And then at the end of all that conversation we vote, but what invariably happens is some of the judges will talk about what rank they had it: "This was my best script, this was my number five, this was my least favorite script out of this batch."

We've had people come into a room and say, "When I started reading this script, I flung it across the room, and I ended up flinging it across the room three times while I was reading it—it's the worst script that I've ever read as a judge in these Nicholl finals." And somebody else in the room said, "It was my favorite script," and that was the script that ended up winning the fellowship that year.

Try a Little Tenderness

When I first started, I thought, "Well, everybody's going to agree." They're going to go, "These are the good scripts, these are the not-so-good scripts, these are the bad scripts." And I found out it's absolutely not true. There are people who love certain scripts and there are other people who will hate those same scripts, and there are lots of people in between on scripts that are loved or hated by other folks. It's just so subjective. There's no way around that.

It takes time to really learn your craft. There are very few people who learn it on a first screenplay. You have to learn to tell stories. You have to learn how to know which stories work for the movies, as opposed to stories that work in other forms. All those things have to be learned by new writers, and they oftentimes submit their first script, their second script. They haven't learned very much.

Can good scripts be overlooked here, at a production company, at an agency, anywhere in Hollywood? Absolutely. There's no question that they can be overlooked. You have to persevere. You have to keep sending your script out. You have to keep writing. That's the single most important thing.

It's extremely difficult to break in as a screenwriter. The Nicholl program has specifically helped the fellows, and it's certainly also helped—if only by way of encouragement—those people who've reached the quarterfinals, semifinals, and finals, and haven't won. Sometimes it helped them get their script to a certain producer who went on to option the script, or a certain agent or manager who then signed them as a client. Sometimes it didn't do any of those things directly, but just reaching quarterfinals or semifinals has served as an encouragement, kept people writing—and the next script was the one that finally broke through.

When I was trying to be a screenwriter, one of the things I learned was how much it meant to me when someone actually wrote a note back to me. It anesthetizes one, to an extent, to going through that experience of mass rejection over and over again. You find out how much just a little human kindness means, so that has run through everything I've done.

3

The Marketplace
of Ideas

Aspirants who survive the onslaught of early rejection have passed their first test. They have put faith in their talent. Their newfound strength must then be put to use solving one of the great enigmas in the entertainment industry: What does Hollywood want? Easy as it may seem to guess which sorts of screenplays will sell based on the box-office returns of current blockbusters, buying trends in the movie business shift with dizzying speed.

In order to sell a screenplay to a Hollywood studio, one must first pass through the gauntlet of the Hollywood reader. Depending on the size of the company to which a writer is submitting material, the reader could be anyone from an outside freelancer to a high-ranking executive. These gatekeepers are barraged with screenplays submitted by actors, agents, directors, managers, producers, and even personal friends. Some scripts rise to the top of the reading pile because money or marquee-name talent is already attached; some scripts go straight to the wastebasket because the writer is an unknown entity. The level of cynicism among readers is predictably high, but most reputable gatekeepers can honestly say that their greatest desire is to discover a masterpiece.

Given that masterpieces don't come along very often, mere greatness is an acceptable substitute. Because greatness, really, is what Hollywood wants—and greatness can take innumerable forms. A comedy that fills a timely market niche is great because it's a safe investment; a horror script that sparks an up-and-coming director's interest is great because it brings two elements together as a "package." Talent and timing must converge for lightning to strike.

Oh, and one more thing—more often than not, established screenwriters court buyers not by showing off their delicately crafted prose, but rather via the dreaded verbal presentation known as the "pitch." As Guinevere Turner notes, there's nothing more bizarre than trying to sell a piece of writing by describing what that piece of writing would be like were it actually written. It's a strange game, but smart writers win it every day by drawing on the same faith that helped them surmount earlier challenges.

Writer, Know Thyself

PAUL SCHRADER: When you look at someone else's films and say, "I can do that," you're in a lot of competition—because everyone else is looking at that hit of the year and they're saying, "I can do that," too. You're gonna be up against all of them, and a lot of them are probably better positioned, and probably even better writers, than you are. So that's kind of rough competition to walk into. But if you look into yourself and say, "What do I have that no one else has, but other people can understand and identify with," then you're only in competition with yourself.

MARK FERGUS: Every time we try to calculate the marketplace and say, "There's the target," we're wrong. You know, we add a little *Blade Runner* here, we put in a bit of *Terminator* there, we add a really strong female lead, and it's all gonna come together, and Angelina Jolie is gonna do this—100 percent of the time, we're wrong. I think in any attempt to be cynical about the marketplace, to try to hit the bull's eye—you're always gonna miss, because the bull's eye has moved the minute you figure out what it is.

Mark Fergus

JOE FORTE: The thing to come to this business with is sort of a respect for it. When you respect something, you try to figure it out in a different way, as opposed to "That movie stunk. I could write a movie." That's probably why that movie stunk, 'cause whoever wrote that movie had the same attitude.

NAOMI FONER: Think of the movies that have come out of nowhere and touched a chord—everything from *sex, lies, and videotape* to *My Big Fat Greek Wedding*. They came from something real in whoever was creating them. You go out every day and you see posters for movies that look like clones of twelve other movies you've seen. Somebody wants to see them, but they're not the movies that are memorable. They're not the ones that change things. They're not the ones that really move people. If there's any advice to give, it's to be true to yourself—to be as specific as you can, and not to worry about what people are telling you to do.

JOHN AUGUST: I wish someone had sat me down right when I parked my car in Los Angeles and told me, "They don't know anything either." What's hard to understand—and hard to internalize—is that just because someone doesn't like something, or doesn't get what you wrote, that doesn't mean they're smarter or better or know more than you know. It just didn't click in their brain right, and they may give you some random bullshit answer because that's all they can think of to say about the situation. I used to try to make everyone happy, so if someone said that they didn't like something and had a suggestion, I would immediately try to incorporate that suggestion—which is one of the worst things you can possibly do.

BILLY RAY: When I started, I was a much more imitative writer than I am now. There were writers that I just revered, and I wanted to be them so badly that I think I made poor choices in terms of not only the kinds of stories that I was telling, but the way I was telling them.

I had a thing for Paddy Chayefsky, so there was a stretch of my career where I was trying to write really biting social satire, which is folly on a couple of levels. First of all, they're very tough to get made. And second, you're chasing an impossible target, because you can't do 'em better than Paddy Chayefsky. There was a stretch where I was trying to be Alvin Sargent. There was a stretch where I was trying to be Peter Shaffer. I think that's typical of being young. I would like to go back and grab the twenty-five-year-old version of me—or, I'm embarrassed to say, the thirty-year-old version of me—and say, "Just find your own voice."

Now I'm at a point in my career where I can draw inspiration from those real heavyweights that preceded me, and yet try to join their ranks in my own way. I'm not there yet. I'm nowhere near to getting there. But I think I have a better chance of getting there by creating my own voice than I would by trying to duplicate what they did.

JUSTIN ZACKHAM: I got an opportunity to direct a movie that I wrote, called *Going Greek*. I wrote it in a couple of weeks, and it was a crappy little fraternity comedy that I made for $200,000 that aired on Showtime. At the time I was trying to write comedy, and I had to go through that process to discover that, really, I'm not that funny. And then I sat back and thought, "If I'm gonna keep doing this, what should I be doing?" So I thought about all the movies that I love, and

I realized that they're much more on the drama side. So I switched tacks, and I went from writing dopey comedies—which I probably just wrote because I thought they would sell—to personal stories.

DANIEL PYNE: It may be that you're the kind of person who is interested in the kinds of stories that are very popular, the kinds of things that studios want to make a lot of—in which case you'll sell a lot of scripts. You may be the kind of person who is interested in telling the kinds of stories that the studios are only occasionally interested in—in which case you won't sell that many scripts. But you can't really change who you are, and you can't really predict what the studios will want. Who would have known that Charlie Kaufman would be able to sell screenplays at all? It just so happened that what he was writing fit a commercial need and turned out to be successful, and that's a great thing.

PETER HYAMS: There are some scripts that may be brilliantly written, except they're about a love affair between a nun and a German shepherd, and then people are surprised why somebody doesn't want to make them. So you can't be nuts. I've worked with a number of different schools, and I remember a script from a UCLA student. I read it, and then I had to go to the class and talk to them. It was a big class. The script began with "E.C.U."— you know, "extreme close up," somebody learned what that was. It said, "E.C.U.—VAGINA." I swear on my kids. It was the birth of a baby, from that angle. When I went to talk to the students, I said, "Who wrote this?" A girl raised her hand. I said, "Ma'am, do you know how big the screen at the Village Theatre in Westwood is? I know, because it was actually built for *2010*. It's seventy-five feet. Do you wanna rethink that shot?"

ADAM RIFKIN: It's always good to write something that you know you can write really well, especially when you're starting out. If you think you can write a horror movie better than anybody else, but you kinda think it'd be cool to write this drama about these nuns going across Australia in search of humanity or whatever, I would say, "Save the nun script for a script or two down the line, and write the script that you know you can nail."

KRISS TURNER: I was a writer on *The Bernie Mac Show,* and I was thinking about writing a screenplay. I knew I wanted it to be about relationships, and a friend of mine, Jacque Edmonds, who was working on another show, sent me this e-mail saying that 42.4 percent of black women have never been married. When I got that e-mail, I was like, *"42.4 Percent*—that's my title!" I remember typin' up the title page—you know, *"42.4 Percent,* Written by Kriss Turner"—and putting it on my corkboard in my office at *Bernie Mac.* It was such a passion piece. I'm telling you, I was so fired up, I couldn't stop thinking about the feature. I had to write it, write it, write it. . . . I wasn't thinking about money. *I had to write this thing.* Once you have something that you really want to say, you can pretty much go. I probably did a first draft in a little over a month.

DAVID S. WARD: When I choose a project, I choose it because it interests me. I know some are probably more commercial than others, but my feeling is that if it interests me, hopefully it'll interest someone else. It's only fun to work on something you really like. It's gonna be hard enough to do if you like it, and it's gonna be impossible to do if you don't like it. If you're workin' on somethin' you're not really into, you're not gonna do it very well. You're not gonna get good ideas. You're not gonna be inspired. You're not gonna be happy to get up every day and go to work on it—and its chances of being made are diminished because of that. Let the audience decide whether it's gonna be successful or not.

JOSH FRIEDMAN: Trying to game the system, trying to write a script that you think is gonna be the next thing, trying to get a jump on some trend—it's a big mistake. You know, people say, "Write what you know." I don't think you should write what you know, because, frankly, I don't know anything. I write what I like. I write science fiction because I love science fiction, and I write drama because I love drama. I think you need to write with enthusiasm, and short of enthusiasm, you need to write with anger. But if you write with indifference, you're gonna fail. Most likely you're gonna be rejected anyway, so at least throw your best pitch.

Stories for Sale

GUINEVERE TURNER: I had no idea that selling oneself was going to be such a huge part of the process, and that your ability to write is secondary only to your ability to walk into a room and present your ideas. Self-presentation is so huge, and I'm so bad at it. I always want to walk in and say, "Just let me do it. I swear to God, it'll be amazing." But sitting there with all of these people looking me and saying, "This is what it would look like," is crazy, because a script is already a description of a thing. It's a description of a movie. So to be describing the description of a thing . . . it's just existential madness to me, you know? But that's how you get the job.

JOHN CARPENTER: I have to confess, I have never gone in and verbally pitched anything in my career. I don't know how to do it. It's always on paper first, or a producer or studio head will say, "We'd like to do this," and I say, "Oh, I think I can do that." But in the broadest general terms, I would never be able to come in and tell a story, because I'm not that much of an actor. A lot of writers can do it really well. I can't.

DENNIS PALUMBO: Most writers are somewhat introverted, and yet we all know writers who are just wonderful salesmen, who bring a lot of bells and whistles and humor when they go into a pitch. You know, it sounds wonderful, and they have a great force of personality. The important thing to remember is that every career has people that are like that, whether they're car salesmen or lawyers or doctors—certainly politicians. There are going to be campaigners like Bill Clinton, and there are going to campaigners like Bob Dole. Don't try to become what you're not. It doesn't matter if by personality you tend to be a little more reticent or introspective. What matters is whether you can convey your enthusiasm for what you're doing to the person who is in the position to buy it. If you think of it less as selling and more as just explicating what's in your mind and heart—letting them know that this is something that you're excited about—then your natural way of being will be compelling.

JOHN D. BRANCATO: Always sit on the couch. That's my advice to wannabe writers when they get in there. Don't take the big chair—let the producer or the director take that. You want to stay out of the limelight. It's different in a pitch meeting, where they're all staring at you and they're hearing an idea for the first time—but even in that case, thinking about the room is smart. I often just shut up and let my writing partner talk, so I'm probably an especially small profile in a room.

Nobody likes a smart-alecky writer. I mean, we're the sort of people they wouldn't invite to their parties. If they could cut us out of the process altogether, they would. We're not like those people. We're sort of the lonely, nerdy guys, and they're the big partiers and the football captains and the pretty girls. Nobody wants to talk to us.

John D. Brancato

JOE STILLMAN: In terms of dealing with people, I would say that I came out of childhood with zero social skills, and I have been learning them slowly over the years—one at a time, skill by skill. It's vital. Even though you spend 95 percent of your time as a writer alone with your thoughts, that 5 percent that you're actually with others is key.

ANTWONE FISHER: You have to be wise. You can't go into a producer's office with a $20,000 watch on. You can't come in with an Armani suit on. You can't look like a rapper or something like that. People are not gonna take you seriously. You have to be authentic. You're a writer. I have a ball cap and a flannel shirt on—that's a writer. You have to be writer-like: eccentric, a little wily, a little confused—but when you answer back, it's so sharp you could cut them with it. They go, "Oh! I didn't know he was gonna do that." Being writer-like is pretending not to be as smart as you really are, and then turning it on.

STEPHEN SUSCO: Pitching is battle. You have a very short window of time to convince someone to spend a good deal of money on you and your idea. You're also pitching to people who hear tons of pitches all day. I do a tremendous amount of work before I go in—I never go in and wing it.

You have to pitch as if you're one of their comrades at the studio, saying, "Here's how we're gonna market the film, here's what the film is gonna cost, here's where we're gonna shoot it, here's what the audience is, here's what the rating is." You need to have all that in your head, and throw all that out in the room.

The second thing is to relax. For me, I just kind of say, "Okay, this is like when I used to go camping with my dad, and he would tell stories." You go in, you imagine everybody sitting around a campfire, and you tell the story. Remembering that storytelling is such an important part of what it means to be human lessens the pressure that you're gonna face, because they generally are very, very high-pressured situations.

ZAK PENN: People smell fear, and fear makes the story seem bad. One of the things that makes people uncomfortable is if you come in and you've rehearsed something, and then you lose your place and you get flustered. On the other hand, if I start to pitch you *Last Action Hero*, and I say, "Okay, so it's about this kid who gets sucked into a movie, and then he uses his powers . . . You know what? I'm sorry. I totally screwed that up. Let me start again. It's about a kid who gets sucked into an *action* movie. I can't believe I forgot that." You know what I mean? Don't be afraid to start over. It's a performance, so that's the equivalent of calling for a line. It's better than having a heart attack out there. Whatever makes you feel more confident is going to make the people that you're pitching to feel that way too, and it makes it easier for them to sit through your dumb idea.

DOUG ATCHISON: For five years, I went into offices and I made the pitch. I got very, very good at pitching *Akeelah and the Bee*. We were never, ever turned down because of the quality of the project—people loved the project. There was no mandate at any of these companies to make a movie about a little girl from the inner city who competes to get into the National Spelling Bee. It was so different from what they'd made, and there is a hesitancy to do anything risky or new by folks who are trying to keep their jobs. There was no upside to anybody in green-lighting this movie. I would go to meetings because they were looking for a writer for something else, and

I'd end up pitching *Akeelah and the Bee*. I would pitch *Akeelah and the Bee* to anybody who would listen, to try to get the film made.

JOSH FRIEDMAN: For *War of the Worlds*, Steven Spielberg came to me, and he wanted me to adapt the book. He said, "Think about it, and we'll talk about it." I worked up this whole take on the thing. I had this great idea, and I called him up to pitch him the idea. I remember he was on Martha's Vineyard, taking his son to a guitar store or something, and I'm trying to pitch him while he's parallel parking. I give him this whole big, great original take on it, and at the end of my twenty-minute monologue, he says, "Mmm, no." I say, "All right," and he says, "Yeah, I don't wanna do that."

I was devastated. I thought, "Well, there goes my chance."

I say, "Well, good luck with the project." He goes, "What do you mean? Don't you wanna do the movie?" I say, "Well, yeah, but you hate my idea. That's all I got." And he says, "Well, I like this one tiny little part over here in the corner—why don't we start with that, and let's go do it."

I got off the phone and called my agent, and I said, "Well, I think I just got the job, but I'm terrified, because I don't have an idea." You know, I find out I'm working for Steven Spielberg, and I don't have the first clue what we're doing.

RICHARD WENK: I had a thriller that I wanted to sell, and there was a famous movie actress who had a production company. The pitch began like this: "The movie's a film noir. It takes place in Palm Springs. It's about a blah, blah, blah." It's a very intricate whodunit, and it's a twenty-minute pitch. I finished, and she said, "That's fantastic, but I hate film noirs." I thought, "You coulda stopped me right there, okay? I didn't need to do the show." But, oddly enough, the next day I went into Gary Lucchesi's office at Paramount, and he bought it in the middle of the pitch. He just stood up and said, "I'll do it," so we developed it there.

ANDREW W. MARLOWE: I had a project at Fox, where I'd gone through all the steps, gone up the ladder, and my agent said, "They really wanna do a deal, but the vice president of production has to hear the pitch. It's pro forma. Just go in and tell the same story." I went in for this pitch, and I waited for an hour and a half for this guy to be ready. I go into his office, and he's on his couch moaning in pain. He had thrown his back out, and was going to go see his chiropractor in an hour to get it fixed. I said, "It doesn't seem like the best time to pitch to you—maybe I should come back when you're feeling a little bit better." And he goes, "No, let's just get it over with." So I didn't sell that project.

LARRY COHEN: You tell your idea, and inevitably everybody says it's wonderful. They walk you to the elevator—their arms around your shoulder—they thank you for coming in, they're all smiles, and the elevator door closes. Then you go home, and an hour later the agent calls and says, "They passed." You've never seen such effusive behavior, and then they tell you no. So I don't pay any attention anymore when people are responsive to something. I just say, "Let's see if they buy it or not." The tragic part is when you go in and pitch something and you do a very good pitch—then the person you pitch to goes down the hall and does a completely inadequate pitch, tryin' to paraphrase all the things you said. So what's getting turned down is not what you pitched—it's what they pitched.

LINDA VOORHEES: The rejection after a pitch is probably my most difficult time. You've gone in and had the personal encounter, so it feels like you went to someone's house and they uninvited you from the table. It's a very sociable event—you're drinking coffee, you're doing a chitty-chat, you're talking about the pictures they have on the shelf.

What's more, you typically like the person you're talking to. You're getting rejected by someone who's pleasant, sociable, letting you in the room, letting you drink their coffee, sit on their sofa. It just all feels dismal.

MICHAEL WOLK: I had many experiences in Hollywood of not pitching original ideas, but of going into meetings with producers who had a property already and were looking for a way to ignite it. It was either something that had lain dormant for a while, or it was a new property, or a sequel they were trying to create, and they were pumping writers for ideas.

I had a marvelous interaction with Dean Koontz, who is somewhat more popular than, let's say, me. He had written a book called *Mr. Murder,* and it was being developed as a script for Bruce Willis. I really liked the book, and I had some great ideas how to make it better for the screen.

I got down to the finals, and I was talking to Mr. Koontz himself over the phone. I was able to impart my story-making magic to Mr. Koontz, who listened. But in the end I was nixed for the job because, basically, Dean Koontz thought he'd written a pretty good story, and he didn't think I'd written a better one.

Michael Wolk

ALLISON ANDERS: The worst thing is when somebody sends you a script that they want you to rewrite or direct or both, and then you go in and pitch them your ideas. Then they use your ideas, and hire some dude that they wanted to hire all along to write it. Don't you think that should be illegal? I mean, shouldn't they have to pay you some money if they do that? I'm almost tempted to take a tape recorder. People tell me you can't copyright the ideas that are flowing like that, but I think you should be able to.

GUINEVERE TURNER: The hardest one was this adaptation of a teen novel called *The Grounding of Group 6*. It's a story about a camp counselor who takes all these kids into the woods and kills them, and all the kids slowly realize that their parents paid this camp counselor to kill them. Awesome story. Still hasn't been made. It was a really hard book to crack, and I came up with this great idea and presented it to New Line. They loved it, and they flew me to New York, and they had me pitch it to whatever executive was there. In the middle of the meeting, she went, "Oh my God, that's brilliant." And they gave it to another writer. They took my idea.

RICHARD RUSH: There are guys who have been very careful about it, writers who have kept their work under lock and key. I've been very casual about it. It's hard to get something sold and financed if you're not willing to show it off to the world and get as many people to read it as you possibly can. And then the question is: Can you get it made before you see it on the screen? I've never done a project without seeing two or three versions of the subject matter onscreen before I could get the picture financed and made. It happened with *Getting Straight*, and it happened with so many of the early exploitation pictures, and so on.

RICHARD WENK: I got a call from Sid Ganis. He was producing a movie called *Big Daddy* for Adam Sandler, and he thought I would be a great choice to direct it. So I met with Adam, who I liked a great deal, but I didn't get the job. A couple years later, I came up with an idea to remake *Mr. Deeds Goes to Town* for Adam. I told it to Sid. He went home and watched the original movie, and then he told Sony. I went to Sony and I pitched the idea, and they all flipped out. They thought it was a great idea. By the time I got home from the pitch, they wanted me off the project.

I don't know the real reasons why. I think that it was an easier sell with Adam and his own guys. But I didn't control the underlying rights to that, so I had no leverage. To their credit, they paid me a good sum of money, and that was that.

Same thing on a movie called *The Girl Next Door*. I heard Howard Stern on the radio with this porn star and a kid from high school who wanted her to come to his prom. I thought, "This is a movie." I pitched it to Harry Gittes, and he got Chuck Gordon, and then we all got together. I kept saying, "I think we should call Howard Stern. I think he's really bright, and it emanated from him." So we got him on the phone, and I told him the story. By the time we got off the phone, Howard wanted me off the project, even though he wasn't involved, and they wanted him.

But this one was mine. I said, "Listen, I don't wanna do a project people don't want me to be involved in. It's not really subject matter that is close to my heart, and I just think it could be a fun movie." They made me a deal, but they did it at the wrong time—they did it after they got a script they wanted to make, and then they had to come to me. I got a nice deal and an executive producer credit.

A Buyer's Market

ADAM RIFKIN: I grew up in Chicago, and I'd always wanted to make films, ever since I was a little kid. The idea of getting movies made seemed like this untouchable magic goal that was impossible to achieve. But I learned that the only difference between making a movie and not making a movie is having the money to make it with.

I didn't realize when I first got here that it was gonna be as hard to get the money as it is. Making movies is extremely expensive. Even low-budget movies cost a lot of money. I mean, a movie that costs $1 million is a really low-budget movie, but if you have to write a $1 million check, that's a big check to have to write for most people, right?

So I was surprised. I figured if you had a good enough script and enough energy and passion for a piece of material, that they're gonna see the quality on the page, and that getting money to get movies made is gonna be a snap. That's not true. It's really hard.

JOHN CARPENTER: I had a project at 20th Century–Fox, and they thought it was too violent, but it was a really, really good script. Later, the guy said, "I really liked it, but I had just come aboard as the production head of Fox, and I couldn't say yes to a violent film like this because I was scared of it at the time." Fair enough, you know? He's doing the job that he has to do as a suit, and I just moved on. It's a complicated deal, this whole issue of you going in and trying to get somebody interested in a project. You have to know what they want as much as what you want. That's the smartest advice I can give anybody: Know what they're looking for in your work. Try to put that in, and get what you want at the same time.

PAUL MAZURSKY: Let's take *Harry and Tonto*. They basically said, "It's a wonderful script, but I don't want to make a movie about an old man and a cat. I don't see the lines around the block." And I would say, as a joke, "What if the cat that he's taking across the country is filled with cocaine? Would you want to do the movie then?" One guy said, "Yeah, that might be interesting." The turndowns were brutal.

GERALD DiPEGO: Before this interview, I thought I would do a little homework. I made a column of original screenplays called "Sold and Produced," and I have three of those. "Sold but Not Produced": I have six of those. "Not Sold or Produced": I have nine. I was a little surprised. I thought, "Wow, that's a lot of pages that stayed on the shelf." You know, nine scripts, 120 pages each—that's a lot of pages that never saw the light of day.

There are some disappointments there. I remember I should have had a signal about this one script called *Rapture.* They bought an option on it at this production company. I walked in, and it's always a great feeling—they loved your script and they put some money on the table. The first thing the executive said to me was, "We really like your script for what it *can* be."

I did notice that the three scripts that were sold and produced are all speculative fiction. Not quite sci-fi, necessarily, but what I call the big "What if?" kind of scripts. Maybe the "What if?" ideas were more fresh, and there was nothing like them in front of the industry at the time. Maybe there's a little bit of a lesson there. I'm not sure.

JOE FORTE: Here comes the cliché—like most writers, I got into writing 'cause I want to direct. *Velvet Underground* was the screenplay that started getting me writing jobs, but simultaneously I was trying to get that film made. What I learned from that script is that every movie has math. And if you can't make the math of a movie work, you can't get your movie made. So that movie was, let's just say, really well written but really dark. It had a first-time director, it had a female in the lead, and it cost $4.5 million. The math of that movie was very tricky. If it wasn't dark, if it had a second-time director, and if it had a male in the lead, it would be a much easier movie to get made. Finally, after a couple of years, it was just impossible.

Gerald DiPego

So I had a new script, and I went out with that script to direct. That, too, didn't have the right math. Both of those films turned out to be heartaches. I had sort of let my screenwriting career peter out 'cause I was focusing on directing, so I sat down and I said, "Okay, I've gotta write a movie for a movie star."

MICK GARRIS: One of the most important things to learn is that there are plenty of good writers who've never been produced. Being produced doesn't mean your work is good. It just means it's filling a need that's had at that time.

ANDREW W. MARLOWE: They're looking at you as an investment in their own career. They're saying, "Okay, if I trust this guy with $80,000—or $800,000—is that an investment that's gonna pay off for the studio, and pay off for me personally in my career?" All these people are worried about their jobs, and if they bet on the wrong horse too many times, they're gonna get fired, and they're not gonna know how to feed their families and pay their rent. I met a lot of writers early on in my career who seemed to have this entitled attitude of "I'm talented. Why won't they invest $80,000 in this story about my grandmother's trip to Russia?" Well, maybe they didn't think that that was the best investment.

FRANK DARABONT: Don't get into this business if it's about trying to make a million-dollar sale. We've got plenty of assholes around trying to achieve that goal. There are more dilettantes in the game than real, committed, I'm-gonna-go-down-swinging kinda people. We need more of the latter and less of the former. We need people who care about this as an art form. Movies should count for more than an opening-weekend gross, because whatever had a huge gross this week, will they be talking about it in fifty years? Will it be credit to the art form, the way we talk about *Casablanca*?

They don't bury you with your bank account. But if you make something great, they'll remember you forever. That's what makes people sit down and develop their skills, and make the most of whatever talent God or the random universe has given you. Don't talk about being a screenwriter. Sit your ass in the chair, and even if takes you ten years—or nine years, like it took me—to start working as a professional, develop and hone your skills. Don't think that the first thing you're gonna write is gonna sell for a million dollars, 'cause I got news for you: It ain't.

I wasn't born into this, and I'm very lucky to be where I am, but it took a lot of effort and a lot of commitment to get there. You know, the harder you work, the more you make your luck. But if I'm any example, I would say that anything truly is possible. It's the Wild West, man. You can ride into town and you can wind up wearing a sheriff's badge if you want. But you gotta believe that that's possible, and then you've gotta work really hard for it, and not feel sorry for yourself 'cause all your friends are out gettin' drunk and gettin' laid and partyin' while you're sitting at home through most of your twenties writing, trying to tell a story that's gonna shock somebody or make somebody cry or make somebody laugh. How much do you love it? How much are you willing to give it? Only the person reading this can answer that.

MARK D. ROSENTHAL: I always get in trouble when I say this: I believe there is no great screenplay that hasn't at least been optioned. I believe there is no great screenplay that doesn't get the writer into the business. Most screenplays are mediocre or just okay. Really great writing always, always gets noticed in Hollywood. When I hear someone say, "It's who you know," or "I couldn't get it to the right agent," that is the consolation of failure. When it really works, it might not get made, because you need a Jupiter effect of a perfect director and a perfect actor—but if the writing is great, you always get into the game.

The Reader's Perspective: Kat O'Brien

Kat O'Brien

Companies throughout Hollywood employ staff and/or freelance readers to appraise incoming material. One such freelancer is Katherine "Kat" O'Brien. A graduate of USC's film school, she worked her way through the assistant and development ranks before becoming a professional story analyst. Her clients include independent producers, mini-majors, nonprofit organizations, and production companies. She's also a filmmaker.

The Reader's Role

My goal is to assess every script that I get from two stand-
points: Is this a strong story and is this commercial product?
I look at the concept and the premise, and then I examine the
execution, the structure, the storyline. Then I'm going to look
at the stakes and the tension, the characters, the relationships,
the dialogue, whether the material is emotionally resonant,
thematically relevant. And then I'll look at the commercial
potential. Where is it set? What are the production values?
Are there trailer moments? Is this a movie that can be made
within the right budget? Is it a good star vehicle for the specific talent that we want to work with?

You know when something is well written. It has a very
specific checklist of well-written things. It's structurally
sound, it masterfully utilizes all the right story mechanics—
and if it doesn't, it does so in such a unique and effective way
that it doesn't matter. The tricky part is that you have to know
exactly what matters and what doesn't matter in order for the
script to be palatable to the bosses.

I wanted to be an actress before I realized that my true
passion was writing and directing. In theater, once you step
on that stage, who you are and what you've been dealing with
takes a backseat, and it's just about the character and being
present in the moment. For reading a script, it's the same
thing. I read a script a couple weeks ago when I was on my
way to the ER with appendicitis. I was miserable. I was in the
worst physical agony I've ever been in in my life, but it was
due and I couldn't get ahold of another reader to pick it up

for me, so I had to do it. It was a good script, and I couldn't ignore that. I gave it a really great analysis.

I love the feeling that I'm out here pursuing my dream, and my dream is to tell really great stories. As a reader, I feel like I'm actually making a positive contribution to helping find great stories.

Write and Wrong

I think there are two kinds of writers. There's the kind who are arrogant about their work: "This is so fabulous, I'm going to revolutionize the world." And then there's the self-deprecating writer who says, "My writing sucks." I feel like a lot of self-deprecating writers don't have the confidence to actually submit their material, and the arrogant writers are like, "I want to be Steven Spielberg," instead of, "I want to be the best me that I can be." I don't think writers should aspire to be legendary. I mean, it's great to dream big, but I think that if you just focus on telling a good story, you'll eventually get to the place where you will have the power and influence to be legendary, if that's what you want to do. The key is finding the balance between those two extremes.

When you submit a script, there's caring, and there's caring too much, and there's not caring enough. If I see a script that has a ridiculously ornate and illustrated title page, I'm thinking, "Why does this writer feel that their words are not enough to get the point across?" Any sort of carelessness in the presentation is a turnoff. When someone doesn't take the time to research script formats, you wonder if this is truly a passion for them.

All of those factors go into giving a script a bad impression. It's just like anything else: If you're going in for a job interview and you show up in a smelly T-shirt and ripped jeans and one shoe that has the toe torn off, someone's gonna be like, "Okay, you don't really want this job."

In my opinion, and in the opinion of most of the people that I've worked with and worked for, putting out a script before it's ready is career suicide. Agencies all have internal coverage systems. I don't want to induce paranoia, but I think that it's really important to know. A script that's not ready to go out can find its way into some sort of permanent record. No matter what you do to revise it afterward, if that draft sucked—that's it.

I was very fortunate to have a really fabulous mentor at one of my internships. He read one of my early scripts when I was still in college, and he brought me into his office and sat me down. He was like, "This script is crap. You need to not show it to anyone. You're very lucky that I like you and I'm willing to read a revision from you. Most people wouldn't care."

Less Is More

A character description should be as spare as possible—one paragraph with the name in capital letters, the age in parentheses if you want to include that, and no more than a four-line description of what makes that character that character. Really focus on distilling it to its core. If a writer thinks of a physical habit that they can give to their character, that's a one-line way to make a character pop.

There are some things that are literary and internal in a good way, and there's some stuff that's literary and internal in a bad way. You just have to use your judgment and really look at the things that you're writing. It could be like, "I've just assigned this action to my character—how would I direct an actor to play that, or how would I play that if I was an actor?" I think that it's really helpful for all writers to take at least a basic acting class, or watch *Inside the Actors Studio*.

A really great screenwriter once told my screenwriting class that the best action should just be four lines. That's it. That's how I like to write, that's how I like to read. I think it keeps things moving quickly. When you encounter a page-long description—which I have encountered—it's miserable. This is not a book. This is a screenplay. Extremely dense, prosaic writing is an impediment, and when writers try to get too flowery or too descriptive, it's often a sign of a writer who hasn't fully matured into accepting what the craft of screenwriting is about.

I'd say it's most important to be passionate about the story that you're telling, and to know the reason for telling that story. Why does this story need to be told? If you can honestly answer that question, I think that's the first huge hurdle. That passion and that emotional resonance and that thematic relevance will come off the page, and will immediately elevate your story, and will engage your reader.

The second thing is make sure that your plot logic is coherent. I think the easiest way to do that is by having characters who have goals. One of the greatest things that Kurt

Vonnegut Jr. left behind was the idea that every single character should want something, whether it's a glass of water or to leave the room. Having all those characters wanting something can really drive your plot.

Writers really just need to understand that it's a long road. It's a marathon. It's a lot of marathons stacked on top of each other. You've just got to have the temperament and disposition to weather that and not get too frustrated by one thing or the other. Understand that there's a bazillion factors going into whether your script is going to get made. Most of it is luck. It really helps, if you get that good luck, that your script is good.

4

The First Yes

Beginning screenwriters must vault one last hurdle before becoming professionals—they must forge alliances with legitimate talent representatives, either agents or managers. Forever satirized as parasites who do little to earn the 10 (or 15) percent of their clients' earnings that they collect, agents and managers actually play crucial roles in the lives of the screenwriters they represent.

The most hands-on managers, for instance, provide comprehensive guidance on how to launch a career, or how to shift an established career into a higher gear. But even the busiest agent, who may have but a handful of minutes to offer any particular client in a given week, delivers not only access to buyers but also several layers of legal protection. Submitting material through agents ensures that ideas are as shielded from theft as possible, and ensures that contracts have the necessary safeguards.

The problem, of course, is that getting an agent is impossible. Or at least it seems that way. Most reputable agents refuse to read unsolicited submissions, because doing so exposes them to legal liability. Therein lies the conundrum: Agents only want to work with established clients, but writers can't become established without agents. Yet new writers land representation every day, either by networking their way to referrals or by earning sufficient notoriety to catch the attention of agents and managers.

Once the two elements of talent and representation are mixed, the conditions are finally right for a rare chemical reaction to occur: the actual sale of a screenplay. Initial success in Hollywood can occur by multitudinous means, as the anecdotes in this chapter prove. From Michael Wolk's fairy-tale experience of selling the first screenplay he ever wrote, to Antwone Fisher's touching realization that a Hollywood paycheck was about to change his life, stories about joining the ranks of working screenwriters are as varied as they are inspiring.

That said, success introduces a raft of unexpected challenges. Frank Darabont was intimidated by the prospect of crafting a follow-up to his Oscar-nominated directorial debut. Shane Black withdrew from public life for several years because of the unwanted attention his record-setting paychecks attracted. In one way or another, every screenwriter who achieves success wrestles with the bewildering sensation that Oscar nominee Richard Rush describes as "free fall."

Don't Call Us, We'll Call You

STEPHEN SUSCO: Getting an agent is the biggest catch–22 that there is: No one will read your stuff without an agent, but an agent won't read your stuff. It takes a lot of work for an agent to break in a new writer, so the things they're gonna look for are really straightforward. One, a really good personality, because they have to put you in a room with people. Two, that you have very strong visions, but you can play ball creatively. Three, that you don't just have one spec script—you've got multiple scripts, multiple pitches, multiple outlines. They want you to make their job easier. If you go in as a creative force with a lot of business sense and say, "I'm willing to work harder than you will work for me," that's the key to maximizing your ability to get an agent.

JUSTIN ZACKHAM: My first manager was my girlfriend's mom. She just represented actors, and she decided to try to take me on as a writer. She got me an agent. Very nice guy, but I knew more having been in Hollywood for two weeks than he knew having been here for five years. I started out with him. I was at ICM (International Creative Management) for maybe two months before they got rid of me, and then I just decided I didn't need an agent. I went for about six, seven years without an agent. Then I landed at William Morris, and, you know, they're agents. They don't do a whole lot. The letterhead gets your scripts read, and studios tell them what projects are available first. Aside from that, in my experience, the whole agent thing is a nice way to throw away 10 percent of what you make. It's the necessary evil.

MIKE BINDER: What you will find out in the long run is that agents have very little power over you. In the beginning, you think you work for them. In the end, they work for you. It's like a bank. You know, once you have money in the bank, they're gonna do their job or you move to another bank. If you don't have any money and you need a loan, you've gotta jump up and do flips in the lobby of the bank. You really don't want to start off with the biggest agent in town, because they won't take the time to believe in you. You want someone who's really gonna be there and walk you through it. What you've gotta have is someone that really believes in you and helps you learn to believe in yourself.

MARK D. ROSENTHAL: The business has gotten too busy. The pace has gotten too fast. It's gotten so much harder to find gigs for clients, so agents can't have the relationship with clients they used to have in the old days: "Let's just go out to lunch once a week and talk things over." There's not as much hand-holding allowed. Obviously if you're Tom Cruise or Tom Hanks, you get hand-held because you're bringing in so much money—but young writers coming into the business today are not gonna get the guidance that an agent used to give. That's a real problem.

PAUL MAZURSKY: My first important agent was Freddie Fields. Famous agent. When *Bob & Carol & Ted & Alice* was made, it was a big hit. And when you've made a big hit, the unwritten rule is you can have five disasters. My next picture was *Alex in Wonderland*, which was one disaster. The next script that I handed in was *Harry and Tonto*, and that was turned down about twenty-five times. Freddie Fields said to me, "You only need one yes." He loved it, I loved it, and we got it made. Art Carney won the Academy Award for the movie, and I was nominated for the Academy Award.

LARRY COHEN: I had a wonderful agent, Peter Saberston, who passed away but who represented me for probably thirty-five, forty years. He wasn't a major agent, but he kept me workin' all the time 'cause I was his primary client. I wasn't just one of a stable of clients; I was the guy who was gonna bring home the bread and butter. If I worked, he was gonna make money. If I didn't work, he wasn't gonna make money. He was out there beatin' the bushes every day, and he got me plenty of jobs over the years. It was an unorthodox way to work. Most writers wanna go with a big agency, but I found that the material speaks for itself. If you've got something good, it can be sold.

Larry Cohen

DAVID S. WARD: It was a bit of serendipity how I got my first agent. I was living in Venice. Small $75-a-month apartment across from a place called the Venice Skill Center. It's a place where they teach people how to be auto mechanics, stenographers, things like that. It's where I got my scripts typed, because I don't type. The guy who ran the place, his wife had had a small fender-bender with an agent, and they'd become friends. He said to me, "I'll give your script to the agent, see what he says." The agent was a guy named Stu Miller, at the Melbourne Agency. He read the script and really liked it, and that's how I got my start. He was actually the agent that got *Steelyard Blues* done, and *The Sting* as well.

SHANE BLACK: Getting an agent or manager is essential. It's the most important thing for a young screenwriter, to have their work made available to the industry by someone with more credibility, so people don't just toss it when it comes over the transom. For me, it was about getting momentum through this group of friends who I was with in college. We all came up together. One of us would get an agent, and then he would reach down the ladder a rung and help someone else up. Then I would in turn help someone after me, and we'd sorta leapfrog up the ladder, each providing whatever access we could by banding together as a group instead of trying to take on Hollywood one by one. It's important to find a group of like-minded people who are on the same wavelength, who wanna write screenplays as badly as you do, who aren't selfish, who support you. If you're sinking or you're drowning, it's nice to have somebody else in the boat.

JOHN D. BRANCATO: I remember that the Writers Guild used to issue a piece of yellow paper with a list of all the agencies on it, including ones with little asterisks that said they will only accept submissions from people they know. The big agencies were all that way. I mean, CAA (Creative Artists Agency) and William Morris and ICM won't accept anything over the transom. But there were a handful of little agencies that would read screenplays, even from a nobody like me. I sent out a spec screenplay to every single one of them, and I met with a couple of them.

I wound up with an agent who had a little studio apartment off Hollywood Boulevard. She had once had a job at an agency, years and years before. She was actually getting elderly and she sorta smelled funny, but she said, "I'll be your agent." She would have been anybody's agent, I think, but she took me on, and she was my first agent. She beat down enough doors that I got a couple of meetings. I got a meeting with Stan Lee through her, and hit it off with Stan right away. I thought he was a great, funny guy, and he hired us to write a draft of *Spider-Man*.

I don't think you get a decent agent until you have some work that's been seen, that people have talked about. Prior to that, anything will do.

JONATHAN LEMKIN: If you don't know anybody, you definitely have to lie. I cold-called everybody on the WGA list who would take submissions and spoke to them. Most of them weren't that useful. Then I read the trades and found out who was opening new agencies, called them, and claimed I knew friends of theirs. Sometimes I would know somebody who would give me a name. Eventually, an agent busted me. She said, "You don't really know this person, do you?" I said no. She said, "I'll read it anyhow."

BILLY RAY: My father was a literary agent and a good one. He represented some of the best writers ever: Alvin Sargent and Frank Pierson and Paul Brickman. . . . Quite a list. Well, he didn't want to represent me because he was my father, so I had to find an agent like everybody else.

There was this one agent who worked at a very small agency, the H. M. Swanson Agency. The agent's name is Bruce Kaufman. I liked him. I thought he was smart and I thought he was hungry. But I didn't want to make him uncomfortable, because I did business with him. By this point, I was not just a gofer for these two TV producers, but I was kind of a junior executive for them, and I was dealing with agents.

So I called Bruce and said, "I've just read this novel that I think you should see." I tore the title page off, and I sent him the novel that I'd written. He called me back a couple of weeks later and said, "I like this very much, who wrote this?" I said, "I did. Will you represent me?" He said yes, and he's been my agent ever since. The joke is that I'm trying to make it through my career with one agent and one wife, and so far I've managed on both counts.

STEPHEN SUSCO: I got my first job while I was still a film student. I got it in my third semester of school, and it was a pretty big job even though we got paid WGA minimum. It was an established director, Ted Demme, and New Line Cinema was producing it, and the whole thing was packaged by CAA. So my writing partner and I said, "This is it. CAA is gonna represent us, and they're huge, and it's gonna launch our careers. We're set."

Right after we got the job, CAA called us in for a meeting. So we put on our best suits and sat in the waiting room and looked at the atrium, and we were just overwhelmed by CAA. The third assistant came down and introduced himself and brought us upstairs. Then we sat in that waiting room, and the second assistant brought us in to the first assistant. We kept getting closer and closer—it was like an airlock.

We finally got brought in to meet the agent, and it was probably a three- to four-minute meeting. He sat us down and he said, "Look, we don't know who the fuck you guys are. We handle Ted Demme, we do business with New Line—that's all great. You guys are brand-new writers and you're getting paid nothing for this, so we're not really gonna do anything for you. All I can tell you is after you leave my office, you should go try to find another agent if you can. And then, years from now, when we're beggin' to have you back, tell us to go fuck ourselves. Have a nice day."

The Right Place at the Right Time

WILLIAM GOLDMAN: I was teaching at Princeton University, and I'd been working on *Butch Cassidy* for six or eight years. I wrote the script over Christmas vacation, and when it went out, for God knows what reason, every studio but MGM wanted it. My late, great agent, Mr. Everett Ziegler, got an auction going. Dick Zanuck at Fox bought it for a phenomenal amount of money, $400,000. That became headline news—small headline news—all around the country: "Screenplay Sells for $400,000." Because everybody knew the directors had all the visual concepts, and they didn't know why this novelist out of New York got that obscene amount of money.

PAUL SCHRADER: I had written *Taxi Driver* as a kind of self-therapy, and then I drifted around to get myself back together. I stayed on the couches of various college friends in Montreal, Maine, North Carolina. And while I was in North Carolina, I got a letter from my brother, who was in Kyoto, Japan. He wrote this long letter about the yakuza films that he had gotten obsessed with. The Bruce Lee fad was very successful at that time, and it occurred to me that maybe the next phase of Asian martial-arts movies would be Japanese gangsters. My brother and I met up in Los Angeles and wrote *The Yakuza*.

The Yakuza was sold for the highest fee going at that time. It got involved in an auction—the first day, there were sixteen bids—and so that immediately gave me a profile. I decided I better write as fast and as hard as I could, so I just started writing. Writing like crazy. Wrote *Obsession*, wrote *Rolling Thunder*, wrote *Hardcore*. Just started trying to knock these things out as quickly as I could. I was only writing on spec. At that time, I felt I could work faster on spec—by the time you pitched an idea and made a deal, you could have written the script.

Paul Schrader

GERALD DiPEGO: After I did *Sharky's Machine*, I had the feeling of, "Well, that's kind of kicked me into the feature realm now." But the features I wrote after that did not sell or were not produced, so the feature career didn't build on itself immediately, whereas television networks were calling me all the time with assignments. There were some assignments I really liked, so I didn't strictly write features after that. It was just a matter of timing. I wasn't able to build on *Sharky*, so it was really *Phenomenon* that kicked me into features to stay, because I was able to follow that up. It made enough of a noise that it pushed me over into features.

ROBERT MARK KAMEN: This is a true story. The day I sold my first novel, I got the call from my New York book agent, and they said, "Simon and Schuster is going to buy your novel, and they're gonna give you $25,000." I had written two chapters, and it was this huge tome about Japan and America in World War II. I figured I had two years of work ahead of me. Ten minutes later, the phone rings and it's Warner Bros. saying they wanna buy my screenplay for $135,000. I never looked back. I never thought about writing another word of fiction. I went straight for the money.

STEVEN E. de SOUZA: I wrote three pilots for Paramount that all sold, and the last one was for the producer Lawrence Gordon. After I did that, it was like the young fighter who gets told, "You know, you're pretty good with your fists and you've got good footwork—I'd like to move you up into the middleweights." He said, "Listen, we have a picture that we've had in development for a number of years, and we wanna do a big rewrite on it. We wanna assign you to this picture." It was *48 Hrs.*

I did the production rewrite of that picture, which was a big change. The script had been around so long that originally the seasoned cop was gonna be played by Robert Mitchum, and the young aggressive punk in jail was gonna be Clint Eastwood. Now it was Nick Nolte and Eddie Murphy, who had done nothing except *Saturday Night Live*.

I did a couple more movies for the same group, for Lawrence

Gordon and Joel Silver. I did *Commando*, and then I did *The Running Man*. One thing led to the other. I was lucky to hit my stride at a time when the kind of movies I liked hit their stride—not just in America, but in the global marketplace.

JOHN D. BRANCATO: The first few years, I was writing low-budget movies. I worked for Roger Corman, worked for other entities making movies for next to nothing. It was great because they actually got made. You finally hear how dialogue sounds in the mouths of actors, and get a sense of how your ideas really don't work when they're finally thrown up there. You learn a lot right away. But after about four or five years, it felt like it was a dead end. Doing another thing from the outtakes of *Iron Eagle* was just so depressing. I couldn't stand it. I thought I owed it to myself to write a screenplay that I really liked—to give it my best shot before I left the industry. I came up with an idea, and worked it out with my partner, and sold it right away. That's the movie that became *The Game*.

MICHAEL WOLK: When I wrote my first screenplay, it was sort of an unusually blessed event. I'd written a couple of mystery novels, and decided to try my hand at a screenplay. I was represented by an agent who had never sold a screenplay. She'd only sold novels. She read it, didn't know what to make of it, showed it to a friend of hers named Raymond Bongiovanni, who was a great literary guy here in New York, and he loved it. They sent it on to William Morris, established a co-agent relationship, and the screenplay sold for a lotta money. It was back in the nineties when there was this wild auction market for spec scripts. When I went to L.A. for my victory tour, people said, "This never happens"—and I must say it never happened again.

GUINEVERE TURNER: Because the world that it represented was so unfamiliar to people, and because the style of it was so scrappy, I think people perceived *Go Fish* to be a documentary, basically, and thought the script was kind of a one-off. And so in terms of being acknowledged and appreciated as a screenwriter, I think the breakthrough moment for me was *American Psycho*. That was complete and utter street cred. The amazing thing about that project was that before it was even made—because Leo DiCaprio was connected to it at some point, and because he had just come off of *Titanic*—it suddenly became, "Oh, you wrote *American Psycho*? We love *American Psycho*." I got jobs off of that movie before it was even made, because the script had buzz.

ANTWONE FISHER: When Todd Black, who produced *Antwone Fisher*, sold my story to 20th Century–Fox, I still didn't get that my life was gonna be changing. Even the money I was paid, I didn't get how much it really was. I'd never had that much money before. If someone gave me, like, fifty or a hundred dollars, I could say, "Oh, that's a hundred dollars." But when someone gives you that much money . . . I had to think about it, and it took a long time to realize that I could actually afford a new pair of shoes.

ZAK PENN: Being part of a spec auction, where your agent is calling, and you have no money, and they're saying, "They just bid a hundred thousand," "They just bid two hundred thousand . . ." It's like winning the lottery for something that you actually did, as opposed to for luck. It's a really, really thrilling feeling. I joke with friends that the time I won the grand prize on a game show was the best moment of my life—then the birth of my kids, then selling my first script. That might actually be ahead of my kids. Then maybe selling my second script, and then maybe getting married. You know what I mean? The thrill that you get from those sales—it just feels like you've been validated somehow. I don't think I'd feel that way now. I'm probably a little too jaded. I don't think I'd be literally falling to my knees. Now the thrill comes from watching the final product.

ANDREW W. MARLOWE: In the film business, there is never one breakthrough moment. It's always a series of moments.

When I won the Nicholl Fellowship for my USC thesis script, that got me a lot of attention. From there, I got hired on to do a couple of jobs. And then my first real big break, I think, was when we got *Air Force One* off the ground—when the script went to Harrison Ford and he said yes.

You never really succeed. You always fail at a higher level. As a screenwriter, the first level of failure is you can't finish your screenplay. I saw a lot of those people in film school. Then you finish the screenplay, and nobody wants to read it. Then you get somebody to read it, and they're not interested. You get them to read it and they're interested, but you can't sell it. Then you sell it, but it's not made into a movie. Or it's made into a terrible movie that you're embarrassed to be associated with. Or, you know, you hit the jackpot. You get the movie made, it's a critical success, it's a box-office success—and everybody turns to you and says, "Okay, you gotta do it again."

You're always climbing that mountain. Sometimes it's the same mountain, sometimes it's a different mountain. But even when you get to the top, there's this realization: "Okay, the view is great, but tomorrow I gotta get up and start climbing the mountain again."

Andrew W. Marlowe

The Catastrophe of Success

PETER HYAMS: There are two breakthrough moments you have, in my opinion. The first is when you actually get in—you know, when you sneak under the flap of the circus tent and actually get inside. That's a breakthrough. That separates you from everybody else who's trying to get in. And then the probably more significant breakthrough is when you do something that's successful.

The first thing that I ever did that was successful was a thing I wrote and directed called *Capricorn One*. We screened the picture, and there was this unbelievable reaction, and I stood in the back of the theater and reacted as I do to most things: I started to cry. I realized that there was a sea change in my life. Somehow or another, things wouldn't be exactly the same again.

I was with a very smart guy named David Picker, who had run United Artists and Paramount and Columbia. After the screening, he put his hand on my shoulder, and he said, "You're gonna have a lot of brand-new best friends tomorrow morning. You better learn how to handle it."

RICHARD RUSH: Most of us have been pushing very hard against a wall, and we've been pushing and pushing for so long, that when it suddenly disappears, we free fall into space. And that is a fair definition of success. You've gotta be aware of the sensation of the tumble—of momentarily losing the resistance you're used to.

ANDREW W. MARLOWE: I've seen a lot of writers who have gotten that first big break, and they have then gone off and partied and hung out and gone to lunch with everybody in town. Six months later, they've been having lunches and they haven't done the work. It's very important to keep doing the work, because you're a writer. That is now your career. I've seen some people fall into that trap. And then I've seen people who have had a lot of success act like they're, you know, the Second Coming—and they never are. Maybe you get one a generation who can afford to be an arrogant prick.

JAMES L. WHITE: I decided to keep the smoke in my ass and not let it get to my head, you know what I mean? Because there's a lotta smoke that comes at you, and if you start believing the hype, then you can't be creative. *Ray* was nice. I'm really, really happy with it. I'm very proud of it. But now I've gotta move on to something else. I've gotta make the next piece I do better than that. Creativity demands that you do something new all the time. You might be tellin' the same story, but you gotta have a nuance in it. It can't be the same licks over and over again. If the next film I make looks just like *Ray*, well, where have I grown?

Doug Atchison

DOUG ATCHISON: Because of *Akeelah and the Bee*, I get sent a lot of stuff about little kids, a lot of stuff about sports and overcoming adversity. I like those kinda movies, but I need to diversify. You know, *Akeelah* is the only spelling-bee movie I'm ever gonna do, and it's an absolutely distinct piece of writing from everything else I've ever written. And yet it is the piece that defines me almost entirely to the business right now. I don't get sent *The Departed*, you know? I would love to write a movie like that. That's not what I get sent. Right now, I have to take advantage of those opportunities that seem like they'll be good projects. But I also need to write some other scripts that I'm not getting paid for, to show folks I can do these other things. You always have to redefine yourself for people, and convince them that you're not a one-trick pony.

JOE FORTE: Having a movie come out, first of all, takes the monkey off your back. No matter what happens to you for the rest of your life, you made a movie. When you're trying to get there, that's a big cloud over your head. You want to have something that's concrete evidence of all the work you've put in. So the psychological aspect of completing your goal is great.

When *Firewall* came out, I felt the pressure to sell the next piece, to get another movie made, to keep it going—and I think I got myself into the position where I had to stop and realize that the person who was creating that pressure was actually me.

Once you get one produced, then you're like, "Well, that's not good enough. I need two produced." You create a consumption mentality, and the way I stopped that mentality was to focus on what I loved. If I write something that people don't respond to, despite my best efforts, then that's just where the chips fall. I think it's really about being on a path that's authentic to you.

SHANE BLACK: With my early deals, there was such insane scrutiny. The numbers were very large. I got this mixed-bag reaction from people, which I didn't expect. Some writers were very angry. I wanted to be invisible and vanish from the equation, and not be accountable for the money I was making. I just wrote the story—it's not my problem who offers to pay for it. I just wanted to disappear and again become a guy who wrote stories. I didn't want to deal with this insanity.

The first time I applied to be a member of the Academy of Motion Picture Arts and Sciences, my friend Dale Launer offered to sponsor me. The criteria for entry is you need at least two produced pieces of work of substantive merit in the motion picture field. At that time, I had *Lethal Weapon, Lethal Weapon 2, Last Boy Scout, Long Kiss Goodnight, Last Action Hero, Monster Squad*—and they turned me down. They said, "We don't feel that your credits warrant membership in the Academy, but perhaps you can reapply at a future date when you have more credits."

This was after all those sales, and I went, "This can't be just about the work." It had to be that money. It had to be these writers sittin' around going, "We don't want *that* guy in here, that one who made all that money."

So for a while, I kind of crawled in a wormhole. I came out again to write and direct a small movie I'm very happy with, and now, hopefully, I'll keep going, but . . . be careful what you wish for. That big paycheck—on two occasions, bigger than anybody had received for screenwriting in history—was a curse that ended up taking me out for a few years. I was scared. Petrified. That kind of money can freeze you up and cause all kinds of unforeseen problems.

FRANK DARABONT: When your first movie out of the gate gets that kind of response—you know, your first movie gets nominated for Best Picture, Best Screenplay—it can be daunting. It can be somewhat crippling. It's like, "How are you gonna top that?" Maybe you shouldn't even try. That was probably one of the reasons it took me about five years to direct another movie, because I was looking for material that had the same kind of meat, the same kind of meaning—and that's not easy to find. Those stories are very rare. It's hard to find a *Shawshank* every time you make a movie. If it were easy, everybody would be making *Shawshank*.

It really just goes to show that the story is the thing that will spark. It's not necessarily the efforts of the actors, or the skill of the director, or the skill of the screenwriter. For something to become special, in a way it kinda transcends and supersedes all of those components. It becomes something greater than itself, and that's not something you can plan for.

BILLY RAY: When I first began, I was a bit of a flavor of the month, and I was writing two scripts for this very powerful producer. It was around Christmastime, and I went into her office to get notes on one of the projects. As I was walking into her office, I saw this computer printer, and it was spitting out a list. I looked, and at the very top of the list it said "AA," and it was the name of her husband and her agent. Then it said "A," and a bunch of other names. I thought, "Okay, this is her Christmas list." A voice inside me said, "Billy, don't look at this list, because you don't want to know where you are. It'll just depress you."

So I went and had my meeting, and a couple of days later, a messenger from her office showed up at my door and presented me with this great silver tray with a gingerbread house on it, and the gingerbread house was inlaid with lights and candies. I mean, it was fantastic. I thought, "You know, I'm not 'AA,' but I'm 'A,' and that's pretty good."

That year passed. And during that year, the two projects that I was writing for her both went into turnaround. Christmastime came, and I thought, "Hmm, something tells me there's no silver tray coming for me this year." So sure enough, a messenger from her office shows up one day in late December, and he presents me with this great-looking gift basket. In the gift basket is, you know, wine and cheese and salami. I thought, "Okay, you know what? I'm not 'A,' but I'm 'B,' and 'B' is okay." You know, I'm still a twenty-five-year-old kid at this point, so I've learned my lesson, and it's fine.

A couple hours later, there's this call from her office saying, "Did you get a gift basket from us?" I said yes. And they said, "Don't open it." I asked why, and they said, "We sent you someone else's gift, and we sent yours to him." I said, "Look, he'll take my basket, I'll take his basket. It's no big deal." They said, "Do not open the basket," so I said, "Okay."

Ten minutes later, I hear this screech of brakes outside my apartment, and this set of panicked footsteps going up my stairs, and then this out-of-breath production assistant knocks on my door. I open it, and he says, "Do you have a gift basket?" I said yes, and I hand him the gift basket, and there was a card on it addressed to some young ICM agent. He takes it, and then he hands me a tin of yogurt-covered pretzels.

When people ask me what it's like to be a young screenwriter in Hollywood, that's the story I tell.

The Agent's Perspective: Richard Arlook

Richard Arlook

Richard Arlook spent eighteen years at the Gersh Agency, eventually becoming a partner and the head of the firm's motion picture literary department, before shifting to his current role as a manager-producer at his own firm, the Arlook Group. His stable of writers, directors, and writer-directors includes artists ranging from emerging talents to established veterans.

The Accidental Agent

I came out here to produce movies. I went from taking any job I could, which was as the contestant coordinator on *Tic Tac Dough,* to my first job in the film business, which was as a foreign sales guy, to getting into the studio area by working as an assistant to Scott Rudin, who was running Fox. I took all that experience, wrote a business plan, and approached some successful commercial producers who wanted to get into the movie business. That's how I became a producer. I started a company in 1986, when I was twenty-four. Two and a half years later, MGM green-lit this movie I had called *After Midnight.* MGM was going through an upheaval, and the minute all the big TV buys and the release plan changed, I knew the movie was going to video. For the time being, it was over for me as a producer.

I got this opportunity to become an agent at Gersh, and I started there in 1990. They needed somebody young who could find new talent, and I had been in all these different worlds where you discover new talent.

In representing writers, my function is to sell their screenplays, secure employment for them, and negotiate the terms of their deals. The time from when I get handed a script to it getting made could sometimes be five, seven, ten years—and the large majority of scripts never get made. I probably sell ten to fifteen out of every fifty scripts. But then, out of every twenty that I sell, maybe two get made. Because those are the stats, every time you've actually gone through that process— from where you're the first one to read the script to actually seeing it projected on the big screen—it's a certain kind of high, you know?

It's a great feeling to discover young talent—that guy working in the video store, or the woman working at a Starbucks. This person who's been on their feet all day to make $25,000 a year, and literally within months you're handing them a check for $50,000 on their first payment, or $100,000, or sometimes even more. I mean, there was a guy that I met, and within weeks, I sold his script and handed him $250,000. He was this close to being evicted. To know that your good work and your brains and your passion have had a positive effect on somebody's life—to me, that's an exciting thing. It doesn't hurt that when you do your job well, you can get compensated well.

The Representative's Role

I'm very concerned about my clients and their lives, beyond just the writing. There are times where you get somebody when they have nothing, and then they start earning money. You see them get married and have kids, and they put the kids in private school, and they buy that dream house because all of a sudden they're making $300,000 to $1 million a year. Then they turn in something and it isn't received well, and they can't get hired. When they start hurting, if you're a human, you start hurting. And so when somebody's hurting, the conversations are, "How are we gonna get the train back on the tracks?"

If somebody's doing really well, the conversations tend to

be more like, "How are we gonna sustain what we have?" You don't speak to every client the same way, because everybody's in a different place.

Because I'm on the front lines, a client will always rely on me to say, "Here's what's going on in the marketplace. This is what they tell me they're looking for and not looking for." It's my job to know that. Having read countless scripts, I can also make an argument that I'm as expert as the next guy on what makes a good screenplay, but the relationships with writers are always different. I have young writers who look up to me because I was reading scripts and selling scripts, in some cases, before they were born. But some established client who's been in the business longer than I have doesn't really wanna hear me feed him lines of dialogue.

I define *commercial* as any script that I can sell. I could also say that a commercial screenplay is something that has a big idea, something that's multiquadrant, something that's a very castable piece, something that's gonna attract a director or an actor. All those things enable the studio to green-light the script. That makes it commercial.

If an agent is good, he's gonna be able to guide a client in terms of what's selling, what isn't selling, what's gonna require an actor, what's gonna require a director. When that agent reads a script, he'll be able to identify what's working and what's not working, and give the client feedback and notes and guidance.

Spotting the Reptiles

There are people that really love being involved in movies, who care about taking the ride with their clients. When they're in a signing meeting, they say, "I'm gonna be there for you through thick and thin," and they view the relationship as a marriage. I think it's very hard for those people to be agents. Those are the warm-blooded people. And then there are the reptiles.

The reptiles are completely cold-blooded: This is a war, so everything is fair. They'll poach other people's clients. They'll say anything to get somebody on their roster, and as long as the client's generating a lot of money, they will find the time to keep the client happy. The minute the client gets cold, the agent can't give them the attention they need at the time they need it most. Those agents tend to be very, very successful people. Those same people go home and read to their children, and are loving husbands and loving wives, and give to charity—I call them the reptiles because they have the ability to cut themselves off emotionally.

When I was a young producer, I never really got the time of day from agents. So when I became an agent, I was like, "I'm gonna treat people the way I always wanted to be treated." I used to be upset that I would call agents wanting material from them, and they'd laugh at me.

And then, when I became an agent, and I would sign a young writer that became hot, all of a sudden I'd get a call from somebody saying, "I want that guy's next script." I'd be like, "I can't give you that guy's next script," and they wouldn't understand. They thought just because they were passionate producers, that was enough. But I'm thinking, "I finally have this hot writer, and he's got an action script. I'm not gonna give it to Joe Schmoe, I'm gonna give it to Joel Silver and Jerry Bruckheimer."

A lot of things happen when you become an agent. You see how difficult the business is, and for survival purposes, you have to become a lot tougher. Sometimes in success, a lot of the reptiles become a little warmer. And sometimes in reality, a lot of the warm-blooded ones become more reptilian.

What Writers Need to Hear

What writers want to hear in a signing meeting and what they need to hear are two different things. If you've written a script, you ask an agent, "Can you sell this?" Well, the honest answer is, "I believe I can because I read it and I loved it, and that's why we're here. But can I guarantee you that I can sell it? No." The reptile will say, "Absolutely! How is this not gonna sell?" It's so infectious that the writer just wants to believe it.

Plenty of people have met with me and met with somebody else—and I'll get them because people can read through the bullshit. And there's plenty of times when they'll go with that other person, and six months later they're calling me because the script hasn't sold and the agent's not returning their calls.

With the scripts I have to read that are sent to me with referrals, the scripts that my clients are creating that I need to give them notes on, the scripts that are being submitted to me for clients to direct or rewrite—that's already three, four scripts a week. There's only so much time in the day. So it's not that I won't read an emerging writer's script—it's that it has to come to me by a referral.

Short of me getting the greatest script in the world that I sell tomorrow for $1 million and then start booking this guy in $400,000 writing assignments nonstop, it's gonna take time to get an emerging writer a job or sell their first script. At this point in my life, that's not a good use of my time when I've already got people in my stable that have established quotes, that are a lot easier to sell.

It's the responsibility of the writer to realize that and to target the proper agent. When I first started off and I didn't have any clients, I would read twelve, fifteen scripts a weekend—or at least attempt to. So it's not that emerging writers can't get their work read. You just need to be smart about who you approach to read your work.

5

What's Yours Is Theirs

Once a screenplay has been purchased, the arduous work of turning it into an actual movie begins. Long before the cameras roll, an intricate dance takes place during which the various parties controlling the script present their ideas for how the screenplay should be modified. This process is known as "development." The fundamental problem with the process is that everyone involved has subjective viewpoints about which suggestions are improvements and which are not. Furthermore, toxic elements—including careerism, personal rivalries, and professional vanity—ensure that other priorities eclipse the best interests of the story. More often than not, scripts get mired in conflicting agendas, resulting in unfilmable rewrites that extinguish whatever enthusiasm the various parties originally had for the piece. When a script suffers this fate, it has been consigned to the netherworld famously known as "development hell."

Writers entering the Hollywood fray need to understand many things about development. First, they must accept that they become temporary employees of companies that buy their scripts. Second, they have to realize that their material will be altered with or without their permission, so the challenge is to make the requested modifications in a way that improves the screenplay, or at least shrinks the blast radius of damaging changes. And third, they need to remember that hundreds of other screenwriters are ready, willing, and able to step in as replacements should the original writer on a given project be deemed unable (or unwilling) to perform the desired revisions. The prospect of getting fired is omnipresent, and the reasons why screenwriters lose their jobs are as maddening as they are myriad.

When entering the development process, the smart Hollywood writer keeps his or her eyes on the prize: screen credit on a movie that actually gets made. Distasteful as it may seem to beginners, the screenwriter's job at this stage is to acknowledge that the same people who bought a script may not yet consider it worthy of being filmed. The individual who embraces this paradox has a shot at not only preserving employment, but also transporting a story from the printed page to the silver screen.

It's Great! Now Change Everything

MARK D. ROSENTHAL: I think the public would be shocked to see how many movies that end up horrific started out as pretty good screenplays, or at least screenplays that you'd say, "Oh, I see why the studio made this movie—it's kinda funny, it's kinda silly, it's stupid but the action's really cool." It's just that in the process of what they do to screenplays, the material gets chopped, and mashed, and turned out.

JANE ANDERSON: The development process is often an opportunity for a studio to pay you for one draft of a script, but get you to write about thirty. There are many executives out there who use writers for what I call "piggyback creativity," because they can't write themselves, but they have something they wanna talk about or explore, and they wanna use your talent to do it with.

NORA EPHRON: Some producers and executives are helpful, and some of them aren't. You can't really generalize, except to say that in the old days, there were very few of them and they were not involved in what is now known as "development." There's no question that movies used to be better before there was such a thing as development. It's a common story in Hollywood that the first draft is better than the second draft, the script having been ruined by notes.

JOHN AUGUST: The thing to remember about development executives is they're not actually trying to hurt you; it just sort of seems like they're trying to hurt you. They don't mean to be jerks, they don't mean to be obstinate, they don't mean to be stupid. They're just trying to get at something, and they can't usually articulate what it is they want. So most of your job in the development process is sitting there, listening, pretending that the things they're saying make sense—and then answering them back in a way that actually does make sense.

ALLISON ANDERS: I remember one moment when my writing partner Kurt Voss and I were in a meeting with people who told us to do two things in a script that were diametrically opposed. I mean, almost everybody has had this experience. And Kurt said, "Okay, we can give you that, but I just want you to know that you just asked for two entirely opposite things. Do you realize that?" They said, "No, they're not opposite." He said, "Yeah, they're really opposite.

You said she's supposed to be here, but she's also supposed to be over here. Do you realize that in the real world of living things, this can't actually be?"

Allison Anders

MICHAEL WOLK: The people who are in the development meetings don't necessarily have the courage of their conviction, but they gotta come up with something, and they gotta lob it out there. Your job, being at the receiving end of a "good" idea in a development meeting, is to handle this turd as if it were a piece of gold.

SHANE BLACK: Their job is not to make the movie better. Their job is to keep their job. At breakfast that morning, they were like, "Yeah, I'm gonna go in there and make my comment." That's their whole day, waiting for that comment to come around so they can say that thing that their boss will hear. And that comment, which to you means nothing—it's like, "Are you insane? Shut up!"—to them, that was their day. It's very important for these people to say something about the script, so it sounds like the studio didn't waste the paycheck they were paid.

I don't go into an operating room and tell a surgeon, "You used the wrong clamp," or "I think you should cut a little more to the left." But any jackwad on a street corner will tell you what they thought was wrong with *Spider-Man 3*, you know? And if they went to Yale or Brown, they could be at a studio and they could have that job. Half the job is having lunches, and the other half is going into a meeting and getting paid to say, "*Spider-Man 3* was bad because of this."

LARRY COHEN: Used to be two people would come into a meeting and work on a script with you. Now eight people come into a meeting, and they've all got yellow pads, and they've all got their opinions, and most of their opinions are bad, and most of them took Robert McKee's writing class. He's given rules to all these people that they seem to have to follow, and they can't judge anything that's original or different. They can only relate to something that they've seen before. There are so many people in these development jobs who have taken that class and other classes, and read books on how to be a screenwriter, with rules and regulations of what has to happen by page thirty, and whatever. It's really screwed up the whole development process in Hollywood.

PAUL MAZURSKY: They like to use phrases like "the arc of the character." It's all bullshit. My daughter is a writer, so I see the notes she's gotten. For the most part, they are criminal, and I have pity for her. Her first script was *Taking Care of Business*. Pretty funny. She wrote another one called *Gone Fishin'*, and it got made with Joe Pesci. She wrote it with J. J. Abrams, who is now the hottest guy in town, and it was purchased. Someone else rewrote it—Pesci, I think—and the studio hated the rewrite. The studio brought Jill and J. J. back. They got paid twice. She's written about four or five others that I've read. They're pretty good. But I've read the notes, and you can't believe them. They're absurd. They wanna change water into wine.

DAVID S. WARD: You have more and more people contributing input. For example, if you're doing a script for a studio, you have notes that are coming not just from the executive and the executive's assistant, but some of the other story people at the studio. So you may have notes that don't even jibe with each other, let alone make sense to you as a writer. So you have to become a bit of a politician, because you can't just ignore the notes. You can't just say, "I think these are stupid—I'm not doing them," because they'll get someone else who will do them.

First of all, try to understand the notes as much as possible, because some of the notes are good. Even in a set of bad notes, there are always some things where you go, "That's true, I didn't think about that." So you have to try to find some common ground. Then your biggest challenge is to figure out how you can do something that satisfies their needs without violating the spirit of what it is you're trying to do. Sometimes you can, and sometimes you can't.

But even that doesn't finish the different levels of development that still lie ahead. You get past the studio notes. Then you get a director, and the director has notes. Then you get an actor, and the actor has notes. It doesn't even stop when you start shooting, because a lot of times there are changes made during the actual shooting. It's never really done until the movie's done.

It's sometimes a miracle that a movie even comes out, given all the different points of view that are sometimes focused on it.

David S. Ward

ANDREW W. MARLOWE: As heinous as they are sometimes, or even as internally conflicting as they are sometimes, the intent behind the notes is always to push you as a writer to do something better. Any writer worth their salt wants to have an impact on the audience. We're all in this business to manipulate the audience's emotions, and if we aren't doing that successfully, we need to take a look at why we're not doing it successfully. Sometimes you'll get a note that says, "Well, this scene is boring—can we put in a car chase?" What you should take from that note is that this quiet, emotional scene that you intended to be emotionally devastating is boring, and that means that you might not have done your work setting up the characters or the relationships twenty, thirty, forty pages earlier.

MICHAEL JANUARY: The object of writing is for someone else to perceive things as you perceive them. And if you haven't expressed it in a way that gets to them, then it's not that they're failing in receiving the message. It may be that you're failing in communicating the message.

ANTWONE FISHER: You know, the development process is the most fun part of writing for me. Sitting in a room by myself, creating the whole thing, is lonely. I like talking. I like getting notes. Writers should be open-minded to the development process, because once you start developing the screenplay, that's when it's moving. It's possible for it to move further, even if it moves out of your hands and into another writer's hands.

RON SHELTON: The cliché about the studio grinder—that it will take an idea and beat it up until it's unrecognizable—well, there's truth to it. There's also truth to the fact that really good screenplays do survive; really good screenplays do get through the system. If you're writing a movie that needs to be a studio picture, then you can't go in thinking it's going to be mangled. You have to go in thinking that you're making a great movie. Mangling is just part of the process.

Write. Rewrite. Repeat.

JOHN D. BRANCATO: Have you ever heard about a study that somebody was doing about the perfect painting, judged on questions that were asked of potential painting lovers across the world? You know, it would have a landscape in it, and it would have an animal somewhere in the front, it would have a pretty girl. . . . It would just have all these disparate elements. And then some artist did the painting, based on the study, which, of course, was an utterly horrible, hilarious painting. That's kinda the way Hollywood generally works. They'll say, "What about the love story?" "Well, it's a war movie." "It's gotta have a love story!" So things do get cobbled together, and you have these horrible Swiss Army knife beasts.

SHANE BLACK: There's no way to protect yourself from a studio if they decide that they want to completely rework your material. They're the ones writing you the checks. This is where writers get in trouble, because they whine all the time. It's like, "The studio can do anything they want with my script!" Yeah, they can. But what if you argued eloquently, like a writer can, or if you spoke out compellingly—and forcefully, and persuasively—for your point of view in a way that influenced the studio? They can do anything they want. Doesn't mean you can't still talk 'em out of it.

DANIEL PYNE: You'll hear a lot of writers talk about how they'll start the development process, and they'll write and they'll write and they'll write, and the script will go in a complete circle. The studio will come back to where they were six months before, with the exact same script. The studio needed to go through that process, which you've already been through as a writer. Sometimes you can identify what they want and explain to them that you already tried that and it didn't work. The writer has an advantage because you know where everything goes, and a lot of times you've taken those paths. If you're patient and you aren't too defensive, you can have a conversation about the note, rather than have an argument about it.

Daniel Pyne

ANDREW W. MARLOWE: It's really the writer's job to protect the material, and that doesn't necessarily mean protecting the specific words on the page. You're gonna get a lot of input from a lot of people, and part of your job is to figure out whether those specific changes are the right things for the material.

JOSE RIVERA: I try not to be intimidated by somebody who's trying to be intimidating. I try not to be manipulated by someone who's trying to manipulate me. I try to deal with the ideas, and filter the ideas through my own standards as a writer, and deal with them in terms of how right or how wrong they feel. It's sort of like erasing the executives from the equation and just dealing with what they're saying: "Okay, in act two, if Mary is an assassin and she falls in love with the guy, is that a good idea?" You have to take yourself out of the equation too.

JAMES L. WHITE: Whenever I talk to young writers, I tell them to park their car six blocks away from where they're going, take their ego out, put it in the trunk of the car, lock the trunk, and give the keys to the first person that's walkin' by. You cannot go into that room with an ego. I go into the room with the objective of making the story good, making the vision come to life. I don't go into the room to compete with the producers or with the execs. That's not my job. I'm there to try to get what their vision is.

JOE FORTE: I like saying this because so many screenwriters hate it when I say this: Look for reasons why the people you're working with are smart. If you look for the way they're stupid and corrupt and moronic, you'll find that. And if you wanna look for the way that I'm stupid and corrupt and moronic, you'll probably find someplace that I am too. You know what I mean? Make people your partners, because they have knowledge that you can download into your brain. If you hear a suggestion from the standpoint of "They're stupid," then you're gonna miss something. But if you hear the note or the suggestion from the standpoint of "How could I make that work for me?" you have a completely different sent of rules. I've gotten the "dumbest" notes, but behind it was a good idea.

RICHARD RUSH: When I was a young man out of the business and a young man in the business, I believed that my opinion was absolutely right, and that I had the right answer to all questions. With age and experience, I learned that I was right on all of those occasions—but that there are several right answers to all occasions. Mine might be the most expedient or the best, but it's not necessarily the only one.

STEVEN E. de SOUZA: You have to remember that there's a whole dynamic in that room. Doesn't matter if you're going in there to talk about your chick flick or if you're going in to talk about your cowboy movie—there are dynamics you don't know about. There's this executive in your meeting, and she's been frustrated that every movie that comes out of this process turns into some kind of movie about teenage boys and fart jokes, and she's trying to elevate the material. Then you have her archenemy, who's not going to make any wussy movies. Then you have the person whose job is shaky, who wants to show off in the meeting. All this stuff is going on, so you want *them* to have a good meeting.

One of the things you can do is leave opportunities for plug-and-play. See, if they can say anything in the meeting, they can think it's their idea. Then they're invested. So for example, you might say, "And I think these villains are doing something to screw with our economy. They want to mess with our money. They're trying to fool people. They have a big suitcase full of . . ." "Counterfeit money?" "Yes! That's right! It could be counterfeit money. Can I write that down?"

BILLY RAY: You have to listen to their problems but ignore their solutions. Their solutions, just by definition, will make your movie more like other movies—that's how studio executives think, and that's not gonna help. I think writers have a knee-jerk response to any notes, which is that they're just stupid, and that knee-jerk response is folly. Not all notes are bad notes. Some notes are enormously helpful. The development process is there to make movies better, and sometimes it does actually work. I've seen scripts of mine get better. Here's the thing to look out for: Sometimes your screenplay—as you go through the second, third, fourth, fifth, sixth draft—will get smarter and tighter. Development always works in that way. However there is a certain raw, organic energy to that first draft—even a certain messiness—that has value. Sometimes as movies get tighter, they get less passionate. You have to guard against that.

DAVID HAYTER: You can fine-tune a script down to the nth degree, and it's uninspiring. It doesn't move. It's too constructed. Sometimes you just need to break all that, and try to reinfuse some of that chaotic energy into it. As William Goldman said in one of his brilliant books, a screenplay is a series of little surprises. If your script has become too solidified in terms of structure and form, then you'll have fewer surprises, just because your average movie-going audience is pretty film-savvy at this point. So you need to find a way to break it up, and to create things that will surprise you as the artist, and thereby surprise the audience as they watch the film.

MICK GARRIS: The genre I work in, mostly, is horror. There probably is no genre that is less understood by studio brass than that. For them, horror is whatever is grotesque, rather than the buildup and the release and all of the tension between those wet spots. The edgy things make horror what it is—not the cat jumping out of the dumpster, not the stalking of the teenagers. But the horror clichés that they're all familiar with are what they think it's all about, and you can't argue these things. All I can say is, "Trust me, I've been doing this for a long time. I know it, I love it, it matters to me." Horror isn't always logical. Horror is something that's very difficult to ask questions about.

Mick Garris

STEVE KOREN: You do become a bit nervous when someone doesn't get the comedy that you're presenting in a script. Maybe it's not the right script for them. I once worked with the Zucker brothers, and they told me that when they went out with *Airplane!* they couldn't sell it—people just didn't get it on the page.

MARK O'KEEFE: Comedy is subjective.

STEVE KOREN: Some people like big and broad, and some people like small and sarcastic.

MARK O'KEEFE: If they want something big and broad, and you're like, "Well, that's not this piece," then it's difficult.

STEVE KOREN: There's a script I just finished that Eddie Murphy is gonna be in called *A Thousand Words*. That started out as a small movie, and then there were some studio changes, and it turns out we decided to make it broader. So suddenly, I had to rewrite everything. But as long as everyone's on the same page, you don't lose your mind. Very often, I'll ask, "Please, could all the producers and executives get together and give me consistent notes?" Because you don't want one person telling you, "Make it small and delicate and precious," and somebody else telling you, "No, have the guy hit in the face with the pie."

NAOMI FONER: I had a moment during *Running on Empty* when I was fired. *Running on Empty* is about a boy who lives with his parents—they're radical, they've been underground, and they're trying to maintain their family in this strange situation. I went in to get the studio notes, and they said, "Oh, we don't like this little boy. He doesn't say anything, he should hate his radical parents, and he should move in with the music teacher." For the first time in my life, I said no. I said, "This story is about something that requires all these things to be here." And I was fired. You have to know when it's not what you started out to do. There are jobs that are gigs—you know, that you're doing for somebody else because they have a vision. The ones that come from your heart have to stay from your heart, and you have to know when you've gone off the track.

ZAK PENN: Being too passive is something that can really bite you in the ass. You can get away with it for a certain amount of time, just letting people tell you what to do. There are a couple writers I've known who treat the job like "I'm here to do what they told me to do," and it can be a career-killer. They're not hiring you because they want to tell you what to do as a screenwriter. They're usually hiring you 'cause they need advice. So even if someone is sitting there saying, "I don't want to hear your opinion," they do want to hear your opinion. You have to fight through that natural inclination that some people have, to just go with the flow. The flow will push you right out the door.

Your Services Are No Longer Required

JOHN D. BRANCATO: If you're hoping to be a screenwriter in Hollywood, you will be rewritten. That's just the way it is. They treat you like you're on a factory line. You'll be fired because "they can't really tell a love story," "they can't do action properly," "they're not funny . . ." You'll be fired for different reasons, but it's the way executives pretty much cover their asses when it comes to the movie coming out. They say, "Look, we hired Frank Blow to do this and Joe Schmuck to do that—we did everything we could to make sure that script was gonna work."

GERALD DiPEGO: They're afraid that the movie might not do well. They're afraid that they might not be giving the right notes. They're afraid that the writer might not be able to deliver exactly what the audience wants. Maybe it was an original script that they loved, but by now they've read it five times, so the thrill is gone. They've been through development, they've seen it go this way and that way, and now their minds are just full of questions and fear. "Should we really trust this writer?" And so, to somehow pacify them, they can say, "We'll bring in another writer just for a fresh look at it," as if throwing various writers at a script is their job.

JOHN CARPENTER: I learned the lesson of rejection with *Eyes of Laura Mars*. They loved the idea, and I could see early on that the way I wanted to do it was not the way they wanted to do it. They wanted a big star vehicle. I saw it coming, but I gave it my best shot. You have to write what you wanna see. I wrote what I wanted to see, and they hired another writer, David Zelag Goodman, who's a very talented writer. He came in and rewrote me—basically the same scene structure, but with a different emphasis—and he gave them what they wanted. That's okay. Not a big deal.

PAUL SCHRADER: Bob Towne rewrote *The Yakuza*, but I didn't know that. I was on the second floor of a bungalow at Warner Bros., and unbeknownst to me, Bob was in the room beneath me writing on the same script.

Looking back at that script, I would love to rewrite it knowing what I know now. It was written as a kind of a gangster movie, and Sydney Pollack wanted to make it more of a love story. In the end, I think it fell between two stools—it wasn't really a gangster film, it wasn't really a cross-cultural love story. I think Sydney would have been better served making the harder choice as to which way that script should have gone.

I wasn't happy with Towne rewriting *Yakuza*, but on the other hand, it was a big Hollywood movie, and it had my name on it, and that was good.

ROBERT MARK KAMEN: I wrote my second script, *Taps*, for Stanley Jaffe, a producer who had just won the Oscar for Best Picture. Very smart, very tough. Every morning I would show up at his hotel suite with the pages from the day before. We'd have breakfast and discuss the day's work. Every day, I had the same thing for breakfast: a big bowl of raspberries and whipped cream.

It might not seem like much now, but back in 1979, having a bowl of raspberries every morning for eleven weeks was a great luxury. I looked forward to that more than I should have, because the day I arrived at his door with the last five pages of the last act, he stood at the door and took the pages there, instead of ushering me in for *the raspberries*.

I looked behind him to the breakfast table. It was set for one. There were no raspberries. He said, "Robert, you have done a magnificent job. You have broken the spine of this thing, given it flesh and muscle, written your heart out." I'm listening to this line of crap, and it doesn't even occur to me I am being shit-canned. All I can think of is the raspberries that are not on the table just beyond the door. And all I can say is: "No raspberries, Stanley?" He replied with the kindest smile, and he closed the door.

DAVID HAYTER: The experience on *Hulk* was difficult, because you have an inevitable proprietary sense over something that you've spent a lot of time working on, even if it's an adaptation of a prior work. I believed that the beauty of the *Hulk* story was that it was our version of the Frankenstein myth. Not only that, but it's applicable to anybody who's ever felt rage inside them that wants to break free. So when I threw myself into that, I grew to love the world and to love the characters.

What happened on that film was Ang Lee signed on, which I was extremely excited about. Ang is brilliant filmmaker, obviously. I really believed in that choice, and for what it's worth, I really backed that choice at the studio. But his producing partner, James Schamus, who's a delightful and talented man, works on all of Ang's movies. They started working on the script, and I sort of faded out of the process. By the end, it really wasn't my script anymore.

That's fine if the movie comes out better than what you had put down on paper, and sometimes it's difficult for a writer to admit that, but I like to be a team player. If the movie's better, the movie's better. On *Hulk*, I kinda felt like they went down a road that undid a lot of the things that I had tried to do to clarify the story for the audience, to make it accessible to everybody. It became what it became, which was more cerebral. That was painful because there were things in my *Hulk* drafts that I felt were great set pieces, or great character moments, or great iconic moments that are just gone. You know, they're gone forever, and that's a shame.

JOSE RIVERA: I did a film for Disney. It was a one-word idea they had: "shadows." I said, "Okay, what about shadows?" They said, "That's it. That's the idea. 'Shadows.' Do something with it." So I came up with this idea about a guy whose shadow is alive. The guy is really awkward with women, and he likes this girl that he works with. He doesn't know how to approach her, but his shadow and her shadow fall in love, and they contrive to get the human beings together. It's a very fanciful sort of thing, and I was happy with it.

Jose Rivera

I wrote the script, and Disney said, "Wow, it's really good, but it's a love story, and what we really want is a buddy film—like, imagine your shadow is Eddie Murphy." And I said, "That's interesting. It's completely not what I wrote." I'm used to getting notes where someone says, "Okay, act two needs some work." I'm not used to getting notes where they say, "Let's change the genre." I just couldn't swing with it. I couldn't do it, and I was replaced.

That was a real blow, I have to say, but I felt it was a complete violation of the idea. I know, intellectually, that they own the idea, but I had invested so much in this magical love story that to turn it into a goofy buddy film . . . I just couldn't do it. The irony is a good friend of mine ended up replacing me. She called me and said, "I'm rewriting you. I hope it's all right." And I said, "Well, if anyone in the world is gonna rewrite me, I'm glad it's you and not somebody else."

FRANK DARABONT: My becoming involved with *Indiana Jones 4* was really a function of having worked with George Lucas in the past and with Steven Spielberg in the past, and also being a huge fan of the whole Indiana Jones mythos. You know, *Raiders of the Lost Ark* is one of those. . . . Are you gonna call it a perfect script? Yeah, let's call it a perfect script. It's a perfect movie in so many ways. So they approached me to become involved in *Indy 4,* and it was really that simple.

The situation had this unfortunate engineering flaw built into it, for my purposes, which is the producer had a certain movie in mind, the director had a certain movie in mind, and what I was able to give them pleased the director, but not the producer. When you're a screenwriter trying to serve a creative vision, it helps if you're not trying to serve more than one master. At the end of the day, I wound up making Steven happy with the script that I handed him, but not George.

You really do chalk it up to creative differences. The movie I had in mind is not the movie that George Lucas had in mind. I have to respect that because George is the producer—and, by the way, it's his character. So do I go through life, you know, holding a grudge or clinging to some seething resentment? No. That's ridiculous. If I did that with every project that didn't go well, I'd be Hannibal Lecter—they'd have to lock me up in a cell with a fuckin' mask on my face.

Here's the thing I've tried to say about this in the past, and not many journalists have really listened: A career is filled with disappointments like that. Every career, no matter who you ask. You could dig up Billy Wilder and ask him. I'm sure he would say the same thing. Every career is filled with peaks and valleys. The only difference between this and other disappointments that I have weathered in this business is that this happened to be a very high-profile project. It had all this media scrutiny on it, and there's nothin' the media loves more than to try to generate controversy.

At a certain point I wanna look around and say, "Where were you guys when that other script four years ago went in the shitter? You weren't paying attention because it wasn't Spielberg, and it wasn't Lucas, and it wasn't *Indiana Jones*."

JOSH FRIEDMAN: This is why I think that screenwriting is the hardest job in town. You're required to put all your passion into it, get on the phone with executives, defend your work—and at the end of the day, you're standing over a trapdoor. And it's not hidden. They say, "Could you move a little to the left? You're not in the trapdoor area yet." So you move over and you stand there, and then have the conversation. That's all you can do.

JOHN CARPENTER: You can't avoid being replaced. You just do the best you can do. If they want somebody else to work on it, there's nothing you can do about it. Learn to love it.

The Development Executive's Perspective: Charles Vignola

Charles Vignola

Charles Vignola has worked with superstar producer Jerry Bruck-
heimer for twenty years. Originally hired in 1990 as a reader for
the production company Bruckheimer founded with the late Don
Simpson, Vignola is now the director of development at Jerry
Bruckheimer Films, the entity behind megahits including the
National Treasure *and* Pirates of the Caribbean *series. He's also*
a screenwriter with projects set up at MGM and other studios.

Head of the Class

A development executive tries to find movies that reflect the company's brand. At Jerry Bruckheimer Films, we do big, four-quadrant tent poles. Occasionally, we will make something like a *Remember the Titans*, but by and large, we do big, commercial, pop entertainment.

The job has two parts. One is like panning for gold—trying to find the material, whether it's an article, a book, a book proposal, a pitch, a screenplay, an idea, a remake. The second part of the job is developing the material to the point where we can attach a director. The process could take years and years. If the studio wants a movie by a certain date, the process goes a little faster. We're working on an accelerated timetable right now to get *Pirates 4* pulled together.

We have a development meeting every week to get a lay of the land—what material we've acquired, what stage we're in with various projects. Jerry's working on production much of the time, so he's traveling to wherever we're shooting. But when a piece of material is far enough along in the development process, it's time for Jerry to give his notes. There's a fair amount of interaction, but the interaction is when it really counts. Material definitely goes to Jerry when we think we could start finding a director.

Like anything, it's the odds. We might buy a project that's very promising, and we hire a writer, and we're very excited—then, amazingly, the script comes in and doesn't resemble anything that we thought it would be. Sometimes we buy something and we think there's promise, but we're not really sure how it's going to turn out, and then the writer gets struck by inspiration—they hand in their first draft, and it's like, "Wow!" To whatever extent we were able to convey what we wanted, they were able to deliver it.

One of the things I've learned is that it really is about the concept. Other things may change dramatically, but the idea always remains the same. So the job is about finding that really unique idea that speaks to the company, and finding the right way to grow the idea into a film. When the writer is able to turn the idea into the blueprint for a movie, it's electrifying—when you're reading, you can actually see actors playing these roles, the set pieces pop, and you can tell what's going to be a trailer moment. Those projects generally jump to the head of the class.

Adventures in Development

We developed *Black Hawk Down* from a series of newspaper articles. We worked with this great writer, Mark Bowden, who brought this true story to life, but there were some things that needed to be worked out structurally. Ken Nolan came in, and we did draft upon draft with him. Ken was really smart, and he got it to the point where we were able to get Ridley Scott attached. Ridley brought on Steve Zaillian, and Steve did his thing. And then Steve and Ken worked on various points right up to production. But that was really interesting to see the project grow from nothing to a great, Oscar-nominated movie over maybe three, four years.

On the *Pirates* series, I believe Jay Wolpert was the first writer who worked on it at Disney. Stuart Beattie wrote the draft that came from the studio to us, asking if we were interested in getting involved. Ted Elliot and Terry Rossio had always wanted to do *Pirates of the Caribbean,* so they had the take of pirates laboring under a curse. That was the creative breakthrough that took the movie in a different direction, and from the time they got on board, they've been the sole writers for the series.

G-Force is one of our latest movies, and that's an example of a project with a number of different writers. That original idea was from Hoyt Yeatman, the special-effects whiz who directed the film. The Wibberleys wrote the initial drafts, and then, because it's a comedy, we had a number of writing teams come on. From the time we bought the idea to the time that the movie came out is probably about three or four years. *Prince of Persia,* the next one after *G-Force,* was something like five or six years. And then we have *The Sorcerer's Apprentice,* which we're shooting right now—that process actually went fairly quickly. From the time that we got involved with it to the time that we started shooting was probably a year to a year and a half. But that was one where the studio wanted it by a certain date.

The extreme would be a movie we made called *Bad Company.* Simpson/Bruckheimer was developing that in the mideighties, when Richard Pryor was a possible actor. It was developed for a long time, and then kind of fell off the map. We revisited it much later on as a vehicle for Chris Rock. So that went through a lot of development.

All Writers Are Not Created Equal

You want to hire smart writers who bring a unique, distinctive voice to the material—a certain flair, a certain élan. There are so many aspects of writing a screenplay, from dialogue to action to character to atmosphere to structure. There are a million things, and a writer might be good at 40, 60, 70 percent of them. Very few people are good at all of them, and those guys work all the time. They write their own tickets.

We're looking for a writer to come in and say, "I know what the movie is." We know what the character is, or we know it's about scuba diving—but what's the movie? Hopefully we find the writer after we read a lot of samples and say, "Okay, this guy's smart. He seems to understand the genre. Let's hear his ideas." Would we hire a brand-new writer to rewrite *National Treasure 3*? Most likely not. But to find the next idea that we're going to develop into a big movie—that's where new writers have their opportunity. We may hire more seasoned writers to execute the version that we're going to shoot, but the new writer will get on the movie.

If you're a writer, you should know your strengths and weaknesses. There are some writers who are very good at coming up with ideas, but they can't execute them. There are people who can execute other people's ideas, but they're not good at coming up with movie ideas. There are some writers who are very good at adaptations, but are terrible at original concepts. Then there are the closers. They're your insurance, and they get paid an enormous amount of money. When there's a hard release date, you really want to go to the guys who come in and knock it out of the park.

It's the writer's job to come as close as possible to giving us what we want. If you're able to make a good case for why we should do it your way, you should certainly do that—but you have to know when you have the leeway to do that. The best thing is to be open-minded to the process, and not come in with an attitude that all development executives are idiots determined to destroy your material.

Some executives think they're being clear and articulate about what they want, but they might be giving something that's more generalized. I'm the unusual sort where in addition to developing movies, I'm also writing movies. I'm able to understand the intricacies of writing, so I can connect with writers. They feel like I get them in a way that other executives might not; therefore, they open up a little bit. There's less guard up, and there's more of an opportunity to brainstorm solutions. For me, the creative problem solving is the fun of the job—that great "eureka" feeling of coming up with something that works on a number of different levels.

6

Power Players

The hierarchy of the Hollywood system is never more evident than when "above the line" talents attach themselves to film projects. Producers have the money to get movies started, directors have the creative know-how to get movies made, and stars have the box-office appeal to get movies seen. These power players have varying levels of autonomy over the film projects with which they become involved, but all have authority over screenwriters.

When everyone works together in a respectful fashion, talents are pooled into a project that becomes greater than the sum of its parts. More commonly, turf wars ensue, during which some of the parts are discarded, especially writers. The insights offered by screenwriters in this chapter explain how to manage, or at least comprehend, the delicate personal interactions that drive every movie production.

Producers are the first heavyweights to become involved. In many cases a producer purchases the rights to an underlying story idea, then hires a writer to expand the idea into a script. Likely the individual whose role in the filmmaking process is least understood by those outside of the entertainment industry, a producer is an entrepreneur who tries to gather all the elements necessary for the creation of an actual film.

Directors generally request and supervise rewrites of the scripts they hope to shoot. In rare cases, such as Paul Schrader's collaborations with Martin Scorsese, the perfect pairing of writer and director becomes the stuff of cinematic legend. The dream of emulating these sorts of partnerships underlies many of the efforts that other writers describe about trying to achieve unity of vision with the directors who bring their screenplays to life.

And then there are stars. As Joe Forte and others note, stars matter because their participation motivates studios to finance and distribute particular projects. Fulfilling the unique needs of movie stars is one of the most crucial skills that screenwriters must develop if they hope to sustain careers at the industry's top levels.

Meet the Moguls

PAUL SCHRADER: I remember years ago, I needed some money, and I was good friends with Don Simpson and Jerry Bruckheimer. In fact, I introduced them. They were both involved in *American Gigolo*. They were on a roll, and they were paying writers a lot of money. We all had the same agent, Jeff Berg, and I went to Jeff and I said, "I'm old friends with them, why can't I get some of this money?" He said, "Why don't you have lunch? I'll set it up." So I had lunch with them on the Paramount lot, and we all talked about doing something. And then a month went by and nothing came up. I asked Jeff, "Did you ever talk to Simpson about those writing jobs?" And Jeff said, "Well, there's kind of a problem." I said, "What's that?" And he said, "Well, Don likes to beat up on writers, and he's not really comfortable beating up on you."

NORA EPHRON: I have had a number of unbelievably painful moments with Hollywood executives, and the truth is that their reasons for rejecting projects were beyond ludicrous—they were willful and capricious, and in several cases meant that the scripts involved, which I had worked hard on and which, I swear to God, were wonderful, were never made. Not only were they unwilling to make them, but they were unwilling to put them into turnaround so that someone else could make them. The very worst moment of this occurred with a man who used to run Fox. He told me he would neither make a movie I'd written, with Alice Arlen, nor put it into turnaround because he was sure it would win an Oscar, and he would be embarrassed the way he'd been when he put *The English Patient* into turnaround.

FRANK DARABONT: I had one producer with his own source of funding—a guy with a lotta dough to spend on movies—offer me a $30 million budget for *The Mist*. He said, "I will write you a check for $30 million, you go make your movie." He literally had his pen poised. And he said, "But there's one string attached. You can't have this ending. You've gotta have another ending." And I said, "What ending would you like me to have?" He said, "I don't know." I said, "I don't know either. This is the ending I've been thinkin' about for twenty years now. And it's not like I haven't tried to think of alternatives, but this is the ending that makes intuitive, creative sense to me. This is the one that I'm most interested in. If you have an alternative to suggest, by all means suggest away. I may love it, I may hate it, I may laugh in your face, but I'll certainly listen to it." He didn't have that. So I said, "Thank you very much," I shook his hand, I walked out of his office without the $30 million check, and I made the movie with Bob Weinstein for almost half of that money—which meant my not taking any salary, et cetera—because I wanted to make my movie.

MICHAEL JANUARY: A producer is someone that lies well enough and long enough until the lie becomes the truth.

BRUCE JOEL RUBIN: I was working on *Deep Impact*, and I had lunch with a president of Disney—someone who had produced another movie I had worked on. We're having lunch in the Disney commissary, and he starts asking me about *Deep Impact*. I just started talking freely and openly. I had no idea he was planning *Armageddon*. He was taking notes on everything I was saying. I wasn't really literally giving him my script, but I was talking to him enough about it that he could pick up the genre, the tone, the character-driven aspect of it. That was really clever, I thought. He was figuring out how to do a movie in juxtaposition to the movie that I was in the process of writing. He was getting all of my ideas. It was really fascinating that there was a kind of subterfuge that was happening with this head of a major studio. When I found out that Disney was doing *Armageddon*, I went, "Wow, that's interesting."

PETER HYAMS: If I want to write, I sit down at the keyboard and write. If I want to draw, I take a No. 2 soft pencil and a blank piece of paper, and I draw. If I want to make a film, I'm asking somebody for money. The only reason why they're gonna give me money is they think they're gonna make more money back than they gave me. If they didn't think they were gonna make more money back than they gave me, they'd be idiots to give me the money. They don't owe it to anyone to make their movie. They have to see something in it.

KRISS TURNER: Producers are only gonna get behind something that can sell, because they only make money when it's green-lit.

GUINEVERE TURNER: The executive who wants the truly innovative, risky idea is a rare breed. There's the lovely and talented Christine Vachon, who produced *Go Fish* and produced my Bettie Page movie, but they are few and far between.

PAUL MAZURSKY: Alan Ladd Jr. was great. I did four pictures for him. You're not gonna find many like him. If you encounter an executive like Laddy, you're in luck. I also had Mike Frankovich on *Bob & Carol & Ted & Alice*. He read it, and I said, "I have to direct it." He said, "What have you done?" I said, "Nothing, but I made a short, I was an actor, and I directed theater. I'm not gonna sell it if I don't direct it." He said, "I'll let you know tomorrow," and the next day he called me. He said, "Okay." I don't think that'll happen now.

RONALD SHUSETT: Dino De Laurentiis said to me, "I want to make a sequel to *King Kong*, but everybody says no, because King Kong is dead. Can you give me a way to bring back King Kong?" So I went home and thought, and then an inspiration hit me. Unfortunately, it was not a correct inspiration, but when you swing for the fences you're going to miss sometimes. I said, "Dino, I know how you can bring back King Kong, and the audience will accept it even though he's fallen a hundred stories. You give him an artificial heart. It's huge—as big as a Volkswagen. It'll be a funny scene, and everybody will believe he can come back to life." He said, "Okay, I like the concept."

So in about three weeks I came back with the story structure. I was trying to do a spoof of *King Kong* and at the same time make it exciting. I said, "After he's resuscitated, he meets the love of his life. It's a giant female version of Kong. He's sixty feet tall, she's forty feet tall." He thinks for a minute and says, "Sounds good, but one thing bothers me, Ron. One thing stops me. People accept one sixty-foot ape. But I don't think they'll accept a female ape this tall. Maybe another male, but a female is too hard to accept."

I thought for a minute and said, "Dino, Kong had to have a mother."

"My God, you're right! We go with this!"

And within months the script was ready and we were shooting the movie. It turns out I did not craft it well enough. It couldn't make up its mind—it didn't work as a comedy and it didn't work as a serious movie—but that's probably the best mistake you can make. There's a saying by Mike Todd, the great old producer. He did *Around the World in Eighty Days,* and everybody thought he was nuts. He said, "He who never sticks his neck out never gets taller than his collar."

RICHARD WENK: I made a short that got bought by HBO, which was not a big thing in the eighties, because HBO had no programming at that time, so they bought anything. It was seen by a producer named Don Borchers, who was working for Roger Corman at New World Pictures. They contacted me, and I came out for an interview. The interview consisted of Roger and Don bringing a poster out of the closet. It was a big poster, and it said *Vamp.* I said, "That's really great." They said, "Now we need a movie to go with it. If you can write a movie that has strippers, college kids, and vampires in it, you can direct it too." So I did. That was my first experience writing a script for a studio, under the guidance of Don Borchers, and it was a great learning experience.

Richard Wenk

LARRY COHEN: The last development deal I had was a half-a-million-dollar deal at Warner Bros., for Joel Silver. After I wrote the script, I called Joel up on the phone and said, "What did you think of the script?" He hemmed and hawed, so I said, "Joel, did you read the script?" And he said, "Well, I was exposed to it." I said, "You were *exposed* to it? Does that mean they held it up and showed you the script, and said 'Look, here's the script that Larry Cohen wrote for $500,000'?"

SHANE BLACK: Joel Silver has been an angel to me because, through thick and thin, for whatever reason, his vision of what he wants to see in movies coincided enough with mine that he trusted me to get what he was saying. At the very earliest stages, we worked so well together that he would literally be in his office and I'd come in five, six times a day and say, "What do you think?" He'd say no. I'd take it back and say, "Okay, now what do you think?" And I'd just keep coming in until he said, "Yeah, that's what I want." That kind of collaboration made me feel very comfortable in the business.

To this day, Joel remains my favorite producer, even though he's so exponentially grown since then—you know, you have to walk beside him on the way to another meeting, and sort of get in as many words as you can.

On *Kiss Kiss Bang Bang*, Joel ran interference for me. It's not that I wasn't trusted at that point by the studio, but I was—well, I wasn't trusted. I hadn't directed anything. Joel was able to drum up a fairly minimal sum of $15 million. He had made the *Matrix* films—you know, the good first one and then the not-so-good next ones—and they all made a billion dollars. So the studio said, "$15 million? Give it to Joel? What are you gonna do? Sit on him, yell at him? No, we're gonna let him do what he wants with $15 million. He's earned that privilege."

I had a unique situation where I had to answer to only one man, because the money was so small. The studio rode off and it was just Joel. If Joel liked it, we filmed it. If he didn't like it, I'd try to convince him. If I couldn't, we didn't film it.

ANTWONE FISHER: I know this producer who never says, "Leave my office," but he sends signals when the meeting is over. Some people in the room don't get the signal. They don't pick up on that, and they wanna be friends. I'm friends with him because I picked up on his signals. You have to know how to read the people you're with. It's like a dance. You have to know who your partner is, and you have so many partners. It's just like a night on the town—you're going to this ballroom, you're gonna dance with all these people, and you wanna dance with them. But when it's time to switch partners, you can't get nostalgic.

Auteur Guide

JUSTIN ZACKHAM: As a screenwriter, you understand that you're providing a document that is gonna be turned into a film, and that is an entirely new evolution of the same story. If you want to write a script and direct it, then you get your way. But if you're just a writer on a project, you are just a writer. As parasitic as it may feel to have a director come in and change your words, that's what you signed up for.

DANIEL PYNE: Directors need to figure out a way to internalize your movie. They're trying to find a movie to base on your screenplay, so their process is kind of outside-in, as opposed to when you're writing it, which is an organic thing.

NAOMI FONER: You have to be able to watch a director do the horrible thing that happens to a script, which is take it apart into pieces and then try to put it back together again. And sometimes they put it back with one sleeve missing. But it has to be their turn. There has to be a single leader.

JOSH FRIEDMAN: Even when directors don't have final cut, they have final cut from you. So you can try to convince somebody of some great idea you have for a scene that they're not sure about, and at the end of the day you may win the battle, but you aren't winning the war.

RICHARD RUSH: The writer's lot in Hollywood has some unfortunate consequences, and I can say that with authority as a director who has run roughshod on writers that I have dealt with. When I say *roughshod*, I don't mean literally. I respect the writer immensely. But when it gets down to the making of the picture, and I want to change dialogue at the moment, I don't consult with the studio or with the writer or with God. I consult with the actor to find out what works well on his tongue, and I change it as needed.

PAUL SCHRADER: It's interesting about directing other people's scripts. I do something that is sort of quasi-unethical, which is I retype the scripts. I change the punctuation, sometimes a little dialogue, sometimes the descriptions. And then I feel like I wrote it. You have to make it yours. When you direct a script, you look at it as a huge problem: "We have this literary event, so how can we rethink it into a visual event?" That shift in thinking, from one side of the brain to the other, is the same whether you wrote it or not.

PETER HYAMS: There's paper, and then there's the logistical phenomena that you have to deal with called "filming." Sometimes things just don't translate, and you have to make changes: "Well, we have to shoot here because we can't make a big move during the middle of the day, and the other place that you want so much would require an extra day." Steven Spielberg can get the extra day. I can't. So you have to make those accommodations.

NAOMI FONER: My best movie is still *Running on Empty*, because Sidney Lumet had a clause in his contract that said he could make one movie a year, as long as it was under a certain budget, that was untouched by the studio. If you have some eight-hundred-pound gorilla who can protect you, then your voice onscreen is probably gonna be close to your voice on paper. Sidney treated me the way a playwright is treated in the theater. The actors were given two weeks' rehearsal—the whole movie, in order, every day—and they were able to voice their opinions about things. Any change that got made, I was involved in making. Such a different process from how most movies are made.

WILLIAM GOLDMAN: George Roy Hill came from the theater, and he loved having that rehearsal time on *Butch Cassidy*. I mean, we would just sit in his office for hour after hour and talk about this line and music and all kinds of stuff. And we had the actors— we had Newman and Redford and Katharine Ross. It was just the five of us in a huge room. The actors loved being able to talk about scenes they didn't like, scenes they didn't feel worked, and get it out of the way in rehearsal. They don't do that today, and it's too bad because you can get rid of a lot of shit early.

BRUCE JOEL RUBIN: When we were doing *Jacob's Ladder*, Adrian Lyne and I fought continually over the script. He had visions for it that were different from my visions, but he was the director, and he's also really talented. I had to learn to accept his visions, and we started to have these very strong, very respectful dialogues about how the film should go. He would listen to me, and I would listen to him. In the end, it's kind of an amalgamation of two different approaches, and in some sense I think the movie benefited from these extraordinary involvements that we had in making the script into the script he wanted to direct.

His rejections of certain parts of the script were very painful for me, particularly the last ten minutes of the movie, which were very much effects-driven. It was essential to me in terms of the theme of the story, but Adrian said to me early on, "I don't do effects." I said, "Well, how are we gonna do that sequence?" He said, "We're not." I said, "But that's the core of my movie." He said, "Find another core." I never did. We shot the movie without ever getting the ending quite right. But what he created had integrity, which is a very extraordinary thing to have a film contain.

JOSH FRIEDMAN: Working for Steven Spielberg on *War of the Worlds* was the strangest experience that I've had, because you have a hard time reconciling the man who made movies that made you go into the film business with the man on the other side of the phone saying, "Put more cars on the bridge!" There's a point where he's just another guy that you're talking to about what you're working on, and I think that's one of the great things about him. He's such an enthusiastic presence—almost boyish—and it feels like he's just as happy to be working with you as you are to be working with him. So it's easy to forget, at least for a while, who he is.

Steven's kind of like your funny Jewish uncle who you're happy to have lunch with, and then he gives you a couple little suggestions for your script, and you're thinking, "Ha, ha, silly Jewish uncle—

that can't work." And then you start working on the screenplay, and you're like, "Oh, that's kinda genius, isn't it?" That happened a number of times, where he would say, "Why don't you try this," and I wouldn't think, "That was the most revelatory, genius, Zen koan screenwriter moment I've had." And then you start implementing it, and all of a sudden the scene or the sequence opens up in such a way that you're like, "Wow, I guess he does know what he's doing. I guess he really is Steven Spielberg. He's not just my Uncle Steve."

Josh Friedman

JOHN AUGUST: I've been lucky to make three movies now with Tim Burton, and everyone assumes that I must have this amazing relationship with Tim, and that we talk all the time, and we're close buds. I've probably spent a total of twenty-four hours in Tim's presence over the course of three movies. The way Tim works is he'll send me something and say, "I wanna do this," and I'll say, "Okay," and I'll figure out what I think it is he wants. Then I'll have iced tea with him, usually at his hotel out in Santa Monica. I'll talk through what I want to do, and he's like, "Yeah, go do that." I'll go and do that, and that sort of becomes the movie. Sometimes there's some tweaking along the way, but it's not this talk-through-every-little-plot-point process. It's been terrific to work on these three movies, and I'm really, really happy about it, but it creates this weird expectation that I must know a lot about what makes Tim work, and what his real goals are as a filmmaker, and what drives him. I don't. I just hope it drives him to keep making movies that I write.

ROBERT MARK KAMEN: Luc Besson and I have had a great relationship now for sixteen years, through thick and thin. Some of the movies have worked sort of well, some have worked really well—*Taken* comes out, it's through the roof, and it's wonderful. This kind of relationship is completely unusual in the world of cinema.

What happens with a writer and a director is that you're working for a single purpose, and the purpose is to make the best film you possibly can. If the director trusts the writer, the director will constantly lean on the writer for ideas. He's sucking everything out of you. He's a vampire. And then at the end of the film, usually what happens is he doesn't take your calls, you don't see each other at dinner, and the free parking space is no longer there. All of a sudden it's a different relationship, because he's onto a different film with a different writer.

Luc calls me every day. We don't even call each other by our names anymore. I call him "Shrek" and he calls me "Donkey," because that's basically us—he's the big green guy who owns the forest, and I chatter. It's quite wonderful for me, because I look at myself as a smart craftsman, and I look at him as a gifted artist and a great businessman. I'm honored to work with him, and I'm honored that he calls me all the time, even if it's just to correct the English in dialogue.

Robert Mark Kamen

PAUL SCHRADER: I've been very lucky with the collaboration with Scorsese. The reason Marty and I clicked, for those years in the past—and I don't know if that applies anymore—was that, in essence, we were sort of the same guy. We were short, asthmatic film buffs with a lot of guilt and anger, only he was Italian and urban and Catholic, and I was Dutch and rural and Calvinist. So even though we were the same guy, we each had different elements. When we connected, he took my elements and exploded with them.

That's just serendipity. You run into somebody who's in the right creative space, and you inhabit the space together, sometimes for a period of years—or, in rare cases in film history, a period of decades. But, you know, we speak of those collaborations with great fondness because in fact they are so rare. When you think of Wilder and Diamond, or Ozu and his screenwriter, you're really talking about exceptions to the rule.

If you had asked me two weeks ago if I would work with Marty again, I would have said no, but something has come up where we might work together, although in a different relationship, as producer and director. We'll see. The truth of the matter is you only make movies with friends when you're starting out, because after you have some success, everyone moves into their own worlds. When you're all out there hustling, you run into each other. But after you're up and running, you're around the people you're working with. I try to have dinner once a year with Scorsese, but that's about it. I'm off making films and writing scripts, he's off making films and writing scripts, and our paths don't cross very much.

FRANK DARABONT: I've noticed that the best directors often are the ones who recognize everybody's contribution as valuable, and that's not just true of the screenwriter. The best directors recognize that the people who have dressed the set or costumed the actors, or the guy slinging the camera from take to take, are just as valuable as anybody on a production. You get that sense of inclusiveness from a really good director. They're the captain of the ship, but everybody else is in the same boat.

JOHN CARPENTER: I always tell people, "Look, it's gonna be great. We'll make this film, but you gotta understand something. There's gonna be one guy at the very end, standing there with film cans in his hand, and you're gonna put all your blame on him: It didn't work because of the director." They're gonna blame you. They always do.

MARK D. ROSENTHAL: I was reading scripts for Mark Rydell, who I learned a lot from, and he was very good friends with Sydney Pollack. They had come through the Actors Studio together. They were sitting in Mark's office at Fox one day. Sydney Pollack had just done *Tootsie* and *Out of Africa*, he had won Academy Awards, and he was one of our most important directors. I said to him, "It must get easier for you." He gave me a look like I was a fool. It's never easier. Every single movie is just as hard.

Performance Anxiety

PETER HYAMS: If you want obedience, get a puppy. If you want actors to listen to everything you say, get unknown actors. If you are lucky enough to work with film stars, you find there's a reason why they're film stars. They tend to be incredibly smart people. Brad Pitt doesn't strike me as the kind of actor who shows up at seven o'clock in the morning and says, "Where do you want me to stand, boss?" If you're lucky enough to make a picture with these people, you're gonna listen to what they have to say, and you're gonna accommodate a lot of what they have to say—otherwise they don't want to do the movie.

WILLIAM GOLDMAN: So much of a movie depends on the casting. I remember on *Misery*, Rob Reiner said he didn't want a star for the Kathy Bates part. He wanted an unknown. And the reason he wanted an unknown was because there are scenes where she does terrible things to the Jimmy Caan character, and Rob's feeling was that if you had had a star—if you had had fabulous Meryl Streep—the audience would know she wouldn't do those terrible things. And so we wanted an unknown person, and we went with Kathy, and she was fabulous. But we could make that decision because Castle Rock was an independent. That's not a decision the major studios could have afforded to make. Obviously, since Kathy Bates won the Oscar, the part had quality on the printed page. We could have gotten a star. Had it been a studio, they would have insisted, and we would have done it. Maybe the movie would have been wonderful with a star. I don't know.

JOE FORTE: The star triggers the financing, and therefore you have to create great star roles that will attract that kind of fish. If I were to define technically what a starring role is, it's that the hero of the movie is impacting every scene. He's making the plot, from scene one to the end. There's characterization and all those other things, but what makes it a starring role is that they are the center.

RON SHELTON: Movie stars like to shine. They like to have their movie-star moments. I will sometimes write a speech that I think I'm gonna cut out later, but it'll attract the movie star. *Bull Durham* has the famous speech. I wrote it just to get a movie star, and it worked. It's not my favorite moment in the movie. It's been quoted, it's been published: "I believe in the soul, the cock, the pussy. . . . Lee Harvey Oswald acted alone . . ." Well, it got the right actor. I thought, "I'll cut that scene." Everybody loved it, so I kept it—and I was probably wrong, and everybody else was probably right. But I think you have to realize, in trying to write a movie-star part, that it still has to be a good part. It has to be honest, the character motivations all have to be appropriate. But movie stars are bigger than life, and so maybe there's something bigger than life about that character you write.

JUSTIN ZACKHAM: David Chase wrote a foreword to a compilation of *Sopranos* scripts, and he was talking about the character of Tony Soprano. He said, "It doesn't matter if your lead character is good or bad. He just has to be interesting, and he has to be good at what he does." The first one is obvious, but the second one is not so obvious. If you think about it, all leading characters have something that makes them interesting, and it's because they're good at whatever it is they do. They're great talkers, they're great firefighters, they're great whatevers.

Stars aren't stupid. They wanna play someone who the audience is gonna be attracted to in some way, or repulsed by in some way, as long as that attraction or repulsion is interesting. And then they have to go on a very clear arc of change. It doesn't have to wrap up neatly, but as actors they wanna be able to show off what they can do.

Change is what drives drama, and change is what causes conflict, so I think if you're writing a part for a star, come up with something that they're good at, that we haven't seen before. "This guy's the world's greatest chimney sweep." Why is that interesting? Why is that real? And let them go through some sort of a transformation that, for better or for worse, is gonna inform their life and give the audience something to think about. For me, that's the trick.

JAMES L. WHITE: The first job that I got was from Sidney Poitier, who hired me to do a rewrite. Mr. Poitier comes out, all sixteen feet of him—'cause he looked very huge to me—and he says, "James, I understand you have a story to tell me." So I said, "Yes, sir." I was so nervous. My mouth was trying to tell the story, but my mind was screaming, "That's Sidney Poitier over there!" So I started at the rear of the story, went sideways and went that way, went down. . . . I couldn't tell a linear pitch. I just couldn't get it out. Finally, just before I was about to pass out—'cause I had hyperventilated—I said to Mr. Poitier, "I have to stop." And he said, "Okay, what's wrong?" I said, "Well, it's you." He goes, "What?" I said, "You've been a hero of mine all my life, and so here I am sittin' in the room with you, and I can't get my story out." He said, "Take your time. You want some water or something? Don't worry, you have the job." Well, I almost passed out then, you know?

ARI B. RUBIN: Sitting down with Robert Redford is an amazing experience. Everybody in a meeting has a different way of expressing himself creatively, and Robert Redford, no surprise, expresses himself by acting. If he has a scene idea, he will act out that idea, and you will literally sit there and watch him do an Oscar-worthy performance of the scene that you have not yet written. So that is a pretty compelling experience.

There's a lot of intimidation walking into the room. Once everybody's sitting, and the water's poured, and the pleasantries are aside, you assume your role. I wear my writer's hat and he wears his—at that point it was his director's hat—and that's what it is. The tension of huge actor sitting in front of you has to fade away, or else you're not going to survive very long in that room.

Ari B. Rubin

GERALD DiPEGO: *Message in a Bottle* was one of the few movies that we had actual rehearsal time built in, and a few of the principals were there for the rehearsals. Paul Newman came all the way from New England to be part of this week of rehearsals at Universal Studios. There were some ensemble scenes that they didn't have enough actors for, because a lot of the actors weren't cast yet or weren't available, so I got to play some of those scenes sitting next to Paul. To hear him talking, speaking my lines, and at the same time being in the scene with him and working—it was one of the real thrills.

SHANE BLACK: Movie stars are gonna give you your best ideas, because they're the opposite of development people. Development people are always saying, "How can the character be more likable?" Meanwhile, the actor's saying, "I don't want to be likable." You know, they give you crazy things like, "I wanna eat spaghetti with my hands." Crazy's great. Anything but this sort of likable guy that everyone at the studio insists they should play.

RICHARD WENK: They are thinking purely from one character's point of view, so there's a lot of insight that can be gained. You like to have those conversations, and it's very rare a writer gets to have them. Mos Def came up with a lot of great stuff on *16 Blocks*. His life, and where he grew up, and his attitudes toward police, and his reactions to things that might happen to him, brought more depth to that role than what was in the script. Because it's from him, you know?

MARK FERGUS: First, a great actor will go through the script and black out all the stage direction. You're like, "But I want you to say that haltingly, so don't cry." They don't want you telling them how to move. Then they will start cutting lines that are emotionally redundant. Great line, great monologue—all gone, because they've said it already over here. They're giving you a gift. They're showing where you've overwritten, where you've hit false notes, where you've tried to be clever but you're full of crap. They're giving you a truth test on your own material.

ANDREW W. MARLOWE: There was this experience on *Air Force One*, where I'd written this little speech. Harrison came up to me and he said, "It's a great speech." I said, "Oh, thank you." He said, "I'm not gonna do it. All this, I can do with a look." And he could.

MIKE BINDER: The reason they're so good is they know what works for them. You gotta listen to them, and you gotta be able to take their knowledge and put it on the paper. You gotta work in their voice.

I'm a big Kevin Costner fan. Loved him in *Field of Dreams,* loved him in *Bull Durham,* loved him in *Dances with Wolves.* When we worked on *The Upside of Anger,* he would call me up and he'd throw ideas by me. "Couldn't I be stoned?" That was his idea, and it was a great idea. It just set the whole thing up. He understood how to do this part.

There were scenes that he would want me to rewrite ten, fifteen times—and many times, I would think, "He's wrong here, but I wanna go way down the street with him and see where we get to." I wanted to see if maybe he got to territory where he's right, or else he gives up and says, "Okay, I liked your idea better." And a lot of times, that would happen. I'd do all these drafts of a monologue, and at the end of the day it was basically the same thing that I was saying, but it was in different words. It was in words that were more comfortable to him.

I never say no. It's not in my vocabulary to say no to an actor.

JOHN D. BRANCATO: In early discussions about *Terminator 3* with Arnold, listening to his feelings about the character, the moments he thought worked the best, what he thought the character was about—that was important, and did help us write. He had a very clear sense of what a Terminator would and wouldn't do, and that really was useful. That was a unique situation, because when my partner Mike Ferris and I were writing, every line that Arnold's character was gonna say, we were able to spit out in his voice. There was one that I really liked. I liked giving him the line "nanotechnological transjectors," which is actually in the final film. Christ, I don't know how many times he tried to say that, but that was just, in a way, a little bit of asserting screenwriters' power—to try to have that line in that Austrian accent. "Nanotechnological transjectors."

MARK D. ROSENTHAL: After the success of the first two *Superman* movies, *Superman III* was really a fiasco, and the cast said, "We don't want to do this anymore." Christopher Reeve came up with the idea for *Superman IV*, so we were asked not just to work with Chris's idea, but to bring the cast back. They all said, "It depends on the script."

Chris was such a down-to-earth star. I remember when we would walk down Columbus Avenue in New York, people would stop him, and he was warm and friendly to everyone. He had no pretensions. He really loved acting. We wanted to get back that feeling of the first two *Superman* movies, and we really worked hard with Chris on that. Luckily, our script got the whole cast back, and he was very happy about that. The great test is we got Gene Hackman back as Lex Luthor, which we thought was a triumph.

Unfortunately, Warner Bros. had made a deal with Cannon Films several weeks before preproduction, and they cut the budget in half, which meant all the scenes had to be downscaled. The movie was supposed to open with this giant action sequence, and it got so pared down that when the movie opened, you knew right away it didn't look right. I think the one sequence in the film that still kind of works is a double date, sort of a farce scene, where both Clark Kent and Superman have a double date with Lois Lane and another character we created, played by Mariel Hemingway. At least you can sort of see what the movie was trying to be.

To watch Chris put himself out there for this movie and have such a terrible product come out at the end was heartbreaking.

Mark D. Rosenthal

ALLISON ANDERS: I had a friend who was one of the most brilliant actresses, Katrin Cartlidge. She was in a lot of Mike Leigh movies, she was in *Breaking the Waves*. She rejected me for *Things Behind the Sun*. I wanted her to play my lead character, and she turned me down. She was notorious for turning people down, because she was not careerist. She completely went with, "What character needs me to bring it to life?" And she told me, "Allison, this character doesn't need me, but I'm gonna tell you exactly who you need to look for, what qualities this person needs to have." And I found Kim Dickens, based on the stuff that Katrin told me. Sadly, Katrin passed away a couple of years ago, but she was amazing. Whatever character called to her—feature, big money, little money—it didn't matter. And so I really take that same attitude. She really taught me that. I feel like there are stories that need me to tell them.

The Director's Perspective: David Dobkin

David Dobkin

NYU-trained filmmaker David Dobkin made commercials and music videos before launching his feature career with the indie thriller Clay Pigeons *(1998) and the hit sequel* Shanghai Knights *(2003). Then came* Wedding Crashers *(2005), which earned over $200 million at the domestic box office. Subsequently, Dobkin has directed* Fred Claus *and produced* Mr. Woodcock *(both 2007).*

A Material World

I believe that great writing makes great stories, and great stories make great films. I start from that, so I really don't move until I trust the material that I have in my hands. I can credit the long, slow boat of my career to being able to build better development skills, because I couldn't get my hands on the material I thought was really great. There's a totem pole in Hollywood, for sure, about who they want to entrust certain material to. The more successful you are with your films financially, the more access you have to better material. It's like anything—if you were going to hire someone to build your house, you'd probably hire the guy who built the house that you really like, or that came in on budget.

I usually get screenplays that need work. It's something that they want to get going, and it needs a director's vision to focus it into what it's gonna be. Then you go out and get talent from there. A lot of times, there's already a start date. The danger with doing that before the material is ready is that you're fighting with everyone for the talent pool in Hollywood, which is not enormous. There are a lot of great actors, but there aren't a lot of movie stars. Once in a while, I have talent that's attached, and they send me the screenplay. That's been a new kind of treat—to be able to get a piece of material with an actor attached—so when you're reading it you're visualizing them in a role. You're able to look at it and go, "I see their voice in it," or "I don't see their voice in it."

A director can read something and be like, "God, this is gonna be a great movie—but it's not what I want to direct."

Something happens when you read something you want to make. I immediately start storyboarding in the margins as I'm reading. I'll start making notes for adjustments to a character, or ideas for new scenes. It happens very organically—either the material starts to pull you into it or it doesn't.

Powerful male bonds always played a really big part in my life. I'm someone who didn't kiss a girl until I was seventeen years old, didn't have a girlfriend till my senior year in high school. I was a late bloomer, so my friendships with guys filled in for that kind of energy. My first girlfriend kind of broke my heart, and it was really my friends who helped me pull it together. With *Wedding Crashers*, I had the opportunity to explore the difficulty that I experienced when my friends got into relationships and all of a sudden part of their emotionality became absent from our friendship.

Nuptial Bliss

For the first time as a director, I found out what the power of telling your own story through a film is—you find a piece of material that lines up with you, and everything starts to resonate at a whole different level. *Wedding Crashers* was the first time I decided I was going to tell my own story in a movie.

I kind of found the coming-of-age story for thirty-five-year-old men, which was my age at the time, and Owen Wilson's and Vince Vaughn's as well. There were scenes and adjustments inside scenes that I brought to the writers, and we created together. The characters sitting on the steps of the Lincoln Memorial, with Vince saying, "We'll look back on this and say we were young and stupid," and Owen saying, "We're not really young anymore"—that was something I actually used to do with my best friend in Washington, D.C., at the end of a long night. I felt that would let the audience understand that Owen was outgrowing this lifestyle.

I added the love-at-first-sight moment with Rachel McAdams so we understood that Owen had an emotional connection. That colors everything in the second act—we understand what his goal is. I added a thing in the beginning where Vince says to his secretary, about Owen, that he's always looked over him, like a little brother in a way; he believes he's holding up his friend, and Owen believes he's holding up his friend. Those were kind of the first contributions to an emotional arc.

Then there was a process with the actors, especially with Vince and Owen, who are both writers. Through a writing/rehearsal/improvisation process, we would work through character intentions and dialogue and stuff like that, and oftentimes come back to about 80 percent of what the screenplay was—with 20 percent of new amazing stuff. You know, Owen said to me very early on, "I think it'd be funny if we go crash funerals." That was his idea. We didn't know where that was gonna go in the movie. Then I realized I needed a bottoming-out moment—an all-is-lost moment for him emotionally. I said, "Hey, I think the funeral could be here."

That sequence was created in a room with Owen writing and riffing, and me kind of being editor to his writing.

Respecting the Writer

I'm a Shakespeare guy. I learned to direct actors through Shakespeare, and Shakespeare's writing is perfect. All the characters are psychologically sound, they're making the right decisions for the right reasons, and they're saying lines that you wouldn't change. So the job for me and the actors, when we're doing Shakespeare, is to discover the writer's intentions—and if we're not understanding it, we keep workshopping stuff until we understand it. But you don't go changing the lines.

In Hollywood, people come in and they wanna change everything. It's almost like they want it to become their own voice—which for some people is very important. It's important for Vince to be in his own voice. You want to see that happen in the process. But not everybody has that. A lot of the time, you want to see the actor become the character.

I do long rehearsal processes, and I want people to find the writing before we go changing things. I like to get the screenplay solid enough that people can come in and participate without it being turned upside down. We'll make small changes on set as we're shooting, but we improvise on the page, you know what I mean? It's like, "Find your way into it, then change a few words here and there." But I really like to stick to the writing, because I know what's there. A lot of people just change and change and change, thinking there's always something better. If it's coming from the writer, I trust it. If it's coming from everybody else, I tend to get a little bit concerned.

I believe in the original writer. I really don't like replacing writers, and I don't think I've ever consciously been the person to pull the trigger on that. I'll roll up my sleeves and get in the mud and go to hell and back with them. I'd rather get in that journey and see what it is. Sometimes the original writer gets burnt out. And by the way, I have many times seen the original writer step off, and someone else comes in, and the original writer comes back and finishes it. What I usually tell somebody, if they're being replaced for a stage of the project, is that this is your baby. Your name's always gonna be on it. These are your characters.

It's part of the process in Hollywood. You shouldn't take it personally, because there isn't a major writer in Hollywood that this hasn't happened to. Hollywood tends to need things on a timetable, and if somebody isn't juicing those ideas, there's not always a lot of time for them to gestate. That's a lot of the reason why different people with different ideas come in.

I don't think it's always necessarily a disbelief in a writer, or a disbelief in their ability to get it all the way there, but sometimes it is. By the way, people can have great ideas but not be able to execute them. You see it with directors all the time, and you see it with writers all the time.

The Collaborative Process

Writing is a very isolated, lonely experience, and then your writing goes out to people, and either it worked, or it didn't work, or it kinda worked. It's the same thing as a director, when you put your movie out in front of people. It's a nerve-racking experience to go through. But, you know, get over it. It's like shooting free throws—you're gonna miss and miss and miss, and then you're gonna start hitting, and you'll hit more often the more you do it.

I like people who are really open, and who understand what their strengths and their weaknesses are. I like people who are good listeners. Listening is a huge thing. I listen very carefully to the writer, and I hope the writer listens carefully to me. I listen to my actors. The actors listen to the writer and the director, and the producers are there to help coach everybody.

The more collaborative people are, the better it is to work with them. You want to have a good experience. Some people can get very defensive and insecure, and that's okay. A lot of people are defensive and insecure and talented. But it's harder for me, personally, to work with people like that.

When you're looking for movies to do, you meet with the people whose writing you love, and you hopefully build relationships with some of them. You try to hire the people you think have the right voices, or people that you know would be excited to have an opportunity to do something different. We meet, and hopefully the writer has the same vision of the movie that I have. It's a little bit of a two-way street. I say, "This is what I'm trying to do," and they have an idea of how to help me get there. Or else they have their own vision of it, and I have to see if that's somewhere I want to go.

7

The Rules
of the Game

If it seems unfair that writers must run the gauntlet of the development process only to discover that even more compromises loom when powerful collaborators become involved, then the fact that other challenges still await must seem patently cruel. But that's the lot of the screenwriter in contemporary Hollywood: The obsessive focus on fast returns at the box office means that writers are expected to deliver blueprints for consumer products, rather than personal artistic statements.

It was not always so. For a glorious moment in the late sixties and early seventies, individualistic storytellers seized power in Hollywood by putting their collective finger on the pulse of the burgeoning youth audience. Almost as soon as that heyday for offbeat screenplays began, however, it ended when studio executives saw the unprecedented box-office returns of effects-driven blockbusters such as Jaws *(1975) and* Star Wars *(1977). As Paul Mazursky and others who flourished in the "New Hollywood" era note, the period during which studios bankrolled personal films was as fleeting as it was precious. The result is the current stark climate, in which corporations scrutinize potential movie productions as closely—and as coldly—as any other items on their balance sheets. These financial pressures lead to an anxious existence for writers who, as Mark D. Rosenthal colorfully remarks, feel like prey trying to avoid the clutches of ravenous predators.*

Adding to the insecurity is this unpleasant fact: Writers who complain too noisily about their status in the creative process quickly find themselves shut out of the process altogether, because they gain reputations for being difficult. The concept that a screenwriter might know best how to tell a film's story simply doesn't have any credibility in Hollywood.

If there's hope in this bleak litany of professional realities, it is the knowledge that pragmatic screenwriters have opportunities to protect their work and to ensure continued employment—if they're willing to compromise. That compromise may take the form of providing gratis labor, parsing unclear instructions in order to identify what powerful colleagues truly want, or even sacrificing beloved story elements for the greater goal of seeing a movie brought to life.

Yesterday's Gone

MICHAEL JANUARY: Hollywood lives and dies on something that seems new and original, but is very much like something that made money before. If you, as a writer, can figure out how to make that formula work, then you can become quite wealthy.

JAMES L. WHITE: The studios are not very receptive to original thought. Everyone likes to say they are, but then they find sixty zillion reasons why there's no audience for this and there's no audience for that, and they keep making the same thing over and over again.

ARI B. RUBIN: I remember when I started out, one of the first questions I asked in every single meeting was: "Do you want original ideas?" They all said no. Every single one of them said, "It's hard to get an original idea produced. If you have a book you love, let us know. If you have a magazine article, we'll option it and you can do it." The money people wanna see something tangible from the get-go.

JOHN AUGUST: You tend to have a lot of ideas you would like to see made into movies, yet the reality is that most things that actually become movies aren't brand-new ideas that I sit down at the computer and write. If I want to have movies in theaters, it behooves me to actually write the kind of movies that are gonna get made. At this point in time, the movies that get made are based on some preexisting piece of intellectual property.

JONATHAN LEMKIN: Things are really brand-identified right now, and if I could pitch *Wheaties: The Movie* tomorrow, I'd have a better chance of selling it than I would with an original idea. "There's already a cereal box, guys!" It's a very strange time.

RICHARD RUSH: A corporate style of conducting business has been imposed upon the movie industry, which used to leave room for the disruptions of talent. It is stunning to see how cleverly everything has been assigned a number value, and any idea is immediately dissected into numbers representing the stars, the subject matter, the possible disposition of it in various media, countries, ancillaries—and it's all a stunning amount of bullshit, because it totally neglects whether it's going to be done well or not.

JOHN CARPENTER: The movie business has evolved from this industry that used to be run by the owners—people like Jack Warner and L. B. Mayer and these guys, back in the golden age. The studios were factory situations, and everything was controlled. Things began to break loose in the sixties and seventies, and more freedom was given to the director. This coincided with a lot of style changes—lighter cameras, you could go on exteriors, and so forth. Nowadays, giant conglomerates own the studios, and movies are just a part of this big company.

John Carpenter

PAUL SCHRADER: There was a crisis of confidence, right around the late sixties. The big studio films had started flopping—*Paint*

Your Wagon; Hello, Dolly!—and the indie films had started making money—*Five Easy Pieces, The Last Picture Show, Easy Rider.* The studios were in very bad trouble. This was the time in which Paramount was actually sold, and they were gonna fold up the lot; 20th Century–Fox sold off most of its lot. There was a real sense of insecurity in the executive suites as to what people wanted to see, particularly what young people wanted to see. So you could actually go into those offices and say to them, like Coppola did, "Today is your lucky day—I have come to tell you what people want to see," and they would actually believe you.

That changed in the early eighties, when Barry Diller came from ABC over to Paramount, and he brought in Frank Mancuso and the whole concept of market research—because the studio executives hated the idea that they had to take the word of artists about what was gonna make money.

Market research used to be a building way on the other side of the lot. When Diller came in, it was right next to his office. Virtually everything went through market research, and that was a great relief to the studio executives, because now they had a system whereby they could tell what people actually wanted to see. But once you introduce the concept of market research, then you start down a road where the filmmakers are moved out of the executive suites, and bit by bit the money managers are moved in. Now the big film conglomerates are run by people who know the money game, but not the filmmaking game.

PAUL MAZURSKY: The seventies were paradise. There was great respect for the auteur, and especially for the director who wrote his own scripts, or cowrote them. They weren't bringing me material. I brought my material to them. In the seventies you were answering to one or two people at a studio. Nowadays it's corporate, so you don't know quite what you're going up against.

The nature of the movie business has changed in some very powerful ways. Number one, when *Jaws* came along, wide distribution became more and more the thing, which led to what I call "opening big on Friday." And if you write a script that they don't think will open big on a Friday, you're doomed to more difficulty. They don't care how good it is, and they used to care.

Paul Mazursky

In the seventies, they all wanted Oscar nominations, so many good movies were made. They weren't thinking about releasing it in three thousand theaters. When they were reading a script, they could say, "Well, if this doesn't cost too much money, if it's really cheap—this guy might be talented, there might be something here. Let's take a shot." And they would open it in maybe fifty or a hundred theaters in the country, see how it did. If it did okay, it would go a little broader, might even get up to five hundred. And if it only cost $2 million, they might end up making their money back and be satisfied.

WILLIAM GOLDMAN: With *Butch Cassidy*, George Roy Hill was a powerful director, and Paul Newman was the biggest star in the world. I think the movie cost $4.8 million. If you were gonna make *Butch Cassidy* today with Will Smith, let's say, and a name director, you're talking $150 million, and that's if you're lucky. That's one of the biggest changes screenwriters have to deal with—everything is so fucking expensive, and it's only gonna get more so.

I was talking to a superpower producer recently, and some studio head just said to him, "We'll make movies for under $20 million or over $75 million. We don't want anything in between." That logic is this: "Under $20 million" means an art film, and they might make money off of an art film, and "over $75 million" means special effects. Well, it's ridiculous to assume that you can't make a movie for $35 million that's a huge hit.

DANIEL PYNE: One of the sad things that's happening in film and television is that this is our mythmaking structure. Culture tends to need myths, and it tends to need storytelling. And I think sometimes we shortchange ourselves by making the kinds of movies that we sometimes make that have no real cultural context except to make money or sell theme-park rides.

STEVEN E. de SOUZA: We've sort of moved into a post-content era now, if you're talking about a studio tent-pole project. And if you're interested in story and human emotion, I would not recommend chasing those kinds of movies. I go to meetings and they're already talking about the sequel. I go to meetings where they're talking about the power of this scene where your leading lady says, "They killed my best friend! They betrayed me! They'll pay!" and they go, "We really think this best friend is an appealing character, and the actor we're thinking of getting is looking for a franchise. Do we have to kill that person? Could that person just be injured?" Well, that's sort of like a different thing. When Scarlett O'Hara says, "I swear to God, I'll never be hungry again," you don't ask if she could say, "I swear to God, I'll never miss lunch!"

KRISS TURNER: You've got *Pirates of the Caribbean 8*, probably, on the way, and I understand it. *Spider-Man 14*. I get it. They're gonna keep comin', comin', comin'. . . . But I've gotta believe in original ideas, because those are what I write.

NAOMI FONER: I do a lot of independent, smaller-budgeted films, and I do those movies that the studios make that are character-based, and I've started to bring things to them to remind them of the movies they used to make. *Ordinary People* wouldn't get made anymore—it would be a Lifetime Television movie. It's not the kind of thing that studios are doing. Those are the kinds of things that I started my career doing, and those are the kinds of things that I think people are still hungry for. This is what we have to convince the studios to make.

RON SHELTON: I wrote *Bad Boys II*. That did $500 million. I think I know how to deal with that marketplace, but it isn't what

I would like to do with my daily life. The need for tent poles kind of lowers the bar to where an international common denominator is the goal of the screenplay, and that just doesn't interest me. But moving over to indies, as I have in the last five years, you run into the issue that independent films are driven by foreign money. Well, none my sports movies works in the foreign market. So that's the juggling act. You know, the business changes. The goalposts move all the time. You can complain about it, or you can try to kick it through the moving goalpost. That's what I do.

Here Come the Writer-Eating Crocodiles

BRUCE JOEL RUBIN: A brief story, just so you understand how Hollywood works. When I had written *Ghost*, I walked out of the commissary with a number of executives, and they turned to me as we were walking, and they said, "Bruce, we just want you to know that *Ghost* is the best script we have ever read." And I just . . . I couldn't quite believe it, but I just thought, "Oh my God, this is extraordinary." I felt so wonderful, and I sort of floated away. About a week later, I was walking out of the commissary behind those same executives, who were walking with another writer. I was listening to them, and they said to the writer, "We just want you to know that your script is the best script we have ever read." And then I got it. I got how the town works, on some level.

NAOMI FONER: I wrote a screenplay called *Triangle*, which I had written for Barbra Streisand about the Triangle Shirtwaist Factory fire, and they hired Jane Fonda to play the other part. She wanted to get rid of me. I didn't yet have enough experience to know that

Tales from the Script

when somebody comes on a picture, they want to bring in their people because they know that if they don't bring in their people, they're in some jeopardy of not being important enough in the process. You know, it gives them power. I was devastated, because I had written a really good script—one that had attracted Jane Fonda, one that Barbra Streisand was happy with. These were a couple of women who I had held in great esteem—who I had hoped would be mentors of some sort or another—but who turned out to be giant pains in the ass when actually encountered in life.

MARK D. ROSENTHAL: Once you're hired for a job, there's a very high anxiety level, which just stays in the background—it's sort of like a white noise of "What's gonna happen to me on this little adventure? Am I gonna make it down the river? When are the giant falls with the writer-eating crocodiles in 'em gonna come? Are they gonna come way down the river? Are they gonna come right away, which they do sometimes?" You know, you turn in a first draft and good-bye. Or maybe you're gonna sail way down the river and get it close to production, and then something bad is gonna happen. Or in the rare case, you're gonna make it all the way through. I once had a studio executive say to me, when we were replaced, "What are you carping about? Nobody goes the distance anymore." As if that was okay.

JOSE RIVERA: Earlier in my career, I was still learning my craft as a writer, and I would think, "I'm not getting these jobs because I'm not yet a good enough writer to get the jobs." Now I don't feel that. Now I feel like I really know my craft, and now if I get rejected, I take it far more personally and think, "Oh my God, these people are idiots. They just don't know what they're doing. They don't know a good thing when they see it." It's much harder to be turned down these days, because I feel that I'm giving it everything I have, and the marketplace has proven that I can perform. When something gets turned down, I feel there's something really wrong here.

RICHARD RUSH: Frequently, I find that if I've written a project, what is going to be attacked is my favorite scene, whatever it happens to be. The one that I know is truly interesting and right, and the reason that I made this piece and the reason it works, is the one that will come under attack, because everybody wants to get in on the glory of what's good about it. They want to change it, and therefore be part owner. I think that's the secret, unconscious motivation that drives it—otherwise the coincidence is too great.

JOHN CARPENTER: Everybody wants to be creative. Everybody. They're trying to influence the movie so they can be proud of it. So you just see how bad the suggestion is and see if you can live with it. If it's not too terrible, you try to accommodate them. If it's the worst thing in the world and it destroys your idea, then you have to stand up and say, "I can't do that. That's just gonna ruin this."

GERALD DiPEGO: I've always stayed with my films. Even when they've replaced me, they've asked me to come back. So when I go into the theater or to the premiere and see the movie, it's not a surprise. I know what the damage is if there's damage, and I know where the thrills are if the thrills are still in there. But it's very hard to be calm about it, because the story is such a personal thing, and you dreamed it up. As people say, it's kind of your child that you're sending out into the world.

I'm sort of toward the end of my career, and that's one of the things I'm so glad to leave behind. I mean, I have a small movie that

I've written, and if it's my last one, that's fine. I'm in business with a man, and we're going to hopefully raise the money and do the film, and I'm looking forward to that. But I'm also picking up my novel career again and writing short stories and so on.

It's hard for me to love what I do, and then make peace with a film that makes you wince and cringe—maybe every twenty minutes, or maybe just twice during the movie if you're lucky. There's always a little cringe factor involved.

DAVID S. WARD: Sometimes you'll write a script and it'll be made into a movie, and you'll feel like the movie is really a pale imitation of the potential that the script had. Other times you feel like the movie not only did the script justice, but it may have improved it. Both of those things are possible. It's not always that the screenwriter winds up feeling like their work has been somehow diminished. There are times when it does, and it's a terrible feeling because everyone works hard and wants the film to be good.

WILLIAM GOLDMAN: Nobody sets out to fuck up your movie. It's not like the director or the stars wake up in the morning and say, "Let me screw up this scene. How can I really cause Bill Goldman pain?" It's just that they're terrified. I wrote a line once that caught on out there in Hollywood: "Nobody knows anything." And they don't. If we knew what we were doing, every movie would be wonderful. If actors knew what they were doing, every performance would be just swell. It's a crapshoot. It just is. There's no answer. I wish there were.

ANDREW W. MARLOWE: I think the hardest situation is when you have a director who gets skittish a few weeks or a few months before shooting. Everybody's loved the script up to that point, but just for insurance, let's bring on a big name, or somebody who's good with this dialogue. They come in and they do work, and the work probably doesn't make the script any better; it's probably a lateral change. That's when it's difficult, because it's not really rewriting to make the project better—it's rewriting to assuage somebody's ego. More often than not, you'll end up with a project that has competing points of view.

ZAK PENN: Particularly on the big blockbuster movies, where you're coming in as a rewriter, I go through that same period of feeling like "This movie's gonna be great, and I have all these ideas, and this is how it's gonna be different from everything else." And then you start to realize: "This isn't my movie." Even if I don't get fired—which probably is gonna happen no matter how good a job I do, because it's the nature of the beast—it's really the director's movie, and the actors' movie, and a bunch of other people's movie. And so at a certain point as a screenwriter, you have to say, "The purity of vision that I'm looking for isn't gonna happen, so what is worth my investment here? How passionate can I be?"

BRUCE JOEL RUBIN: Writers don't own the very product that makes this whole business flourish—and that's not right. It's not fair. It's never been fair, and every writer knows it. There's a kind of underlying anger in every writer in Hollywood at how misused we all are by the business. It is really cruel on some levels that writers have so little participation in the work they create. You know, to be a writer and to have to fight to go to the premiere of your movie, or to be allowed on the set where they're shooting your movie—it's not right.

MARK O'KEEFE: This was at the *Bruce Almighty* premiere. It was my first movie. There was some sort of VIP area with the actors, and I'm like, "Oh, let's go in there and say hi to everybody."

STEVE KOREN: The security guard wouldn't let us in. He didn't know who we were. I got mad. I'm like, "You have a job tonight because we had an idea once!"

MARK O'KEEFE: Steve's freaking out. I'm getting a little testy.

STEVE KOREN: I'm like, "Come on! We wrote this movie! Please."

MARK O'KEEFE: And then Stacey Snider comes out, and she's like, "Oh, let them in." So we go in there.

STEVE KOREN: She was very nice to let us in.

MARK O'KEEFE: Yeah, and we're like, "We're here! We did it!" It was very emotional being denied access to . . .

STEVE KOREN: . . . to your own movie.

MARK O'KEEFE: Yeah, this is our own premiere. And so Jim Carrey's in there with his daughter and her friends. There's a few other people—I think Will Ferrell was there. But it's very empty. And the only other person in there was some woman. We go up to her, and I'm like, "What involvement did you have with this?" And she's like, "I trained the dog."

STEVE KOREN: The urinating dog in the movie.

MARK O'KEEFE: Yeah. And she says, "So what did you guys do?" I say, "We're the writers." And she says, "Oh, wow. It's so cool they invited you to this."

Mark O'Keefe and Steve Koren

Your Reputation Precedes You

MICHAEL JANUARY: If you do things that get you a certain reputation, when you come up in a meeting or a discussion, you can get shut off very quickly. If you have a reputation for being difficult, if you have a reputation for threatening to sue people, if you have a reputation for not being able to deliver, then when there's a discussion around a table, someone will say, "I heard this," or "I heard that," and they'll go on to the next choice. You will disappear from the conversation, sometimes with an expletive.

JOHN D. BRANCATO: Being really pissy about things doesn't help. One of the great blow-up stories happened with a close friend of mine. He's in a development meeting, and somebody's saying, "We want this character to have more of a Judd Nelson feel—you know, from *Taxi*." My friend turned to the executive and said, "That's Judd Hirsch, you fucking moron." That wasn't really good for his career, but the story was told repeatedly, and I think people love him all the more because of it.

PAUL SCHRADER: I have a very troubled and problematic reputation. I'm known as somebody who will cause you trouble. I'm not that good at taking orders. I'm not that good at, you know, shufflin' my feet. I have friends who are. I was just talking to Richard Price, who worked on *American Gangster*, and he was talking to me about the hard time Denzel Washington gave him. I thought to myself, "My God, I would have walked out of the room if someone had said to me the things that Denzel was saying to Richard." But he didn't walk out of the room, and he pulls down bigger numbers.

JOSE RIVERA: If you're starting to feel like you're hot shit and you don't need to play fair with others, I think that can really hurt you—feeling that you can be a one-man band, that you don't have to listen anymore. You know, the root of the word *hubris* means that you stop listening. I think that's the biggest danger you can get into—when you think you've got all the answers, or you've got all the experience in the world.

MICHAEL WOLK: I think there are ways that you can handle your career to cultivate relationships with the people that have the power to make your movie. And I think I did everything I could absolutely wrong. I was about the work, I was about the script, I was about transmitting my vision—but I wasn't so much about schmoozing and hanging out. One factor was that I was a New Yorker. I couldn't wait to get on the plane back to New York.

There's a line from the marvelous light comedy *Mourning Becomes Electra*: "Rottenness is born of sunshine." That was kinda my feeling about L.A., and so when I would go out there, I would stay there until I started to rot, and then I would come back to New York, which was usually no more than ten days. So the idea that I would cultivate relationships with the Hollywood community was kinda . . . I was thinkin' they would reach out to me 'cause I was an artiste. But they stopped reaching out for some reason.

I think it's very, very important to cultivate real personal relationships, because those are the things that really count when people are starting to put projects together. Who do they like? Who do they wanna work with? Who do they wanna hang with? You know, that's very important. Even if they don't get you what you want right away, just keep workin' the rooms, and keep in touch with people. And if they ever do somethin' good for you, let 'em know that you're really very grateful.

DAVID S. WARD: Hollywood's a small town. People pretty much know what goes on. It's very hard to keep a secret. Most people know what movies really cost, as opposed to what people are saying they cost. How does this affect screenwriters? Well, you can get a fairly good reputation as a screenwriter without really having a lot of credits, because people may have read work you've done that was actually very good work—it just didn't happen to get made.

There's all kinds of reasons why scripts don't get made. They may be too expensive for what people think the commercial return could be. They could have gotten caught in a change of management at the studio, where somebody else comes in and doesn't wanna have anything to do with the slate that was developed before.

But because the script may have circulated, a lot of agents around town may have read it, a lot of executives and studios around town may have read it, and a lot of financing entities. And they may have liked it. They may have thought, "I'd like to work with this writer sometime." Maybe that script doesn't get made, but that script will get you work doing something else.

Taking One for the Team

FRANK DARABONT: Look at the credits on the end of any given movie. Even a simple film that was shot in six weeks, like *The Mist*, has hundreds of people bringing their contributions to the table. That the initial vision on the screenplay page remains intact by the time it hits the screen is miraculous considering how many fingerprints get on it along the way—even when those fingerprints are well-meaning fingerprints. So when you see something intact, you really have to take pleasure in it, if you're the guy who put the words on the page in the first place. It's a very bizarre process, what we do. So when you see a great movie . . . man, I find it very inspiring to see somebody's work that really speaks to me. To see those components having all sailed in the same direction and landed safely, instead of hitting the rocks, is fantastic. I love that part of what we do.

JOHN AUGUST: I think what newer screenwriters fail to understand is that about 50 percent of the job is how well you write. The other 50 percent of the job is how well you can understand what the people making the movie—that includes the producers, the studio, and, most importantly, the director—need in order to make the movie. I think one of the reasons why I'm able to keep working with some of the same filmmakers again and again is I can sort of intuit what it is they really need. Sometimes they don't have the vocabulary or the specific answer to explain what it is that's not quite working, but you're listening very carefully and figuring out what they need. There's a social aspect to screenwriting that's very different from being a novelist or almost any other kind of writer.

DAVID HAYTER: It's my job to be positive. There are some times when I'm going into a meeting that I know is gonna be miserable, but to a certain extent it's my job to go in and power through it—to keep it afloat, you know? Even if you have to force your enthusiasm going in, it's contagious, and it will pick you up, and it will pick up the people you're meeting with. Studio executives with stone faces will suddenly start being drawn in by your energy and by your enthusiasm. It'll make your life easier, and it'll make the movie better in the long run.

JOE FORTE: As a writer, the only power you have is persuasion. That's it. You can stamp up and down and you can scream, and eventually people are not gonna want to be around you. And so you try to stay as close to the process as you can, because that's your only ability to influence it—to be in the room and try to persuade people. People want to change scenes or dialogue. You work with that. But the thing that I try to influence is the theme, that emotional through-line. That's what the movie's about.

If you don't know what it's about, for you, then you can't influence anybody, and your arguments don't make sense. They won't track. But if you can always return to that through-line, that's what the theme is there for. It orients everything. It's the registration mark that goes through your movie. And if you can bring people back to that, that's why you try to stay involved as much as you can—or are allowed to be. Then, you know, the chips fall where they may. Because it's such an expensive business, it's collaborative.

ADAM RIFKIN: A movie that costs $70 million, $80 million, $100 million just to make is gonna cost another $100 million just to promote. That's a $200 million risk. So of course everybody's nervous. Everybody's gonna second-guess everything, and everybody is gonna run around like chickens with their heads cut off, panicking.

But you have to be professional. You have to be easy to work with. Because let's say that you're working on a project that you know is going south. You can rant, you can scream, you can be difficult in the room—and then you can be guaranteed that you will never work at that studio again. But if you are working on a project that's going south and you do the best job you can, they're gonna remember that you worked hard, that you are creative, that you're easy to work with. And when something else comes up, they're gonna think of you for another project.

If you're difficult, believe me, they're gonna remember you—they're gonna remember not to hire you. I know a lot of writers who do this, and get themselves systematically banned from studio after studio after studio. It's not worth it. It's one movie. If you're a writer worth his salt, you've got a stockpile of scripts. You've got a hundred books that you think would make great movies too. You want to be involved in as many projects as possible, because it's a numbers game. Of the thirty movies you get a chance to develop, maybe two of them get made. You know what I mean? You want to keep working.

Adam Rifkin

DAVID S. WARD: I think the most difficult behavior is to be defensive about your work—to simply say, "No, I'm not gonna change it. You're stupid. Your ideas are stupid." Word gets around that you're difficult to deal with, that you're not professional, that you're not a team player. That can really hurt your career, because it's just a fact of life in the movies that changes are made to scripts. Nobody ever turns in a script and they just go and shoot it.

LINDA VOORHEES: When you're on an assignment, you are contracted to do three rewrites and a polish. So the first draft that you turn in to a producer is their first draft, but you have rewritten it between six and twelve times. So you've already done six to twelve rewrites, and you're calling it "Draft One."

Then you sit in a meeting and they do notes on their "Draft One," and you go back and you rewrite for the "Draft Two" that you're gonna turn in to them per the contract. To get to that draft, you again rewrite between six and twelve times. Then you do another set of notes.

The third time, you rewrite again, and hopefully it's in pretty good shape, so you're only gonna rewrite between three and six times. Then you want the green light. If you don't get the green light, then you give them their polish. If you do get the green light, then you do the polish with a director. So either way you're gonna do the polish, and that polish is a true draft. It's never a real "polish."

So you're doing a lot of freebies along the way, and the reason you're doing the freebies is because you have pride as a writer, because you want to turn in your best writing, because you want to work again, and because you want that paycheck again. The other thing is, quite frankly, they let you know that you can be replaced. You want sole writing credit if possible, so you hang on to it with everything you have by doing those various iterations as you're calling it "Draft One," "Draft Two," "Draft Three." By the time you get to the polish, you've rewritten easily twenty times or more.

If you're lucky enough to be in preproduction with a director, you can do another six drafts.

BRUCE JOEL RUBIN: I worked on *The Last Mimzy* for eight years, so you have no idea how many drafts were done. I mean, beyond understanding. And in the last year toward production, more drafts than I had done in the seven years before. It was exhausting and difficult. I was removed from the project. I was brought back to the project. In the last months of it, I was told to cut the script from 120 pages to, like, 95. The people who were putting the money into the project wanted a shorter movie.

So I cut it, and we got it down to a very skeletal length, and then we had the cast reading just before we started shooting. Everybody sat around the table and read the script, and my heart just sunk. I said, "This is the outline of the movie. This is not the movie. It's not there." I didn't know what to do, but I knew that they had planned every day's shooting—there was a schedule, and they weren't going to change any of that. But within that schedule, I could look at every scene and I could give it a little bit more tissue, a little more fat, a little more heart—whatever was required to make it richer. And so I went home that night to the hotel. I worked all night, and I rewrote the movie. I gave it more life.

Working on *Mimzy* was a great experience for me, because I finally understood how much you can cut away, and then how much you have to add back to make sure it's alive. It was one of the great lessons because I didn't know you could pare away that much and still have it work. That was really astounding. One thinks that all of one's words and all of one's scenes and all of one's dialogue is precious, and has to be there to make this thing work. That proved not to be the case.

Bob Shaye, who directed the film and produced it, knew this. He kept saying, "Cut more, cut more." And I kept thinking, "It's gonna die, it's gonna die." Not only did it not die, it found a kind of musculature that was very powerful. I did need to come back in at the end and add the little bit of flavoring, but it finally all worked. I really loved that I could learn so much about movies, even at this late stage of having written a fair number.

JANE ANDERSON: I wrote a spec script called *Cop Gives Waitress $2 Million Tip*. It later was turned into a film that they renamed *It Could Happen to You*. I went around pitching the idea to various studios before I wrote it. The idea I pitched was a cop can't pay his tip at a diner, and he tells the waitress, "I'll split my lottery ticket with you." He wins, they split the ticket, the cop and the waitress fall in love, and the cop's wife is so furious about this that she sues them for everything they have—takes all their money away.

Originally, I said, "The cop and the waitress realize that even though they lost $10 million, they found love, and that's where their true happiness was." I remember the executive at this one studio looked at me and said, "They don't get the money?" I said no. "You mean they walk away poor? Can't they have some of the money?"

I knew that, as is, the idea wouldn't sell, because these executives felt that in order for the film to be satisfying, the characters had to have money. So I thought to myself, "How can I have the cop and the waitress have money in the end, yet still relate what I want to say—which is that generosity of heart is what counts in this life?" I gave it a different ending, which was: The cop and waitress lose all their money to the greedy wife who sues 'em for everything they have, and then every New Yorker who fell in love with the cop and waitress's story hears that they're penniless, and every New Yorker gives them a dollar. They end up with $10 million again.

In that way, I was able to hold on to the integrity of my story and yet please a studio—thus the film got made.

The Screenwriting Guru's Perspective: Richard Walter

Richard Walter

Carving a path through the Hollywood jungle is so challenging that writers often enlist the guidance of so-called screenwriting gurus. These charismatic personalities of varying professional experience present seminars; offer one-on-one counseling, often for substantial fees; and appear at conventions such as the annual Screenwriting Expo. One of the most respected veterans of this circuit is Richard Walter, co-chair of UCLA's screenwriting program. Walter is the author of several books, including The Whole Picture: Strategies for Screenwriting Success in the New Hollywood *(1997), and a popular commentator on entertainment industry topics.*

It Pays to Embrace Spontaneity

I came to California about forty years ago, fell into film school at USC. That was the turning point for me: Irwin R. Blacker's class. He's long gone now, God rest his soul, but he was the teacher of many, many famous writers, including the likes of George Lucas, John Milius, John Carpenter. In his class, I wrote my first screenplay. I never would show that script today. It looks like what it is, a first effort. But it had some spark, it had some style, and it got me a lot of work. It won me a career, such as it is.

I worked for all the studios, writing assignments. I was at, like, the top of the second tier. I'm the original writer of the earliest couple of drafts of *American Graffiti.* That led to a great deal of work for the studios writing coming-of-age stories. Mostly they were not made, but I was well paid for them. It's frustrating, but a lot less frustrating than starving to death. I wasn't naïve at all. I was absolutely savvy that there's no way you could get into the movie business—it just can't be done. I always tell writers to expect the worst in life and in Hollywood. This way you can guarantee that your surprises will be exclusively of the pleasant variety.

What I really think pays off is stumbling around blindly and stupidly, and grabbing on to that which you really like. That's true in your life narrative, and it's also useful in your screen narrative. You have a clear goal, where the story is going to go, and then the story runs away from you. I never knew a writer who wasn't surprised by dialogue that a character spoke by circumstance. That's where the real fun is.

That's where the spontaneity and the naturalism are. That's what audiences respond to, and the biggest mistake you can make is try to hold to some preordained plan that you intellectualized at some time in the past.

When Colin Higgins was a student here—before *Silver Streak*, before *Foul Play*, before his great successes—he entered the Goldwyn competition hoping to win first prize. First prize in that era was $4,500. And in that day, you could actually live pretty comfortably in Los Angeles for a year on $4,500. That was his dream, to win $4,500 so he wouldn't have to have a day job. But alas he only won second prize, which was $2,500. And so that meant he had to supplement his income with a day job.

He went to work for a swimming pool cleaning company. And the very first pool that he's cleaning is in the flats of Beverly Hills—great big, fancy house. As he's vacuuming the pool, sitting under a beach umbrella at the pool is a guy who clearly owns this house and he's reading a screenplay. They get to chatting, and Colin tells him about this script that won the Goldwyn prize. And this producer agrees to read it, and ends up producing it. It's *Harold and Maude*. So you just have to stay open to the surprises. You have to be in the stream of things.

The Privilege of Suffering
So many people come between you and the ultimate work. It's true they may mess it up, but there's every chance they'll make it even better than you imagined it could be. That's what's unique about film—the opportunity to belong to the

family of artists and craftspeople. If you can't stand what goes on in Hollywood, then write novels. But if you're working in film, you have to not merely tolerate or even accept this collaborative nature, but you have to rejoice in that.

The important thing is to stay open to everything, no matter how ridiculous it sounds, because there may be something useful lost in there. Sometimes it takes some time to really get it. But the important thing is to stay open. If all you do is glean a small percentage of useful stuff, then it was worthwhile.

Everything means no except yes. That means 99.999 percent of what you hear is no. There are two calls that every writer should want to hear. The first is a producer wanting to know who is your agent. That's a good call. The best call is from some anonymous person at an accounting department for a movie studio that just wants to know your social security number. That means they're cutting you a check.

Don't be such a crybaby. Expect it all to go to hell. Right now, as we're sitting here, David Mamet is teaching a workshop in another building. David Mamet is a gigantically successful screenwriter and playwright. But he's a bitter, dark soul who carps about how he's been betrayed by this, that, and the other—how tortured the business is, and what idiots the producers are. David Mamet is this way! So that never goes away. You have to accept that or you must do something else.

It's a privilege to be permitted to suffer in this business.

They have this ceramics program here at UCLA. In the beginning, each student creates some kind of an object, preparing the clay and sculpting it and glazing it and baking it in the kiln and so on. Then they analyze them all at the end of the quarter. And then the last thing they do is they line up and throw them against the wall and smash them to bits. The professor is trying to get them to understand that it's just clay. There's more.

Screenwriting is not about the sale. It really is about the process. I'm a hard-boiled New Yorker. I can just imagine my friends back East saying, "Richie, you've been baking your brains in the sun too long out there in California if you're talking about 'the process.'" But it's true. It really is about getting into the process, and not becoming goal-oriented. Writers get paid for what other people get scolded for: daydreaming. We're supposed to wander. You know, Faulkner supposedly divorced his first wife because she didn't understand that when he appeared to be gazing idly out the window, he was really hard at work.

What could be greater than just spinning your tales, telling lies, making up stories, and having people actually pay you money for it? Feed your family, pay for your kid's fancy private-school tuition, simply because you told some crazy story that you made up?

There is something so unique about the human condition that has to do with creativity. You know, beavers don't do it, termites don't do it—not plankton, not krill. Humans do this, and if you don't do this you are not entirely fulfilling your purpose as a human being.

8

Slings and Arrows

Thus far, screenwriters have illuminated what could broadly be termed the predictable obstacles associated with their profession. Beyond these challenges, however, lie minefields laden with unpredictable obstacles. Some writers will encounter each of these pitfalls during their careers, and some fortunate souls will avoid them all. But every person who attempts a career as a Hollywood writer needs to be aware of how bad things can get; better to learn survival skills and never need them than to need them and never learn them.

The topic of being fired has been discussed previously, but in this chapter scribes reveal the breadth of this unfortunate reality, describing the regularity with which writers are replaced as well as the politics associated with being asked to revise another person's work. This unflinching survey of life on the Hollywood assembly line leads directly into one of the thorniest subjects in the world of screenwriting: arbitration. Facilitated by the Writers Guild of America, arbitration is the process by which the multiple writers who contributed to a given screenplay contend for screen credit on the resulting film. As David S. Ward notes in his startling remarks about The Mask of Zorro *(1998), arbitration matters because the financial and professional stakes involved are quite serious.*

Even more serious are the catastrophes that befall unlucky proj-ects, either on the way to the screen or once they reach theaters. Some screenplays aren't fated to become films, and some films aren't fated to become successes. Writers including John August and Richard Rush describe projects that spiraled into disappointment, and William Gold-man uses the story of Year of the Comet *(1992) to underscore that paying audiences are capricious about the stories they embrace. If a writer of Goldman's experience and stature can get blindsided by an unexpected flop, such a fate can (and probably will) befall any screen-writer at some point in his or her career.*

Finally, this chapter explores the harshest obstacle of all, the one that's virtually impossible to confront head-on because it so often man-ifests behind closed doors: prejudice. Whether ageism, homophobia, racism, or sexism, the small-minded preconceptions that infect every other aspect of society infect Hollywood as well.

The Assembly Line

JONATHAN LEMKIN: I had a funny experience a few years back, where I got called in for a production polish. The studio had a big director, and they had a spec script written by somebody who was new to the business. Really good idea, no third act. We were on the edge of getting the movie made, and I wasn't entirely happy with the third act myself.

I called up the original writer. I said, "I'm not hunting credit. All I'm trying to do is polish this so the studio's gonna give this guy $30 million to make your movie. Here's what's going on with the third act. Help us, because it's gonna be your movie." He cursed me out for a while—he was gonna buy the movie back, and "How dare I," and all this. The movie never got made.

I met him about four years later. We kind of avoided each other, and he finally crossed the room. He said, "Look, I've never gotten a phone call like that since, and I am so sorry, because I didn't know it was the course of business, and I didn't know that what you were doing was actually incredibly respectful. Nobody makes those phone calls! You made that phone call, and I blew it."

I've been the last writer, I've been the first writer—it just happens. It doesn't make you happy, but you can't fight the process.

JOHN AUGUST: You're like the architect, but they're building the building, and sometimes they decide, "You know what? That's not quite the building we want. We're gonna bring in somebody else to design the new gazebo." I've replaced writers and I've been replaced. The times it's gone well have been when everyone's a grown-up about it.

While it was a really bad and frustrating movie, *Charlie's Angels: Full Throttle* was a good experience in that process. I reached a point where I just couldn't keep working on that movie, and the Wibberleys were brought in to rewrite me. Before they took over, we talked through how the whole movie worked. Ultimately, I came back in and rewrote their draft. We talked through the whole thing again.

We never actually met in person until the premiere. They were seated a row behind me, so we finally got to talk face-to-face. We ended up doing the writers' commentary together on the DVD, which was fun because we could explain why the movie made no sense at many, many points.

DAVID S. WARD: *Sleepless in Seattle* demonstrates that a movie can be written by more than one person. There were three of us on it: Jeff Arch, who wrote the original screenplay; Nora Ephron, who directed the movie; and myself. Each of us made significant contributions to the movie. Even though we didn't write together, that was a real collaborative effort to make that movie what it was.

NORA EPHRON: I think when you're hired to do a rewrite of a script, you don't really think that much about respect for other writers. You're just trying to get the script to work for whoever hired you.

JOHN D. BRANCATO: Toward the end of *The Game*'s process, we were fired. David Fincher hired another writer, who I actually think improved a few things, and came up with a couple of lines we hadn't. In that case, it was actually additive rather than subtractive.

ANDREW W. MARLOWE: When I've been rewritten, oftentimes I've been on the project too long. We've reinvented the main character a couple of times, and the main character that I'm dealing with now is haunted by the ghosts of the previous main characters, so there's no clarity in my mind as to what the main character should be doing in a particular scene. As we all know, structure comes out of what your main character wants. When you lose that clarity, there's not much you can do, except bring in somebody else.

ROBERT MARK KAMEN: Genius in Hollywood equals how much money you make for the studio, so for twenty minutes after *The Karate Kid*, I was a genius. Several of my friends came to power as senior executives at Warner Bros., and they said to me, "You can write fast, you work really well with directors—we have a great job for you. Come work for us."

In the eighties and nineties, Warner Bros. put out all these big action movies, so I came to work as the in-house guy. I'm taking other people's stuff—and they've worked really, really hard—and I'm saying, "That sucks. I'm gonna change that." And because I had the studio mandate, I could change it, kind of like a script assassin. For instance, when I got *The Fugitive*, the movie started in one place and it went all the way across the country. I said, "No, no, no, the movie shouldn't be that. The movie should be, like, on a racecar track. It should start out in Chicago, and it should go all the way around and come back to Chicago." And they said, "Okay."

So I'm doing all these pictures at Warner, and I was sitting on a plane flying back from L.A. to New York. I sit down, and a guy next to me opens a script to read. I said, "Oh, are you in the movie business?" He said, "Yes, I'm a writer." I said, "Me, too." He said, "Oh, my name is so-and-so," and he puts his hand out. I said, "My name is Robert Kamen." He pulls back his hand, and I said, "I rewrote you, didn't I?" He looked at me with venom, and he said, "Twice." It was a five-hour flight, and he didn't talk to me for the rest of the flight.

BILLY RAY: When a rewrite is offered to me, I ask myself three questions. The first question is, "Does it inspire me?" Do I wake up thinking about it, which is the simplest litmus test that I can apply? The second question is, "Is it set in a world that I can write about credibly?" Do I have any knowledge about this world, or is it the sort of world that I can do some investigation into, like the FBI or the *New Republic* magazine? The third question is, "Is this something I can make better?" That, really, is the most important thing.

Sometimes I'm the fourth or fifth guy that's brought in on a project. If you're going to take money to jump into that line, you have to be absolutely certain that you're going to make that movie not just better, but demonstrably better, because other smart people have tried and failed.

Billy Ray

When you come into a room with a bunch of executives on a rewrite, there's a pretty fair level of panic in that room, because they know that they have no idea what they're doing—and yet they have to look like they know what they're doing. So you walk in, and for that one moment you have a little bit of power, because they're looking at you, saying, "Will you make us okay?" You can say to them, "It's gonna be okay. Here are your four drafts. Here's what's not working about them. Here's what I think we can do to make them better, and I know how to do it." And they all relax.

For just one second, you're the man. It goes away the second you're actually writing, and they can start doing their usual studio and producer routines. But for that moment, you do have a little bit of power.

JOE STILLMAN: I was brought on to *Shrek* because of my animation experience. Even though they had been in the process for about a year and a half, or maybe two years, they were still working from an outline, and fundamental things still needed to be done—such as find a way to make an ogre likable, because ogres are inherently pretty disagreeable. So a lot of what I was doing was character work, and trying to find that love story. I definitely see things that I contributed—thematically as well as dialogue—and that makes me feel good, 'cause I like what the movie is trying to get across.

FRANK DARABONT: You can take enormous pride in a film, whether your name winds up onscreen or not. That I felt I'd made a very solid contribution to *Saving Private Ryan* takes nothing away from Robert Rodat's work, and it also takes nothing away from Scott Frank's work—'cause Scott came in after me and targeted a few areas that needed targeting. *Private Ryan* was one of those experiences where I remember watching it and thinking, "Damn, this is good, and I'm really proud of what I brought to the movie, but I'm just as proud of what the other writers brought to the movie."

Robert brought something very important to the table to begin with. It was a privilege to work on that script. It was a genius idea. It was a beautifully focused, simple, elegant, potent idea. So to help that process along was awesome.

DANIEL PYNE: When I rewrote *The Sum of All Fears*, part of the assignment was, "We're gonna get a younger actor to do this movie, so are you interested?" And I thought, "Yeah, this is a way for me to get into it. I can write a character that Tom Clancy hasn't written before, that the franchise hasn't written before." Even though there was a script that preceded me that was pretty good—Paul Attanasio's script—I could add something to that by creating this new version of Jack Ryan, by going back before the books start, and taking his history and finding a new character that I could own. It's hard, though. It's not an easy process. But usually, by asking the right questions in the first meeting or two, you can ascertain what they like about the script that they have and what they don't like about the script that they have, and you can decide whether that gives you any breathing room.

DAVID HAYTER: On *The Scorpion King*, which was the prequel to the *Mummy* movies, Universal called me up about three weeks before they started shooting, and asked me if I would take a look at the script, because they weren't satisfied. So I did, and I gave them a sort of a two-page proposal. I said, "Look, I would do this and do this and do this." And so they said, "Okay, great, we want you to do all of that. You can't change any of the locations or the sets or the characters or the basic course of the story, because that's all set up and storyboarded. But you can change the dialogue, and you can

change the events, as long as they take place in the same locations."
I was like, "Okay, well, that's great . . ." And they're like, "We're
shooting in three weeks. Go."

Name Value

LARRY COHEN: When you take their money and sell them your
material, they have the right to change it if they want to. I hope they
won't. I hope if they do change it that it'll be a positive change. I'm
certainly not saying that no one's ever improved upon anything that
I wrote. Probably 90 percent of the things that I have written, I have
gotten sole credit on, so I'm pretty unusual. That doesn't mean there
weren't changes, but they weren't significant enough changes for me
to have to give up the credit to somebody else. So I'm happy to take
credit for somebody else's work if it turned out to be good. Why
not? What am I gonna do, make a disclaimer? "That was a good
scene, but I didn't write it?" So God bless—thank you very much.
Of course you have to take the bad with the good.

JOHN AUGUST: Sometimes when there are multiple writers on
a project, you go through a process called arbitration. That's to
figure out who deserves the "Written by" credit on a movie. It's
all handled by the Writers Guild, and it's an incredibly screwed-up
system that's probably the best system that we can manage given
all the variables involved. Arbitration is handled by an anonymous,
one-time-only panel of three different screenwriters who read all
the drafts and figure out who should get credit. I've been through
arbitration a couple of times where I was trying to get credit, and

it's not *Law & Order.* It's not a legal proceeding, but you're trying to explain in your arbitration statement exactly why you deserve the credit you think you should get, and talk the panel through the logic of why this other writer deserves a different credit.

GERALD DiPEGO: Sometimes the statements are so intense that you know there's a bloody situation going on. You know there are people who feel outraged.

PAUL SCHRADER: I didn't arbitrate on *Close Encounters of the Third Kind,* because Spielberg said to me, "There's nothing left of your script," and he was very anxious to get the credit. That was fine with me. I thought, "Well, I'll be a nice guy. I won't arbitrate, and he'll be my friend." The truth was he resented me all of the time for even saying that I had written the script. So when the next opportunity came, which was *The Last Temptation of Christ*—Jay Cocks had written for that, and Marty wanted to give Jay a second-position credit—I said, "Marty, thank God for arbitration. We don't have to have this discussion. We can remain friends. Take it off the table. Let the WGA decide. This is not something we should talk about." Ultimately, I got the sole credit and Jay didn't get credit, and my relationship with Marty stayed the same. So I wish I had just arbitrated with Steve. Probably would've been cleaner and better.

DAVID S. WARD: On *The Mask of Zorro,* I rewrote probably 85 percent of the dialogue, and I didn't get screen credit on it. It was a huge deal with the Writers Guild; it was on the front page of the *Los Angeles Times.* The director, Martin Campbell, was upset about it, and I was upset about it. The guild said, "Dialogue doesn't count."

And I said, "Wait a minute. If people are saying different things—and in many cases because they're saying different things, they're doing different things—why does that not count?"

So to me, it's a very flawed system. You have no idea, really, the way it works—you just get a letter saying you either got credit or you didn't.

The thing about arbitration is it's important to your career. If the movie does well, that credit translates into money—not only residuals from that movie, but other jobs. People say, "He was involved with that movie. We've got a movie he'd probably be very good for based on his involvement in that movie." Most people know that I worked on *Zorro*, but in pure monetary terms, not getting credit on that movie probably cost me half a million dollars.

DAVID HAYTER: I was very lucky in the arbitration process to get sole credit on *X-Men*. Amazing, significant writers had worked on it, so I was very fortunate there. I got what I felt was the proper credit on *X2* and *Scorpion King*. I did not get credit on *Hulk*, which was fine—it wasn't really my movie at that point, but I did do a lot of work on it. I can't speak for everybody's experiences, but arbitration seems to be a pretty effective process. It seems to me that if you really deserve the credit, you'll get the credit.

JOHN D. BRANCATO: *Catwoman* was probably the single worst thing we've had an opportunity to work on, other than maybe a Roger Corman film long, long ago. Actually, no—those are better than *Catwoman*. In that case, I think in the final arbitration there were twenty-eight writers, of which we were writers number fifteen and seventeen, because we'd been fired and rehired on the project.

Everybody fought for credit in the same old way. You read the script and think, "Oh, well, this is really terrible, and yet a piece of it is mine." You never knew. I mean, just from the script, maybe it would have worked. There must have been fifteen arbitration letters from the different writers saying, "Oh, please give me a piece, I should have my name on this." I wrote one of 'em, with my writing partner, and we prevailed and had a shared credit on screenplay and story. Then I saw the movie, I guess the week after I wrote that letter, at some early screening. Wow, that was depressing.

DENNIS PALUMBO: A writer friend of mine once described screenwriters as "egomaniacs with low self-esteem," and that's a great description. It was me when I was a screenwriter, certainly—where on the one hand, you have that hubris that Goethe talked about, where you had to believe that what you wrote was so great everyone needed to read it. And at the very same time, the moment a studio executive or director replaces you, you go, "God, I knew I was crap."

What arbitration does is it kind of forces a writer to confront what he or she has actually done, what the contribution was. Is the person coming along who wrote behind them better than them? And what does "better" mean? In Hollywood, "better" doesn't mean anything. If Angelina Jolie accepts the screenplay and then brings in a writer she likes to beef up her character, that doesn't mean the script becomes "better." It becomes different.

There is no "better," because the reasons scripts get rewritten and fooled around with have very little to do with the quality of the writing. They have to do with what's required.

RONALD SHUSETT: When Dan and I created the first *Alien* movie, we got net points for giving up the right to write all sequels and prequels. We never lost identification with the series, because on every single *Alien* sequel it always says, "*Alien* characters created by Dan O'Bannon and Ronald Shusett." This lasted through the present day, with *Alien vs. Predator*. And I must say, when they first said, "*Alien vs. Predator*," we kinda groaned.

What happened was the director turned to several original ideas that we had written for the first *Alien*. We overwrote the original script, like most young writers do—there were about twenty-two pages that never even got filmed. Paul Anderson, the director, noted that some of those things could be very valuable for *Alien vs. Predator*. Fox owned those ideas, so the studio didn't have to pay us more money—but what was at stake was the credit. So that became an arbitration.

Arbitrators read our original script of twenty-five years earlier and read the shooting draft of *Alien vs. Predator*, and voted us in as story credit. "Story by Anderson, Shusett, and O'Bannon." It's a rarity. The credit was entirely arbitration.

ZAK PENN: When it comes to the issue of credits, I think a lot of my attitude was determined by my first experience, which was *Last Action Hero*. I felt betrayed. I was pretty angry that we lost credit on our own first screenplay to Shane Black. To defend him a bit, I didn't really know that this was par for the course, that everyone gets rewritten. But I was shocked when people were applying for credit on a movie that we had thought up. It seemed weird to me.

Because of that experience, I think I've been much more cognizant of other writers than many of my peers. I always call people when I'm rewriting their scripts, to talk to them before I take the job. I make sure to let them know. A number of times, I've turned down credit on movies, because I felt that the original writers were not getting their fair share. I don't do that because I'm trying to be a martyr. I just think that's fair. I often feel like, "You know what? I'm getting paid well for what I do, and there's someone who wrote this original script who's much more upset than me. What right do I have to cry over not getting credit?"

Do I think the system is a good system? Not particularly. When someone writes a short story, it says "Based on a short story by," and then "Screenplay by." So when an original screenplay is rewritten, why wouldn't it say "Based on an original screenplay by," and then "Rewritten by"?

But short of that, I've got a lot of credits so I don't worry about it as much. I have the luxury of not sweating it. And there are times when I kinda don't want to take credit. If I've written a script, and then I've been fired and it's been rewritten by eight other people, if I end up getting screenplay credit on that movie, I'm gonna have to answer for that movie. I still have to answer for *Last Action Hero*.

The Best Laid Plans

WILLIAM GOLDMAN: I love red wine. I drink red wine every night of my life, thank God. I wrote a movie about red wine called *Year of the Comet*, and it was written out of blind passion. It's a thriller about a chase after a legendary bottle of red wine. The movie had gone very well in the shooting, and the first sneak we had was out in California. The opening sequence was a wine tasting in London, and people were hopefully funny and phony and spitting and all that stuff. As I'm sitting there, I watch the audience get up to leave. Now this is a sneak preview—they didn't pay any money—and in the first five minutes, 50 people left out of probably 250 people.

Zac Penn

They hated us.

We changed the movie, got rid of the tasting.

They still hated us.

They didn't want to be anywhere around a bottle of red wine.

But who knew? I mean, it was written with great passion. The reason it was called *Year of the Comet* was that the most legendary year in the history of wine in France was 1811, and a comet went over France that year. The most famous wine at that time was Château Lafitte, and I made up a story of a legendary giant bottle. Well, if you could find one, it would be worth millions of dollars. So I thought,

"That's a good idea."

It wasn't! It was a horrible idea!

ALLISON ANDERS: With *Four Rooms*, there were four filmmakers who were friends trying to do something. It was an exercise for us. We didn't make it the big thing that it was. We're not the ones who came up with Bruce Willis and all the stars. We were happy to have them, but originally, it was just gonna be a little teeny-tiny movie. What happened was that we didn't work hard enough on the script, and part of that was the fact that Miramax wanted to do it immediately. It was turned in as a first draft, and it's a complicated thing to try to put four stories together. I was like, "Really? We got the deal already, and we've only written one draft? Aren't we gonna work a little bit harder on the script?"

JOHN AUGUST: I came on to do an adaptation of *Tarzan* at Warner Bros., and the one thing I said to everybody before I went in for my first meeting was, "I really wanna do *Tarzan*, but set in modern-day Africa—so not khaki-and-pith-helmets Africa, but civil-unrest Africa." And they said, "That sounds really exciting. Why don't you do that?" And then three drafts in, they said, "You know what? Maybe we could do a period piece." So it was essentially a year of my life that I wasted trying to do this version that wasn't ever gonna get made. It's another reason why you need to get paid enough to make it worthwhile—if you're gonna be spinning your wheels, at least you're getting paid for spinning your wheels.

DAVID HAYTER: I had a very solid relationship with Marvel, having worked on a number of films with them, and I was looking for something to write and direct. They brought up *Black Widow*, and I knew the character very well from the comic book. So I spent about a year working on the script, and I was extremely happy with it.

Essentially, the story is a young Russian girl's parents are killed, so she's given to the KGB to be developed into a super spy. In her early teen years, the Soviet Union crumbles, so they decide to kill her. But at that point, she's too tough to kill, so she escapes and makes her way to America. Then, years later, we catch up with her in present day. She's a freelance mercenary, and she's called back to where she was brought up to face her past. What I tried to do was use the backdrop of the splintered Soviet Empire—a lawless insane asylum with four hundred some odd nuclear missile silos. It was all about loose nukes, and I felt it was very timely and very cool.

Unfortunately, as I was coming up on the final draft, a number of female vigilante movies came out. We had *Tomb Raider* and *Kill Bill*, which were the ones that worked, but then we had *BloodRayne* and *Ultraviolet* and *Aeon Flux*. *Aeon Flux* didn't open well, and three days after it opened, the studio said, "We don't think it's the time to do this movie."

I accepted their logic in terms of the saturation of the marketplace, but it was pretty painful. I had not only invested a lot of time in that movie, but I had also named my daughter, who was born in that time period, Natasha—after the lead character in *Black Widow*. I named my daughter after a movie character that I wasn't working on anymore.

RICHARD RUSH: I had run across a project that fascinated me. It was a nonfiction book about Air America. Air America was the biggest airline in the world, owned and operated by the CIA, with more planes and pilots than all the rest of the airlines combined. Their job was fighting the secret war in Laos, dropping goods and supplies to our allies while they bombed the shit out of our enemies.

The whole airline was run on the basis of dirty tricks, because it was a CIA invention.

I researched the screenplay for four or five years, and it's the best screenplay I ever wrote. Better than *The Stunt Man,* which is saying a lot because I got an Academy Award nomination for *The Stunt Man.* I got a commitment from Sean Connery, and other actors were dying to do the second role.

I went to Southeast Asia to scout the locations. I came back with a production that was so well put together, the commanding generals of two countries were willing to bomb any other country I wanted so I could get it on film. To my amazement, someone else had taken over as head of production for the company during my absence. He had gone through the back materials that they owned, read the screenplay, and fell in love with it. He decided he wanted it for himself. They announced to me that he was going to take over the screenplay.

Now there are two absolutely vital rules to observe when you take over a project in the industry. The first one is to fire everybody connected to it, because they will turn out to be your enemies. The second is to territorially urinate on it to make it your own. So he had a new screenplay written. It turned out badly, and he couldn't cast it. They lingered for a year or two trying to cast this screenplay.

What they had done is terminated me and paid me off. It was a handsome payoff, and there was no way I could reject it. As a matter of fact, I couldn't even take my name off the screenplay, because if you get more than $400,000 for a screenplay, you're not allowed to take your name off. As soon as I was out of the picture, Sean Connery left, which I thought was classy. Finally, the head of the studio came to me and said, "Will you do the movie with Sean Connery and Patrick Swayze?" And I said, "I told you about that cast two years ago." He said, "Patrick's coming in this weekend. He's interested. I want you guys to meet."

I guess the new head of production got wind of that and got desperate. That weekend, he offered the movie to the two actors who did it—at twice their regular salary. It was burned and gone, and I had to live with having my name as co-screenwriter on the bad reviews that ensued.

Richard Rush

MICHAEL WOLK: Something that really made me feel like I was suffocating in a glass box was the fact that I sold three screenplays for considerable sums, and nothing ever happened with them. Nothing. The feeling I got from that was really a deathly feeling of suffocation. It's like, "In Hollywood, no one can hear you scream." I think that was one of the motivations for my exodus from Hollywood. I couldn't deal with the fact that you write something, and it may be really good, and it might be very producible, but it just sits there. I mean, writing is communication, right? If you're communicating to this little mafia of Hollywood people, and beyond that no one ever gets the story, and you have no right to disseminate that story yourself, it can make you feel as if nobody is listening to you. You are a tree falling in the forest.

Small Minds, Big Obstacles

LINDA VOORHEES: For one pitch, I immediately knew that the executive hated me the minute I walked in—because I was a middle-aged woman from Orange County, dressed like I had just come from the country club. I wasn't edgy, I wasn't the cool chick, I wasn't Goth, I wasn't the sweet young thing just out of college. It was like, "If she's not fuckable, then what are we doin' this meeting for?" That was the expression on his face.

I thought, "Well, he hates me already, so I may as well make him *really* hate me." I became like a mass of gravity in that room. You could not get me out if you put dynamite under me. I had a ten-minute pitch. I stretched that into maybe about forty-five minutes. And if he stopped me, I would start over again. You know, I was just gonna torture him.

There is a compartmentalized rejection, and it has to do with gender, and it has to do with age, and it has to do with ethnicity. It's very subtle, and it's very unintended. Well-meaning people have a bias that they often aren't aware of, because they won't permit themselves to be aware of the bias. No one's ever gonna fess up to it, and I wouldn't expect them to.

GUINEVERE TURNER: There's an incredible need to prove yourself if you're female, and even vaguely attractive, and also my age. I feel like most successful female screenwriters are at least ten years older than I am, and Lord knows what their war stories are. But also there's a "lesbo" dynamic that goes on. I did this one pitch with this director, where he was like: "Have you always been a lesbian? What was your first experience with a woman?" And I was like: "What the fuck are we talking about here, dude?" The script wasn't gay. So this prurient need to know about my gayness comes up a lot, which is just lame and boring.

NORA EPHRON: It's very hard to get a movie made in Hollywood whether you're a man or a woman, but it's harder for women. This is just a fact. Someday I hope it will be different. But you can't pretend that it's easy for anyone, except maybe Steven Spielberg. As my friend Sean Daniel often says, "This is not a business for sissies."

NAOMI FONER: According to our film culture, you'd think everybody's wife was between twenty-two and thirty-five, and they were all incredibly beautiful, and they never struggled with any of the things that people struggle with. And then they disappeared for some reason—they were sent off to some kind of boot camp—and they became perfect grandmothers. This is garbage. I admire terribly my friend Jamie Lee Curtis, who gets on the cover of a magazine naked, showing people that she has cellulite, and that all those touched-up pictures are touched-up pictures, and she just looks just like them. That's the truth, and women need to know that. Real people need to be in movies, and when they show up, people respond. They respond in droves. But for some reason, the fantasy makers don't want much of that to happen.

GUINEVERE TURNER: I feel an incredible pressure and obligation and responsibility to create women characters who are not victims—and if they are victims, telling a raw, true story about victimization. It's something that I come up against all the time. Something I'm working on right now, all they want to know is why—"Why is she so powerful and great? What happened in her childhood that made her this way?" And I say, "What happened to Jack Bauer that made him the hero of *24*? Nothin'. He just is." Male heroes are just badass, and women are always like, "Well, you know, she was beaten and raped, and then she became a superhero." I'm like, "What if she's just awesome for no apparent reason?"

JANE ANDERSON: In *The Prize Winner of Defiance, Ohio*, the main character is a woman. The studio gave me a green light with Julianne Moore to star, and we hadn't cast the male part yet, which is a great role but secondary. I remember going from star to star to star—every male star said, "Oh, it's a great project," but they turned it down because the film wasn't about them. Female stars will take anything, because there are so few parts to act that have any kind of quality to them.

I knew we were going to be able to cast a really wonderful male actor, and I did eventually with Woody Harrelson. But halfway through the project, the studio pulled the plug because they were afraid I wouldn't be able to get a big-name male actor. I found that to be just a stunning example of Hollywood sexism, because if you're trying to get a go for a film that stars a male lead, and you have your male star in place, you can cast the female secondary part the day before you start shooting!

Jane Anderson

ANTWONE FISHER: If they feel like they can make money from what you have to offer, they don't care about your race. I also think that there have been opportunities that have been afforded to me because I'm African American. If there's a story that has African-American people in it, they come to me to say, "This is a cultural thing that the original writer doesn't understand. Can you help us straighten this out?"

KRISS TURNER: I would say that I have made a career out of being a black female writer. You know, if you have a black female in your sitcom, I'm probably gonna get a call to come in for a meeting. Now that there are hardly any of those shows, I'm more aware of the obstacles. I mean, there were so many black shows in the nineties. I can look through my credits: *Cosby*; *Living Single*; *Sister, Sister*; *Bernie Mac*.

Even in my feature career, it's like, "Oh, we have this black sorority movie," or, "We have this black comedian we wanna do something around." I'm pretty sure that the next spec I write will be color-blind. If they wanna do it black, they can do it black. If they wanna do it white, they can do it white.

I don't know how much my movie made, but I think it made $14 million. I don't think I'm gonna get that movie made again. You know, when we went in, we were stoked. We were like, "Look, you haven't seen this since *How Stella Got Her Groove Back*, about a professional woman looking for love. It's been a while, and let's do it . . ." Not big box office. That's the honest-to-God truth, you know? So I don't think studios are like, "Oh, let's get another *Something New* goin' on."

JAMES L. WHITE: The big obstacle that you face is that when you humanize your own people—instead of making caricatures, you're making characters—Hollywood has a tendency to go, "I don't know if there's a market for this." For me, telling the story of black life is

Kriss Turner

like going to see *The Godfather*. I didn't know that much about the mafia or about Italian life, but at the end of two hours and fifty-five minutes of sittin' in that darkness, Michael Corleone kills seven people, and I was very, very happy for Michael, 'cause he had saved the family. So I said, "If they can do that, I can now write a drama explaining black life." You know, explaining black life—not hittin' them over the head with "you evil white people," but inviting them in and allowing them to spend two hours inside the skin of a black man or a woman, to see what that world is about.

JOSE RIVERA: Early in my career, part of the problem with being a Latino writer was being stuck in the clichés of what that meant— and that usually meant you're gonna write about drugs, gangs, crime, prostitution, maids, that kinda stuff. I think it's gotten a little bit better. What's happened in the last couple of years has been a huge influx of really fantastic filmmaking—you know, from *Amores Perros* to *Volver,* even *Pan's Labyrinth*—that explodes the possibilities of what Latino filmmaking can be about. On the other hand, you know, if you go to the Writers Guild and look up the statistics, it's still abysmal—the number of Latino writers who are show runners, or who are on staff, or who have deals to make movies.

ARI B. RUBIN: The WGA threw an event about a year ago that I was involved with, called "The 101 Best Screenplays." It was a great event, and I would say about thirty screenwriters got up on the stage to be celebrated. I was there with a couple of people, and one of them is an agent. He said to me, "You know, that's some great writing talent on that stage. I hate to say it, but I don't think more than one of them could still get a job in L.A. today."

How is it that thirty Academy Award–winning screenwriters could not get a job in L.A. today? There are several elements involved, according to this agent. One is they've priced themselves out of the market. And two is that they're just—what's the word he used?—"stodgy." They're not staying current with the tastes of the audience. I think it's a matter of, "Are these writers still telling original stories, or are they fitting every script they have into their own formula?" You do see breakthroughs in writers who've been around—every now and then, a writer who's gotten caught in a rut comes up with a great idea.

My father's an interesting example. There were several films he wrote that I thought were so-so. They weren't produced. He has multiple homes to support, and he very much writes for a living now, less so than pleasure. Then recently, he came onto a project called *The Time Traveler's Wife*, and out of the blue he wrote this script in, I would say, three weeks or a month. It was a really good script. Completely reinvigorated, completely different. If you look back at his life recently, he's been getting out of a rut in his own life, and that was reflected in his writing.

LARRY COHEN: They say ageism exists in Hollywood, but I haven't experienced it, because I'm eternally youthful. If you're excited about what you're doing, if you have fresh ideas, I personally don't think age matters. If the script's good, who cares who wrote it? When you go in for assignments, that's a different story. If they're gonna do *The Fast and the Furious* or something, obviously they're gonna wanna hire some young guy to write it, who they think will have an understanding of those characters and that milieu. But for spec scripts, the material speaks for itself. I've had all these young actors—Katie Holmes and Colin Farrell in *Phone Booth*, Bijou Phillips in the remake of *It's Alive*, Elisha Cuthbert in *Captivity*, Jessica Biel and Chris Evans in *Cellular*. I'm getting a lot of young people in my scripts, so obviously I'm writin' stuff that young people can play.

BILLY RAY: When I first started, I was the flavor of the month, and that happened partially because I was twenty-four. I can't now complain about ageism, since I benefited from it at the beginning of my career. I have no doubt that ageism exists, but I think it's more complicated than people think. Studios are trying to make movies for fourteen-year-old kids, and so there's the assumption that a fifty- or a sixty-year-old man is less qualified to write something for fourteen-year-old audiences than a twenty-five-year-old kid is. I don't think that's true. I think either you can write or you can't.

RICHARD RUSH: A couple of years ago, I had a heart transplant, and the heart was from someone who was decades younger than me. So now my legendary sense of the youth market has become virtually infallible. At least that's what I tell the studios.

The Writers Guild Arbitrator's Perspective: Jonathan Lemkin

Jonathan Lemkin

When multiple writers compete for credit on a movie, the Writers Guild of America's arbitration process begins. Jonathan Lemkin has an informed perspective on that process, having prevailed in a complex arbitration and served on numerous arbitration panels. A working Hollywood writer since his early twenties, he spent over a decade writing for television series, including 21 Jump Street, *before notching feature credits on* The Devil's Advocate *(1997),* Lethal Weapon 4 *(1998), and* Red Planet *(2000). Then he raised his profile considerably by adapting the script for* Shooter *(2007) from notoriously difficult source material. Previous writers on the project included such heavyweights as William Goldman, John Lee Hancock, and Nicholas Kazan, but the final movie bore only Lemkin's name.*

Hitting the Target

Shooter transcended at least three regimes at Paramount. It was associated with someone who was no longer there, and everything he had touched was then considered tainted, which happens all the time. You know, a president leaves, and the whole development slate gets trashed. Constantly. You need a buffer zone in the middle, sometimes, for a project to come back to life. When the regime changed again at Paramount, a friend of mine, Lorenzo di Bonaventura, was able to keep the project moving forward. He had a producing deal at Paramount.

Shooter is based on a book by Stephen Hunter called *Point of Impact*, which had been developed at one point for Robert Redford, another point for Keanu Reeves. And some very prominent writers had worked on the script. You know, people who have gold statues on their mantelpieces.

The book is 550 pages long, and has an A, B, C, D, and E story in it. It's pretty complicated. I read the previous drafts of the screenplay, and, you know, bless those guys for going down all those blind alleys. I said, "I can't do any of the sub-stories. I can't even tell the whole A story in this book, but it's a great, great story." Then we had to move the book from a Vietnam setting to current day. And then there's just stuff I wrote in the middle of the night to amuse myself, which I never thought would end up on the screen—and all that stuff ended up on the screen.

That was one of the things I found most fascinating. The stuff I expected them to cut, there were never any notes on.

You know, Mark Wahlberg's character saying he wanted Bono to step into a negotiation—I thought, "They'll never let me do this." Never got a note. The wildest things that we had Michael Peña's character say never got a note. The notes always tended to be on plot points, and they left the character stuff alone.

One of the things that I do, which I think always surprises the studios, is I demand to go back and redo the primary research. I don't want to write based on someone else's research. I got ahold of the guy who trains a lot of the mercenaries—or, excuse me, "contractors"—who are in Iraq, and I said, "I want to learn how to shoot at 700, 800, 900 yards." *Point of Impact* is known in that community, and the sniper's the good guy, so they were really welcoming.

I went out to Pahrump, Nevada, where there's a six-hundred-acre course, and I crawled around in the dirt for a couple of days, and shot and shot and shot and shot. I learned how to clean a rifle. I learned a little about how to disarm somebody. I went down to Camp Pendleton, hung out with the Marines. It's not that the book isn't well written or the material isn't there, but unless I experience something, I'd be writing it based on somebody else's experiences. I think redoing the primary research is key to making something your own.

A Complicated Process

Early on, I arbitrated something without understanding the process, and I'd even gone to the next step beyond that, which is a "process review board." I lost the arbitration but learned a lot about the rules of the guild. Now I've been in arbitration, I've been the arbitrator a lot of times, I've written arbitration statements, I've read arbitration statements. I've actually done it enough where I will get phone calls from people and guide them through the process.

I'm a very strong supporter of the union, and so I was flattered to get the call the first time. It's like, "Wow, I can actually help out here. I can give something back." I tell everybody I know who's in the business, and who can be an arbitrator, "Do it." It's a lot of work—you may get twelve scripts and a novel. I've gotten these FedEx boxes, and it's like, "Oh my God, this is so much to read." But if not us, who?

There's a lot of money attached to this, especially in residuals and in production bonuses. I mean, there's a certain pool of money that's set aside for production bonuses, and that gets split among the writers who are credited. There's no question that your production bonus can be a significant amount of money.

You take it very seriously. You want to do the right thing. You sit down, you read all the rules, you consult with the person at the guild who's coordinating. The arbitration process is confidential almost all the time. I'm generally judging writer A, B, C, D, and E. You know, on *Shooter*, I believe I was writer G, and I got full credit, which is not a common occurrence, as you can imagine.

Your job is to ask questions about what are called "essential elements." And if writer A chose essential elements, writer A's decisions as the first writer mean a lot, even if there was a book or underlying material. Even if someone did a great job or a great draft—or even if some of their work or a single character remains in the final work—you have to ask yourself, "Are these essential elements or something else?"

The arbitration panels I've worked on—90-plus percent went where I would have expected them to go. Very rarely have you seen a truly crazy arbitration. I worked on one where I actually protested to the guild. I was angry about the standard we were being asked to apply. The underlying material predated the guild agreement, and I was really upset that the underlying material wasn't credited. Because of the weird rules in the guild, I felt someone's work was being ignored. But it was outside of my control. It wasn't wrong in the sense that the rules weren't being followed. I just thought the rules were wrong.

I have certain problems with the way the arbitration system works. My biggest problem is I think it's not been updated to represent what goes on in the industry today. In the arbitration system, there are two classes of writers: original writers and people who do adaptations. With the original writers, the second writer needs to contribute 50 percent or more to receive credit, and subsequent writers need 33.3 percent or more to receive credit—which is a throwback, I think, to a really early phase in the guild's history. Because way, way too many projects now are based on underlying material, be it Legos or a video game or a television show. So, really, all writers are equal—except some writers are more equal than others. And that's a problem. I would like to see that change in the guild. I'd like to see one standard applied across the arbitration process.

I think it's a difficult, complicated, messed-up process, but it's the best one we've found.

9

Taking Control

After enduring years of cavalier rejections, catastrophic battles, and capricious terminations, it's only natural for writers to crave the autonomy that comes with the director's chair or the producer's corner office. As far back as the studio era, legendary screenwriters from Preston Sturges to Billy Wilder took up directing to ensure that their stories were not butchered on the way to the big screen. But the transition from one job to the other is more easily imagined than accomplished, and the responsibilities that accompany directing and producing can sometimes outweigh the rewards.

As John August explains, the earliest challenge writers face in trying to raise their profile is establishing a profile in the first place. August is one of the industry's most proactive screenwriters in terms of ensuring that his contributions to movies aren't lost in the shuffle, and he's just one of the many accomplished scribes who has leveraged his success behind the keyboard for broader opportunities.

For writer-directors such as Mike Binder and writer-producers such as Ronald Shusett, the transition to hyphenate status is graceful and permanent. But for others, such as Bruce Joel Rubin, the experience of taking the helm led to the realization that being in control is a lot less fun than it sounds. And for some screenwriters, notably William Goldman, the idea of being in control doesn't sound like any fun at all.

Anonymity Is a Choice

JOHN AUGUST: I don't think there are any famous screenwriters. There are some screenwriters who film students have heard of, but your mom probably doesn't know any screenwriters other than you. That's because screenwriting is kind of invisible. If screenwriting is done really well, it seems like the actors made up their lines, and that the director knew to put the camera there, and that the movie sort of came together all by itself. So a lot of times it feels like the screenwriter is anonymous.

It's tough to be known for anything as a writer if there's not a consistent body of work that people can associate you with. The writers you tend to hear of are writer-directors. They're consistent, and they have a brand identity: A Kevin Smith movie feels like a Kevin Smith movie. Increasingly, I think there's an opportunity for writers who are interested in writing one kind of movie to do that. Charlie Kaufman is sort of a brand. No matter who's directed them, his movies feel like they're one body of work. It's an opportunity for certain kinds of writers to be consistent in the type of work they're gonna do and the presentation of who they are. The degree to which that might protect you from rejection is that if someone doesn't like a certain one of your movies, at least it fits into an overall body of work, so you can say "I wasn't a fan of *Jersey Girl*, but I can see how it's a Kevin Smith movie," and it becomes part of your overall canon.

I actively try to associate myself with the movies that I've written, so that more people out there might actually have an understanding that the director directed the movie, and this person wrote the movie, and that there is someone behind the curtain who helps get the movie up on its feet.

John August

JUSTIN ZACKHAM: You write a film called The Bucket List, and Jack Nicholson and Morgan Freeman are in your film. How nice. Suddenly you're a genius to all the people who barely could spell your first name, let alone know your last name. So I partnered up with a guy I've known since I was ten years old—one of my best friends on earth, trust him completely in a way that I would never trust anyone in this town. We're using the fact that I have a writer's credit on the movie, and the fact that I had something to do with the production of it, to say, "We have these other projects now that we wanna get done." We're producing our first film with this writer named Jessica Goldberg. It's this great little script that she wrote, and we were able to find $3 million for it. I think she's doing it with us because I'm a writer, so she knows that she's got a producer who's gonna approach it from an empathetic standpoint. Writers very, very rarely get those little points in time when we can leverage something, so I spent the last year building on the perception of The Bucket List to get other projects going.

RICHARD RUSH: Here's the biggest trick I learned and pulled off throughout my entire career. In order to make a movie, the studio's position is "We take a screenplay, we find a bankable director, and if a top director says yes, he will attract the actors." I learned early in the game not to put my name on the screenplays. I worked with a collaborator named Robert Kaufman. He would turn in the screenplay, and the studio would give it to me. I would walk into the studio a few days later and say, "I got bad news, guys—I think we're gonna have to make a picture. I like it." And they would say, "Hurray!" We got away with that a few times. I would have been suspect if I liked it because I had written it, but if somebody else's name was on the script and I said yes, that made a "go" picture.

MIKE BINDER: I'm in a unique business. I run a very small boutique firm that makes my movies. I'm never lookin' for development deals, and in fact, you can't buy one of my screenplays. There's no money except for the entire movie. I write a script and I package the actors, my brother budgets the movie, and we take around the complete package. I'm not lookin' to make $100 million. I'm just lookin' to make movies that people really like. I'm an entertainer. Even in *Reign Over Me*, people are cryin' several times durin' the movie, they're laughin'—but they leave with hope, and they feel good about the ability to handle loss. You gotta know the spot on the horizon you're going for in so many ways. You gotta know where you wanna go, 'cause you can't hit the spot on the horizon if you don't know where it is. You've got to ask, "What kind of movies do I want to make? What kind of movies do I want to see?"

RONALD SHUSETT: Especially after *Total Recall* and *Alien*, I was getting big fees, so I had money to option material. I couldn't compete with the studios, but I could come up with $25,000, even $50,000, in front money. And there were plenty of properties that could be had. So I would option it myself, if I didn't have an original I had faith in at the time. And then I would shape it up with my partner. I would always do it on spec until I had it in a form that I felt I wanted to sell, and then I would go to the studios. I put in my contract that I must be either producer or executive producer, and I must be on the set. It's not in my contract that I can overrule most people, but I have the power of persuasion because I'm in a position of a functional producer—not just a name-only producer. I'm there helping make the movie. And if things I'm saying are coming out right in dailies two or three days in a row, they're like, "I think Ron's right about that." So I have an unfair advantage since I would never sell any script, no matter how much they offered me, without being either producer or executive producer.

PAUL SCHRADER: I was a screenwriter for maybe two years, and I realized that I really wasn't a writer—I was a screenwriter. I had to decide. If I wanted to be a writer, I should write things that people actually read. It could be articles, it could be nonfiction, it could be fiction. But people don't actually read your screenwriting—they watch a film adaptation of your screenwriting. So I said, "I'm really not comfortable being half of a creator. I think I want to be a whole creator. I want to be a filmmaker."

I've never been very good at taking orders. Even as a kid, I must have had ten jobs during high school and college. I got fired from every one, because sooner or later, somebody always says to you, "You should do this," and you say, "I think I have a better idea," and they say, "You're fired. We don't want your better idea. We want you to follow orders." The only jobs I never really got fired from were the ones I created. The films I've put together, I can't get fired.

To Direct or Not to Direct

LARRY COHEN: Why did I direct twenty-one pictures? Because I wanted to control every aspect of my own movies, and have a great time making them. So of the forty-six produced pictures that I've gotten made, twenty-one of 'em I made myself. I had a good time making 'em, but I still had to deal with all kinds of vagaries of weather and sound and crew and actors. It doesn't have the purity of simply painting a picture, composing a song, or sculpting, or writing. That's something you do all by yourself.

NORA EPHRON: There were several things that clearly made me want to direct. The most important were that it was a way to make sure my scripts were made the way I wanted them made, and to make sure they got made at all—something to think about at all times, but especially after turning fifty—and to put some muscle behind scripts that interested me and probably weren't going to interest other directors, most of whom were men.

RON SHELTON: *Under Fire* was my first produced script. Roger Spottiswoode directed that. It was Nick Nolte, Gene Hackman, Jean-Louis Trintignant. I directed second unit on *Under Fire* and *The Best of Times*, and there was a lot of action in *Under Fire*, and I got to work with actors a little bit, so I had a fairly impressive reel for only two movies. The great John Alcott, who did all of Kubrick's movies, shot *Under Fire*, and working for John was really a baptism of fire. He was a brilliant guy and very demanding, so I had to learn very quickly what lenses I wanted at five in the morning, and where I was gonna use 'em, and defend my positions. So after those two pictures I felt I was ready to direct.

The only way I could ever get a job was if I wrote about a subject that I knew better than anybody in the movie business. Whatever arguments they made against me, it can't be "He doesn't know this world." So I wrote *Bull Durham*.

JOHN AUGUST: We were very lucky that Doug Liman signed on to direct *Go*. He's a person who tries to do fifteen things at once, and of those fifteen things, some of those aren't going to get done fully. That gave me an opportunity to help out a lot more in making that movie than I would have otherwise been able to do. So the first day I showed up on *Go*, I was surprised by all these trucks, and I couldn't believe they were actually making my movie. By the fifth day, I was directing second unit, 'cause we had already fallen a day behind. It showed me I can actually tell somebody where to put the camera, and get stuff to happen the way it should happen to make a movie.

JOSE RIVERA: The Oscar nomination for *The Motorcycle Diaries* gave me some momentum, and I immediately started working on trying to get a project made that I could direct myself—a project called *Celestina,* which my wife is part of as well. With all my experience in the theater, I know how to direct actors, and having produced *Eerie, Indiana,* I know what it feels like to be in production and to be in post. But the fear that people have of a first-time director—that follows you. That's real. And people have not financed the film, based largely on that. People just don't want to take chances with their money, with their time, with everything. And so regardless of having a great script and a great cast, it's a real challenge to become a director. For instance with *Celestina,* I've had to rework the script to make it far less expensive to produce, hoping that with a lower price tag, then they will say, "Okay, we'll write you a check and take a chance on you."

GUINEVERE TURNER: I honestly feel like if I wanted to direct a feature right now, I could probably raise a scrappy little $500,000 and do it. I'm not ready. I didn't go to film school. I didn't go to screenwriting school. I just continue to make short films because it's school. It's incredibly important to me to understand what I'm good at and what I'm bad at, because I don't wanna fuck it up. When I direct, I'm gonna rock it. I don't want it to be like, "Hmm, well, that was a nice effort." When you hear the word *effort,* you know you're in trouble. That was me on the track team—which I joined as a high schooler because I was in love with someone on the team—crying, trying to finish the relay. "Good effort! Come on, Guin, you can do it!" I don't ever want to feel that again.

Guinevere Turner

PAUL SCHRADER: You have to enjoy your own company, and the solitude that's necessary to hatch an idea and dwell on it and go back and forth in your mind, sometimes for months—and then you also have to enjoy stepping out on stage, which is what happens when you walk out onto a set, and a hundred people are there, and they're saying, "What shall we do today?" You have to entertain them, in a way. You have to motivate them. You have to try to make them creative as a group. You can't just look at your shoes. So you have to like both things. Usually if you've been writing for a while, you're really lonely, and you hunger for the social aspect of directing. And if you've been directing too much, you're really getting sick of people, and you're anxious to spend some time alone writing.

WILLIAM GOLDMAN: I never had any interest in directing, from the very, very beginning. First of all, I don't like being on the soundstage. I find it very boring. I've done my work, for the most part. I also tend to fuck up scenes. I'll find a spot out of the way and stand there and watch a take, and just before the shot, the director will say, "Bill, that's where the shot finishes. Please move."

There's a scene in *The Princess Bride* where the hero is taking the heroine in the fire swamp, and there's smoke and there's fire, and her dress is on fire. The hero, Westley, puts it out, and Buttercup's okay, and they continue on. And though I wrote the book and I wrote the movie, I'm watching as this thing started—wonderful Cary Elwes brings in wonderful Robin Wright, there's the puff of smoke, her dress is on fire—and I scream, "Her dress is on fire," totally destroying the shot. And Rob Reiner turns to me and says, "Bill, it's supposed to be on fire."

I don't like being around actors. I don't know what actors want; I don't know what they mean. That doesn't mean that I dislike them all. It's just in a work situation, I have no idea how to please them.

I don't know why directors want to be directors. I don't think it's a good job. I never did. And I think most of them are not very happy people—not that writers are, because we know writers aren't happy—but I think directors go through a lot of shit.

When we worked on *Butch Cassidy*, I came out in the middle of shooting to watch several hours of dailies. It was before they went to the South American part of the movie, which was shot in Mexico. I'm walking with George Roy Hill, and a guy comes by and says, "Hat okay?" Hill nods, and then suddenly George, who was a Marine pilot—very tough—almost went to his knees, because he realized the guy had said, "Is this hat that I am holding in my hand all right, because we're going to Mexico in the morning?" And if it had been the wrong hat, which it was, it would have delayed shooting for at least a day while they came up and got the right hat.

I've always thought about that little thing, because when you go off and shoot somewhere on location, if you don't have the right hat, baby, you're fucked.

Life Behind the Lens

JANE ANDERSON: What I learned is that film really is a director's medium. The script is essential as the beginning of a great story, but there's a whole other element to a film, which involves the visual—and even more importantly, there's what the actors bring to the script. I learned that as a writer, I have to release my script to my fellow collaborators. When I direct my own material, I'm ruthless about cutting what I think is nonessential. Directing has made me a very spare writer.

ADAM RIFKIN: I've been fortunate in that I've been able to have kind of a dual career. I get to write big studio family movies, which I love to do, and to a lot of people in town, I am the go-to big family-comedy writer. But luckily I'm also able to write and direct movies that are more personal to me, that aren't necessarily comedies and aren't necessarily family fare. The studio movies—*Underdog* and *Mouse Hunt* and stuff like that—those jobs afford me the freedom to be able to spend the time on the projects like *Look,* which are small passion projects.

RON SHELTON: I've written a number of movies that I didn't direct. Some came out better than others. But you have to understand that when you write for another director, or you write it on an assignment and somebody else is gonna interpret the material, you just have to let go of it. It's not yours anymore. Because when you hand it off to a director—even if you're the director—it's now time to interpret the music. The screenplay is the sheet music, and the problem is that unfortunately it only gets played one time in its life. Whereas, you know, a Duke Ellington suite that was performed sixty times on the road and never recorded properly can be reinterpreted endlessly.

The old cliché is true—you write one movie, you direct another movie, and you edit a third movie. You have to embrace the process that in the beginning was the word, but is gonna end up pictures.

I care about the words on the page as much as any writer who ever lived, and I try to get 'em right. But when we're shooting it, if there's a better way to say it or do it, I'm the first guy to say, "Let's try it that way." Preston Sturges used to tell the actors they couldn't change a comma. I go in prepared to not change a comma, but like jazz music, if you know the chord changes—the musical text that I call the screenplay—you have to let the discoveries and inventions happen. I think a good director does that. You have to also know when to say, "No, get back to the text." It's a dynamic process.

I want to have discoveries. I want something to happen that I don't anticipate—hopefully something that I can build on, not something that causes me to go to my trailer with an actor and have a serious talk. But that's the excitement when I'm directing—looking forward to something I didn't know was gonna happen.

Ron Shelton

ZAK PENN: I've directed two very independent movies, where I've had total freedom. They're actually improv movies, so not only was there freedom, there's no script, so it was totally up to me and the actors. And I think that's made it a little bit easier for me to return to the kind of heavily structured world of rewriting, because I remind myself, "Okay, this is a different thing now. I want this scene to be in *The Incredible Hulk*, but maybe they don't want it to be in *The Incredible Hulk*—or maybe they do but they wanna change it—and I'm just gonna have to accept that."

BILLY RAY: I'm a dinosaur. The things that I'm trying to achieve are not things that are terribly valued in my business. The window of opportunity for the movies that interest me is literally getting narrower and narrower by the day. If I could be happy making comic book movies, my life would be a lot easier. If I could roll out of bed and come up with an idea as singular as "There's a bus, and if it goes less than fifty miles an hour, it blows up," my life would be a lot easier. But I don't think up ideas as good as *Speed*, and I'm not turned on by movies that are just sort of glorified comic books.

The movies that made me become a writer are *Ordinary People*, *Kramer vs. Kramer*, *Tootsie*, *The World According to Garp*, *Network*, *Rocky*, *Fiddler on the Roof*, *Jaws*, *The Godfather*, *All the President's Men*. . . . Those movies are almost impossible to make now, and yet those are the movies that I gravitate toward.

I made a teeny movie called *Shattered Glass*, which was that kind of movie, and I just made a slightly larger movie called *Breach*, which is that kind of movie. Grown-up drama. Those are very tough to get made. You make it easier on yourself if you are also the director, because it's one more element that you bring to the party. The flip side is you've gotta make it for a price. If you wanna make *Breach*, you can't go out and spend a jillion dollars. That's fine. You don't need a lot of money to make a movie like *Breach*.

However, there's also the pure screenwriting part of my career, where the range of opportunities is a little bit wider. I can write a movie like *Flightplan*, and now I'm writing the remake of *Westworld*. Those are ideas that totally turn me on. They're big popcorn ideas. They're not ideas that I think I'd be any good at directing, so they give me freedom—when I'm writing them, I don't have to worry about how much they cost, and I don't have to worry about how difficult they're gonna be to shoot. Someone out there, in about a year, is gonna be standing on top of a moving train shooting a fistfight between two characters. It's not gonna be me, but I will have been very happy writing that scene for them.

Once you've directed, people always assume that all you want to do is direct, and that is part of the hierarchical nature of our business. I don't consider it to be a step back at all, having directed, to write for someone else. I got into writing with the idea that I wanted to work with great directors. I am not a great director, so it would be stupid to limit myself to only working with me. I want to write for Ang Lee. I want to write for Peter Weir. I want to write for Scorsese and Spielberg and Stephen Frears and Ron Howard. I could learn something from writing for them.

PAUL SCHRADER: I began as a kind of a Hollywood hustler and a Hollywood whore, and the first four films were studio films. Then I went off to Japan and made *Mishima,* and when I came back the industry had changed. The kind of films I was making were now independent films. I did not fight this phenomenon. I just bent with the wind, lowered my profile, lowered my price, and made smaller films, made independent films. I had no desire to keep playing a game that I felt no longer included me.

I've probably pursued too lonely a course as a director. I think maybe I should have concentrated more on doing projects that appealed to a wider audience, rather than just doing things that I cared about, and assuming that a wider audience would find them. You know, it's made my whole course as a filmmaker kind of difficult, and it's always been a struggle to get films made. *Affliction* took six years. *The Walker* took six years. Looking back on it now, I wish it had been an easier path.

But I'm glad I took the journey I did. If it hadn't been for the arts,

I'd probably be very rich, because I have capitalism in my bones. But the arts came along, and now I'm a more modest writer and director. I don't regret it for a second.

BRUCE JOEL RUBIN: I was very proud of *My Life* as a screen-play. When I directed it, I realized that I was what I would call a mediocre director. Okay director. Good enough director. I got it on the screen. It's a movie.

Directing a film is fascinating because you put all of your scenes on celluloid, and then you put them all together just as you wrote them, scene by scene by scene. Then you sit down to watch what's called the assembly, and you go, "This is the worst thing I have ever watched in my entire life. How did I ever think I was a director? How did I ever think I knew what I was doing? The script doesn't work at all—it worked in all the little pieces, but now it's just awful. There's no emotional thrust." It was the most depressing day of my life, watching the assembly of *My Life*.

Then my DP, Peter James, looked over at me and said, "Now you get to make your movie." And that was a wonderful piece of infor-mation. Whatever was on paper didn't mean anything.

I sat with Richard Chew, who is a wonderful editor, literally every day. I made him a little crazy, but it taught me a lot. We rewrote the movie on film. We found the rhythm. We found the tone. I watched *My Life* come alive, and it was a great learning process. A lot was lost from the literary element of the material, but a lot was gained from the truth of the performances.

I realized that the script for me is still truly the creative birthright of the movie. It is the writer who gives birth to a movie, not the director. I don't care what anybody says. A director is an interpreter. They come in and refashion the script, but it wouldn't exist without the writer.

The Maverick's Perspective:
Duncan Tucker

Duncan Tucker

Screenwriters who finance the production of their own scripts get to purchase the autonomy that eludes peers who toil in the Hollywood vineyards. The catch is that most people who bankroll themselves are neophytes prone to overestimating their ability to generate professional-quality films. Furthermore, the likelihood of landing significant distribution is infinitesimal, because outsiders, by definition, lack the necessary industry connections.

Every so often, however, someone gets it right. Consider Duncan Tucker, who made the crowd-pleasing dramedy Transamerica *(2005) with $1 million that he cobbled together from various sources. Released by the Weinstein Company, the picture earned a solid $15 million during its theatrical run, and netted Oscar nominations for leading lady Felicity Huffman and theme-song composer Dolly Parton. Tucker won numerous prizes for the film's screenplay, including an Independent Spirit Award.*

Countering Clichés

Gay people used to be represented in movies solely as queens or serial killers. And then, in movies I greatly admire, *Boys Don't Cry* and *Brokeback Mountain,* the noble hero is murdered by a society that misunderstands him. I wanted to move beyond that really fast, and make a story about a person who happens to be trans, but the subject matter is not transsexuality. It's about growing up and coming to terms with one's self. In the end, my character lives and is perhaps on the road to finding some kind of happiness, which is the best any of us can ask for.

When I did the initial research for *Transamerica,* I interviewed trans women and street boys. I was putting together the outline, and I realized, "I'm not sure I know how to direct." I wrote a little twenty-minute movie based on some of the street boys' stories, and made *The Mountain King* with a crew of, like, three people. I had some success with it, and it turned out well enough to give me confidence to proceed with *Transamerica.*

It was pretty much impossible to find financial backers. For a year and a half, we were trying to choose actresses who could mean money for us, but Felicity was somebody I always envisioned as being a wonderful choice. The money finally came from me. I saved, mortgaged the house, borrowed from my mother, borrowed from both my brothers, borrowed from family and friends, maxed out credit cards. I was ready to be in debt for the next ten years. When we finally made that decision, I was free to offer it to Felicity. Thank God she read it and immediately responded to it.

She said that she had to reshoot a TV pilot twelve weeks from when I hired her. I was like, "Holy shit." I called my producers and said, "Can we possibly get this thing done in twelve weeks?" They did some quick calculations and said, "We can if we start working this afternoon." I called Felicity back and said, "You're on." That afternoon, we started hiring location scouts, talking about budgets, talking about DPs and costume people, and getting everything together. It was this amazing race against time. We finished shooting on July 3. Felicity went home, spent her holiday looking at firecrackers, and then on July 5, she went into production with the reshoot of the pilot for *Desperate Housewives*.

We were editing when *Desperate Housewives* became a big hit, and we still couldn't get the movie out there. She was becoming more famous, but distributors still weren't knocking on our doors. Finally, we got it done in time to submit to Sundance. Felicity's husband, William H. Macy, called the people he knew there. They looked at it and they said, "No way." I thought, "Oh my God, I made a crappy movie!" A week later, we heard we were in the Berlin Film Festival.

The Momentum Builds

At Berlin, we had four screenings in huge theaters that were sold out to the point where there were people standing like sardines in the back of the theater. And we *still* couldn't drag distributors to see our movie. Then we won a jury prize at Berlin, which was a shock to me, and a few days later, Variety.com ran an amazingly good review. Suddenly everybody wanted to see the movie.

We were the first acquisition by the newly formed Weinstein Company, so that was newsworthy. We weren't eligible for Cannes because we'd already premiered in Berlin, but we were in the Cannes market to sell the film internationally. The first day of Cannes, the headline in *Variety* was "The Weinstein Company's First Acquisition is *Transamerica*." We sold to, I'd say, three-quarters of the international territories, and we kept raising our price. That was amazing.

Just before the film was going to be released, I signed with some new agents, and I said, "It would be so great to have an original song over the end credits." They said, "Who would you like?" I said, "I think Dolly Parton would be amazing—she's this symbol of life energy and self-transformation." They got it to her desk, and she wrote a song for me.

The distributor sent me on tour. I was in a different city every two days. Over nine or ten months, I think I was home maybe a total of two weeks. Talking in front of audiences was something that I hadn't done before. My first time was at Berlin, and there was an audience of six to seven hundred people. I had a double scotch just before having to go up there, because I was feeling jittery. Luckily people were really respectful and they seemed to be delighted with the movie, so it wasn't too painful.

I must have done it a few hundred times. Some of the same questions get asked over and over, so you learn what gets a laugh. You come up with something extemporaneously that works, and then you use it again and make it sound extemporaneous. You have to be a bit of an actor. Some people can do it, some people can't. There are probably wonderful directors, far more talented than I, who distributors might not want to send on tour because they can't speak in public.

Reaping Rewards

Spending a few months out in Los Angeles for award season was completely surreal. I was living in a little sublet studio apartment in West Hollywood that my producer found for me, and every day I'd have to do a radio interview or a print interview, I'd have to work on the DVD bonus features, I'd have a party for Felicity, a party for Dolly, a party for *Transamerica*. I can't remember very many things about that time, because it was a blur—but it was a fun blur. I went as Dolly's date to the Oscars. She was a vision in pink, and she sent me a pink handkerchief made by her dressmaker to match her outfit.

I remember going to the Spirit Awards and sitting between Felicity and Fionnula Flanagan at our table. I think my award was announced first. Fionnula and Felicity jumped up and hugged and kissed me. It was so great, and I was shocked and delighted.

I don't fool myself. The thing about *Transamerica* is that the characters are unconventional, but the story itself is . . . I don't like the word *conventional*. How about the word *classic*? It's a road movie. The hero goes on a quest, and comes back home changed after having met friends and enemies. *Transamerica* sets out to entertain, because you can't be subversive if they don't see your movie.

My task was to make audiences love the characters immediately. I wanted to give audiences permission to laugh, and permission to feel for these characters. The first time you see Felicity in *Transamerica*, she is an odd-looking character, but I hope that by the end of the movie, people aren't aware of the way she looks. They just see her as a human being, and they've completely brought her into their hearts.

Because I was paying for it myself, I got to make exactly the movie I wanted to make. I got to choose every last song, every last cut, every last bit of casting. Everything was mine. I know there are a lot of mistakes in the movie, but they're my mistakes.

10

No Is the
Path to Yes

Even with the considerable financial rewards that screenwriting can offer, having scripts repeatedly rejected, rewritten, and regurgitated by an unforgiving factory system is enough to challenge the optimism of the most emotionally balanced individual. And since artists are trained to become as emotionally sensitive as possible, the ease with which screenwriters can turn into cynics is immediately apparent.

As writers including John D. Brancato note, a certain degree of cynicism is helpful, because laughing at the preposterous extremes of the movie business is an effective defense mechanism. On a deeper level, learning to separate one's professional life from one's creative life is among the most complex growth experiences that any working artist undergoes. Those who find this delicate balance can retain enthusiasm for their work. Those who do not run the risk of derailing themselves, because few writers can remain creatively viable after becoming jaded about their own craft.

Leavening cynicism with optimism is just one of the coping strategies that screenwriters employ in order to sustain long careers, because each individual wrestles with demons in a different fashion. Some focus on the finish line, viewing rejection as a distraction along the path to acceptance. Some empower themselves by declining lucrative offers in favor of personally fulfilling endeavors. Some, like Shane Black, cling to vestigial traces of the "childish hunger" that drew them to screenwriting in the first place. For many writers, wonderment at being able to make up stories for a living is the greatest balm of all. James L. White reveals that the dream of becoming a screenwriter was so powerful that it helped him defeat an insidious personal hardship.

Perhaps the most brilliantly counterintuitive advice comes from John Carpenter. If the previous chapters have revealed any underlying truth, it is that the writer's lot in Hollywood is unlikely to change anytime soon. For some, fighting that fact fills them with the strength of righteous indignation. For others, blocking out that fact allows them to remain upbeat. But for Carpenter, simply acknowledging that fact is a means of moving past adversity and focusing on what really matters: the work.

Rejecting Rejection

JUSTIN ZACKHAM: The problem with this business is that you are always a hair's breadth away from being a millionaire—it's just the widest lock of hair on the planet.

JOE FORTE: A lot of times, I describe what I do as being a bank robber. You know, there's a vault out there with your name on it and money inside. You can have it if you can figure out how to open that vault.

NORA EPHRON: I think the most important thing you have to know is that it's a very, very hard business, full of rejection and setbacks. If you don't want to succeed really badly, you won't. But, of course, if you get a movie made and it works, there's nothing like it. Nothing.

ROBERT MARK KAMEN: Rejection is easy. Having the knives surgically removed from your back is hard. I have had my fair share of knives removed. There are still one or two that I leave embedded as a reminder that getting too comfy can be hazardous to your creative health.

JANE ANDERSON: The secret to longevity is to ride this crazy roller coaster, and just know that it happens to the best of us. It happens to the most famous artists in this field. It happens to the stars. Careers are broken only if the artist allows it to be broken.

ALLISON ANDERS: You should never take rejection personally. You should just say, like, "Okay, they didn't want that—maybe they want this." Try to keep those relationships going, if you like the people. If they suck, fuck them—you don't ever have to go back to them again. Go to the people who are open to your ideas, and who you feel compatible with, and you will come up with something together.

JOE STILLMAN: I gotta say, going to writers on the topic of rejection is just great. It's like going to an alcoholic to ask about beer.

I think all rejection is ultimately justified on some level. I'll give you a "for instance." In the last few years, I went for a few projects—some of them were rewrites and some weren't—where I felt like, "Okay, I just need the job, so I'm gonna *kinda* go for it." In one

o cases, I lost out to somebody who had come up with the right
.e. What I realized was that I was spending a great deal of time
ursuing something that wasn't my passion, and that was not the
best thing to do. That's caused me to make a real sea change in terms
of what it is that I'm willing to pitch on.

Joe Stillman

MIKE BINDER: You can focus on what's gonna go bad or what's
gonna go right, so I'd just as soon focus on what's gonna go right.
You wanna take your dreams and make 'em reality. You wanna
be a storyteller. So you gotta be thinkin' about your own stories,

your own dreams, in a positive way. I think that the more positive you are—the more you're thinkin', "This is really gonna be a good project, and I see it happening"—the more you're gonna have the energy to get it done. If you can't do that—you're more like, "Ah, who's gonna want this?"—you never finish anything.

DANIEL PYNE: One of my mentors was William Sackheim, who was a legendary television producer. In television, you're usually getting rejected at a higher rate. You could write three pilots in a year, and they could all get rejected. I watched Bill go through this, and I realized that he had this marvelous ability to just forget. When it was time to develop new ideas, he just started all over again. I think that's what sustained him. It's what made him have a fifty-year career. I've tried to emulate that a little bit, to not fall into that trap that writers tend to fall into, where you say, "They're not gonna buy this because it's a thriller, and they're not making thrillers now." I love writing, and I love filmmaking, so if I focus on the parts I like, there isn't room for the rejection to take hold and defeat me.

NAOMI FONER: From the beginning, I did this because I thought there were stories that had nothing to do with me, but needed to be told, and that if I could be the instrument of telling them, then they could keep me going. If you do it to be rich and famous, that's a terribly wrongheaded idea. If you're doing it to tell stories that need to be told, you can get yourself through the bad moments, because you're doing something bigger, something that transcends you.

JAMES L. WHITE: Hold on to your dream, and do what you have to do. I was a city health inspector in Boston. Do the necessary work to pay your bills and take care of your family, and you'll get there. Talent has a way of workin' itself out. Hollywood will find you. Eventually.

One of the things that Ray Charles and I had in common is that I used to use heroin like he used heroin, but we both were creative at the time. Of course, he did a lot more with his creativity than I did. But I imagined being here—that's what kept me going, and that was one of the ways in which I was able to kick drugs. I knew this is what I wanted to do. In a drugged state, I could never accomplish this—I'd write a page or two, and if you didn't get it, man, you weren't smart enough. I was high. When I sobered up, I read it, and I didn't get it either.

I imagined getting to this. But I'm glad I got here sober.

James L. White

MARK O'KEEFE: All you really need is a good idea, and to execute it in a good way, and you have a movie.

STEVE KOREN: There is a sense of being in the Old West here—it's like panning for gold. Generally, if you have a great idea, someone will buy that idea. You're always one script away from a career. But you have to be prepared. It could take many years before someone will bother to consider your work.

MARK O'KEEFE: Basically, anyone who is relatively bright, and is taking the trouble to read this book, and is going through the process, and considers themselves a writer, and is going to keep doing it, and is willing to critique their own stuff, and is willing to take criticism . . . I think there is a place for everyone.

STEVE KOREN: There's a giant group of people who want to be writers, and a smaller group who actually write, and an even smaller group who are actually going to strive so hard that someone's going to pay attention to them. And when you get to that smaller group, you have to really commit yourself. I don't know about Mark, but I was obsessed at one point. I took every course, I read magazines, and I just kept going to movies. I remember at one point, I sat down and wrote down *Rocky* beat by beat.

MARK O'KEEFE: Wow.

STEVE KOREN: I wanted to understand the structure of what was happening, you know? I wanted to take myself through what those writers had gone through. You have to commit.

MICHAEL WOLK: Going through no is the way to get to yes. Going through no also means, I think, understanding why people are saying no, and being proactive in getting toward the yes, and listening to the feedback, and moving forward so that you're getting rejected by a better class of people as you work your way up. The more gracious you are in handling rejections, the better you can develop relationships that are initially based on rejection. You got the door open half an inch because they liked the idea, but they thought you couldn't write dialogue. Next time, you send 'em a thing and say, "I've been brushin' up the dialogue, and I took your words to heart." A no can be really the start of a yes.

KRISS TURNER: My pastor at church says, "A setback is a setup to a step up." That's what I believe.

ADAM RIFKIN: I was hired to direct a movie called *Barb Wire*, which starred Pamela Anderson. I had made a number of independent films. This was a bigger film, she was a high-profile figure—on paper, it seemed like the smart career choice, even though some voice inside of me said, "This isn't what I feel passionate about." Ultimately, I got fired off that movie. I got caught in the middle of a political battle between Dark Horse Comics, who owned the character, and Propaganda Films, who was financing the movie.

All the people who had called to congratulate me for getting the job wouldn't return my calls after I'd been fired, because it was on the front page of the trades. I thought to myself, "I could either sit around and feel sorry for myself, or I could use the only power I have in Hollywood—the ability to generate material."

I sat in a room and went on a writing frenzy. The first script I wrote didn't sell. The second script I wrote didn't sell. And then I had an idea for a movie. I had never written a family movie before, and I told Brad Wyman, the producer I've worked with on many films, "I have this idea for a movie, but I think it's too stupid. I shouldn't write it." He said, "What is it?" I said, "It's about two brothers who inherit an old drafty house that's worth a lot of money, and there's a mouse in the house, and they become obsessed with killing the mouse. But the mouse is much smarter than they are, and the mouse ruins their lives. It's kinda like a live-action *Tom and Jerry*." He said, "You should write that immediately. You'll sell it for $1 million."

I wrote it really fast, and I thought, "There's no way this is gonna sell. This is too stupid." But I just got into all the cartoons I loved when I was a kid, went to that well for inspiration. While *Barb Wire* was still in production, *Mouse Hunt* went out as a spec, got into a bidding war between a number of studios, and DreamWorks bought it for $1 million.

If there's any point to this story, it's that Hollywood is all about rejection. Everybody in Hollywood is rejected over and over again. The only thing you can do is love what you do and keep doing it— because eventually it's gonna pay off. For me, that was an example of ignoring the rejection and plowing forward, and it turned out to be the best thing that ever happened to me.

The Better Part of Valor

JOSE RIVERA: One of the things that kept me sane earlier in my career was saying no to certain things I didn't want to do. Being a Latino writer, I was pitched gang movie after gang movie. People wanted me to write a movie about a Salvadoran gang. I said no. Then they pitched me a girl gang, and I said no. And then they pitched me a deaf gang—a gang of New York kids who can't hear. I said no to all that stuff. I said, "I don't want to write about gangs, I don't want to write about drugs, I don't want to write about any of that stuff. I think that's a Latin cliché, and I don't want to be part of it." One of the healthiest things a writer can do is to know where to draw the line for themselves and say, "You know what? I don't care how much money you're offering, I don't do that kind of work."

ROBERT MARK KAMEN: I called a producer yesterday and I passed on a job. I'd already been talking about "This happens in this act" and "This happens in that act," so I was a little nervous about calling because I didn't want to be yelled at, or to hear this again: "You'll never work in this business again, you son of a bitch!" I called them up, and I said, "I don't really feel this," and they said, "There'll be something else." They don't want to give me a big paycheck, and have me go into a studio and pitch, and then have me turn in something that is less than inspired. That won't be good for them; it won't be good for me. I get paid a lot of dough to do this, and the expectations are very high. If I don't meet those expectations, I won't get a job next time.

RON SHELTON: I learned early on that I can't write anything if it's not about me. I don't mean that in a sense of megalomania. I mean about my experiences, needs, fears, desires, whatever. So even if it's about a photographer in the Nicaraguan revolution, like *Under Fire*, his issues have to be issues that I care about personally. I would make a lot more money if I was a good mercenary—you know, somebody says, "Here, we'll pay you $3 million to write a script about aliens and space stars exploding . . ." I can't do it. I want your money, but I don't know how.

JOHN D. BRANCATO: A couple of times, we've had movie deals, and then had disagreements early on in the process, and just said, "Look, no harm, no foul—let's go separate ways. You don't have to pay us. We're outta here." I'd like to think that I can always do that. A lot of people don't have that luxury.

JONATHAN LEMKIN: If you let your lifestyle expend your last check, you then say yes to a really bad project to keep the checks coming. The quality of your work goes down, your reputation goes down, and it's harder to get the next job. I've definitely taken the wrong job a couple of times, and it's very hard to do your best work if you're feeling like, "Oh, this is the wrong job."

PAUL MAZURSKY: If I had needed jobs desperately, I might have behaved differently. But I made a great deal of money on *Bob & Carol & Ted & Alice*, so I had "fuck you" money. It gave me courage.

LARRY COHEN: I made some mistakes over the years, but I don't know that they were really mistakes in the long run. When I was doing television, I created *Branded* and *The Invaders* and *Cool Million*—I created eight television series. ABC came to me and said, "We'd like to set you up as a supplier." They were tryin' to turn me into, like, an Aaron Spelling.

The opportunity to become a supplier for a network is a multi-million-dollar opportunity. If I had taken that job, my career might have moved off into a different direction. I wouldn't have been writing anymore. I would have been supervising other people, and would have made a lot of money—probably much more than I ever made. But I wouldn't have been doing what I wanted to do, which was writing.

So that was the big crossroads in my career—whether I was gonna take that chance to become a supplier for ABC, or whether I was gonna continue just being the lone wolf out there writing scripts, trying to sell them in the marketplace, and never having a big suite of offices and a bunch of employees.

You know somethin'? I'm happy I didn't take the job.

MICK GARRIS: David Cronenberg recommended me to write *The Fly II*, which was great. However, there were four other writers after me. It's not a movie I love, and when I saw the first sneak preview of it, I kinda sank down in my chair because it was so far removed from what I'd written.

I had come up with an idea that I thought was meaningful and scary and interesting. It was all about Veronica Quaife, the leading lady from the first *Fly*. She has her pregnancy, and she decides she's got to get an abortion. She runs into a clinic, there are people who say, "Don't abort your baby," and all that. It turns into a religious anti-abortion kind of situation. My idea was sort of political and dramatic and adult. Scott Rudin was the production executive on *Fly II*, and he really liked this edgy take, which was trying to continue what Cronenberg had set up in what I think is one of the great horror films.

At that time, 1986, there was a lot of teenage horror, so the studio wanted to turn it into a teenage monster movie. Fox was being run by Leonard Goldberg, and there were big fights between Goldberg and Rudin on the direction they wanted to take. I got about halfway into the next draft when I was offered a movie to direct. Because there was so much infighting going on at Fox, I chose the moment to make my exit—and to make my feature directing debut.

SHANE BLACK: I jumped ship on *Lethal Weapon* in kind of a fussy way, because I had my own vision for the series. I didn't think that the first movie violated it too badly. There was one sort of outrageous scene in the first movie, where there's a hundred cops on the front lawn of Danny Glover's character, watching a man beaten to death and cheering like, you know, *Thunderdome* or something. I didn't like it then, and especially in view of later LAPD high jinks, it became very difficult to watch. But at least they managed to avoid straight comedy.

Shane Black

When doing the sequel to *Lethal Weapon*, I tried to think of something that would make it seem like it had come full circle— what if it was one big movie, number one and number two? What would the run be? It came out that the Riggs character would die at the end, and they didn't like that. They didn't like a lot more too. They changed the tone and decided it was going to be a feel-good cop series about funny people doing funny things. I couldn't write funny, and I couldn't write cute, and I couldn't write feel-good just for the hell of it—especially in a cop story. I was used to *Dirty Harry*, and they wanted *Dirty Harry 4*, where he's got a farting dog.

So I hopped ship. Turns out the next movies made a great deal of money, and that's fine—I'm happy to take the paycheck for having gotten this thing rolling. But, man, I didn't wanna write comedies.

MARK D. ROSENTHAL: When the filmmakers are giving you ideas that you just find preposterous, you're very tempted as a writer to call up your agent and say, "Replace us." You know, let's walk off, and we have our integrity. We have found over the years that that's a very dangerous form of self-pity. It's okay to be pushed out of the plane, but don't drop a parachute and jump, because by staying on the plane, at least you might win little battles.

MICHAEL WOLK: After I first had my flush of success out in Hollywood, I was assigned several things by a studio. After that, I tried once again to write an original screenplay to sell. It didn't sell, and I was really downhearted because I was expecting it to sell. There was a nibble, but no bite. A few weeks later, my agent said, "What are you doing now?" I said, "I don't know." He said, "Look, I just had a guy who wrote *The Poseidon Adventure* meets *Jaws*. It's called *Tentacles*. Write something like that."

Something that will always sell in Hollywood is high concept, and it's usually, "You take this and you match it with that, and then you got a movie." Like with *Innocent Blood*, it was, "Mafia? Vampires? Hey! It's a movie." Well, there's your high concept, and then there's the studio's high concept. As an artist, your idea is going to be satisfying to you, but when you're told a high concept that sounds pretty low to you, that is very hard to invest your energy into.

I went back to New York. I just said, "I'm gonna write a novel and say good-bye to Hollywood for a while," thinkin' it would be there when I got back—which is not the way to do things. My advice to screenwriters would be to stay in L.A., and take as many meetings as you can, and work the community, because eventually the jobs will come around.

My initial success, and the striking level of it, didn't prepare me for the reality of the marketplace. If I had really thought about the future, I wouldn't have been so much of a diva. I took my chips and I left, and I spent a lot of the chips—and by the time I realized that I wanted to court the Hollywood community again, they had moved on.

All About Attitude

GUINEVERE TURNER: Everyone's like, "Oh, you have a cushy life—you just sit around and write." I'm like, "No, it's actually really hard." As I like to say, I wish that my job was being a bricklayer—because I would lay the bricks, the wall would be built, and that would be it. Nobody could deny that it's a fucking brick wall. Nobody's gonna come along and say, "Mmm, I think that brick should be over here."

I stay positive because most days, I don't have to get up until I want to get up. I also work in my pajamas for most of the day. I get to go to movie premieres, and have people vaguely acknowledge my contribution. I stay positive because I love my life.

You know, I had an office job once, for a year and a half, and I was suicidal. I was twenty-two—maybe I was suicidal anyway. But I mean, I love that I actually get paid, more or less, to do what I do. And whenever I'm feeling whiny and sorry for myself, I'm like,

"You're not homeless, you're not dyin' of cancer, you slept until ten, you get to go out and party tonight. Your life rules."

MICK GARRIS: Our complaints mean nothing compared to the complaints of people who are pipe fitters for a job, or working on ships, or fighting overseas in the military. You know, those people have the right to complain, and they're the least likely to complain. And here's a bunch of people who live in Beverly Hills or whatever, with very comfortable homes, cars, partners, a good income, and the like, bitching about somebody making them change their script and having that give them ulcers and sleepless nights—it's just not worth it.

MARK O'KEEFE: You forget that compared to a normal standard, you're doing very well. It's easy to get caught up and in the L.A. socioeconomic scene.

STEVE KOREN: That could actually affect your writing. Suddenly, you want to write a movie about a guy who's having problems with his investment banker.

MARK O'KEEFE: Yeah, exactly.

STEVE KOREN: You're like, "Yeah, that's relatable. Everybody I know has this problem." You forget.

MARK O'KEEFE: Yeah.

STEVE KOREN: I actually keep my dad in mind when I write. He was a mailman. He came home at night and he loved watching movies. So what could he relate to? That's what we tend to write. The ones that we've talked about, that excite us, are ideas that everyone can relate to.

BILLY RAY: The best writing advice I ever heard, I actually read in a book of interviews with screenwriters. It came from Paddy Chayefsky, who you'd have to rank as one of the best screenwriters of all time. His advice was: "Don't think of it as art, think of it as work."

Because when a screenwriter is stuck, and he calls in another screenwriter to help him, that second screenwriter doesn't come in and say, "What is the art problem?" He says, "What's not working about your script?" And they push up their sleeves and they start to fix what's not working, as if it were a car with a broken engine. You need to approach it like work. If you are an artist, it will come out as art anyway, but at least you will have done your job.

I write every morning the same way. I take my kids to school. I'm at my desk by nine. Someone feeds me at one. I get back behind my computer at two, and I write until five. My nights and my weekends belong to my family, but basically I'm at work all day long, like a plumber, or a guy who cleans pools, or a secretary.

JOHN AUGUST: One thing you have starting out that you don't have later on in life is abundant time and energy. I was just sitting down with a kid who had just graduated from college and who had moved out to Los Angeles looking to be a screenwriter-director-filmmaker-everything. I encouraged him to do everything all at once. Because there's something about those first couple of years, where you're broke and poor and sleeping on the floor and eating Top Ramen, where anything is possible. You have very little to lose. You sign on to be a PA on a no-budget short film and maybe meet somebody great, or maybe that film ends up being something terrific, or it leads you in a new direction.

The challenge comes as you get older, and you develop more responsibilities. You have to balance things you didn't have to balance before. I have regular hours. I work from nine to six, and then I need to be home, because somebody needs to give the baby a bath and put her to bed. I can't work weekends. So it's a very different kind of life.

Your natural instincts are to treat your job kind of like finals in college—screw around for a couple weeks, and then spend a couple of all-nighters writing that paper you really need to get written. As you get older and develop more responsibilities, that's not practical anymore. You find yourself having to budget your time and make a plan, and do all those things that are sort of the anathema of what you think a freedom-loving writer should want to do. It becomes much more of a job.

The luxury of experience is that you actually have craft. I can just muscle through things where I used to have to sit around and wait for inspiration. You have new skills that are different from what you had at twenty. In exchange for all the energy you've lost, you have a focus and a precision that you lacked early on.

JOE STILLMAN: The number of rugs that can be pulled out from under you in this business is vast. I kind of know that intellectually, so when those times happen, I think, "I'm in the film business. I chose to be here. I'm not a victim." You know, "You can't get the ups unless you get the downs." But then you take a few more downs, and it starts to feel like, "Oh my God, what am I doing here? One more, and I'm outta here."

A lot of us get a sense of who we are based on what we do. So when I'm riding high—forget riding high, when I'm actually employed— yahoo, I'm great! And when the opposite is true—I've pitched three or four things and haven't gotten anything—I must be utter crap, and I can't stand it anymore. It's a hard way of looking at the world, and it's very common here. I think that attitude is even fed and nurtured while we're here.

One way to deal with that is to recognize that whether up or down, neither is who you are. I'm working to consciously develop other aspects of my life so that I'm not quite as emotionally dependent on the ups and downs.

Joe Forte

JOE FORTE: If you just define yourself as a screenwriter, and you have a bad day as a screenwriter, then that's your whole world. You're building your life on this very singular pylon. It's important to remember that you're a brother or a father or a boyfriend, and also that you have interests and hobbies that feed you and nourish you, and bring ideas in and balance you out. If I have a bad day screenwriting, I can come out to my studio, and I can paint and connect with myself. It's important to build a broad life that feeds you, that nourishes you, that gives you stability.

DOUG ATCHISON: It's wise to stay out of situations where fellow artists are grousing about Hollywood, because you can get into a circular conversation about how messed up Hollywood is, how inconsiderate the people that run Hollywood are, and how they don't get it. That's not healthy. The film business is a hugely difficult thing to pursue, so you have to realize that this is impossible—but you do it anyway.

BRUCE JOEL RUBIN: I meditate every day. I sit down and I let go of my mind. I let go of the struggle, I let go of the tension, I let go of the anger, and just, in a sense, immerse myself in this very still pool. That pool is very reviving. It's very loving, very joyous, very full of life, of newness. It's always about what is in the moment, as opposed to what was and what will be. It's so present and refreshing.

I go there every day. I often go back there many times a day, because it is the place from which real creativity can come, and from which your revival as a person—after all the onslaughts of degradation that occur in the Hollywood sphere—can come. It brings you back to you. It brings you back to what you're about, why you do what you do, and it completely reinvents your life, in a sense, on a daily basis.

I have my anger. It definitely comes up, but I don't live in it. Sometimes I get caught in it for a period of time, but because I practice this thing every day of letting it go, that's where I get relief. The problem, for most people, is that they never go there—they don't even know it's there to go to. They go to, you know, Prozac or Johnny Walker Red. They go to whatever they can to kind of diminish the pain. I go to a place where there is no pain to diminish.

Don't Let the Bastards Get You Down

JOHN D. BRANCATO: Once you are seduced by the pleasures offered to you, you kinda lose whatever edge you had, and you start to say, "Well, I'm doing this one for the car," or "I'm doing this one so I can have a long vacation." The thing you want to avoid is waking up and saying, "I have become exactly the hack that I most loathed when I first started to write screenplays."

Somebody says, "We're gonna pay you $1 million to write *Bug Boy 3*." You think, "Well, okay . . ." Even though you know it's not gonna be a good movie, you find a way to say, "*Bug Boy 3* could say something about the human condition that hasn't been said." You have to lie to yourself. You have to have amnesia. You have to do a lot of things to really succeed as a screenwriter.

On the movie *Catwoman*, at some point in the process I started to get curious about the whole notion of a day self and a night self, and the opposition between the two, and archetypes of women as good girls and bad girls, and the interplay between them. Trying to write stuff that would play to that set of concerns became interesting. Forgetting Halle Berry, forgetting movies, forgetting all the attendant crap on the project—from a writing perspective, it was exciting to think about those issues. So even on the most threadbare, hideous, stupid project, you can still—if you're any good at all—find something that's interesting and fun and worth some creative energy.

I've read screenplays, plenty of them, where the writer obviously hates what he's doing, and thinks it's bullshit. That kind of cynicism is pernicious. It hurts the project. It hurts movies in general. So I try not to be cynical about the thing itself—about the screenplay, about the movie—while being cynical about every single other thing attached to it. Staying innocent in the creative process is the thing.

NAOMI FONER: I remember Alvin Sargent saying to me when he saw *Running on Empty,* "This makes me want to do my own best work." I never got a compliment better than that, and whenever I see something that makes me feel that way, I try to say it to the person whose work I've just seen. That's how you should feel enough of the time to keep going, 'cause there's so much stuff that happens that wants to push you back.

MARK D. ROSENTHAL: I have gotten better at picking up the signposts, like, "I think they're out looking for another writer," "I think he didn't like this draft," "I think something bad is gonna happen"— you know, the zombies are gonna break into my psychic room and rip my throat out. I feel, "Well, I'm a professional. I can see that coming." But when they rip your throat out, it doesn't feel any better.

DAVID HAYTER: To continue to justify working in the business, you have to start saying, "They don't know what they're talking about." Once you start to go down that road, that's pretty danger-ous. I mean, a lot of them may not know what they're talking about, but a lot of them do. There are a lot of smart people in this industry. Once you start to create a divide in your mind between you and them, that divide will only widen and widen and widen.

JONATHAN LEMKIN: What I try to do to maintain my sanity is alternate between artist and whore. If I was just an artist, I'd be broke, and if I was just a whore, I'd be sad. So I go back and forth. It's not quite "one for them, one for me." Sometimes it's "two for them, one for me." But generally, after I've done some rewrite work, or I'm just feeling burned out, it's like, "I've gotta do something that's original."

ZAK PENN: If you don't have a good coping strategy, you probably won't last. I mean, some of the typical ones are alcoholism, drug addiction, nymphomania—I've managed to avoid those. I play a lot of video games. Killing people on the safe field of the Internet is a good way to get your aggression out.

DANIEL PYNE: I get incredibly frustrated and bitter and cynical. How do I stay positive? I try not to go to movies. I try to stay away from Hollywood parties. I have friends outside of the business. I try not to read the trades. . . . I shouldn't be saying this on tape.

ANTWONE FISHER: I have written a lot of screenplays, but only two of them have actually been made into films—the ones that came directly from me, only two in sixteen years. My job, as a screenwriter working in Hollywood, is to give the producer and the studio what they want. Whether they make the movie or not, that's in someone else's hands.

RONALD SHUSETT: Quiet periods are torture. The older you get, the more painful it is, because you're afraid they'll never give you another shot. If you don't get movies made for several years, it's worse than having flops. You disappear. It just gets harder and harder to get your movies made. And I never imagined that. I thought making bad movies was gonna hurt you more. From 1992, with *Freejack*, to 2002, with *Minority Report*, I didn't get a movie made as a writer or a producer. And it looked like I didn't have the stuff anymore. During that time, I had movies I could have gotten made, but I didn't believe in them. I had offers from studios. Keep your oar in the water, and keep rowing—because if you don't, they think there's something wrong with your talent just by vacancy.

Ronald Shusett

MICHAEL JANUARY: I was fairly depressed at one point that I was getting these action movies made, and was not getting paid a lot of money. And so I went to therapy. Some guy was offering a little therapy thing for creative people, so I said, "Okay, I'm feeling bad. I'll go and sit and talk it out with some other people in the same situation."

So I'm going to therapy because I'm getting these movies made and not making a lot of money. In this session is this other guy who's working over at Warner Bros., getting paid an awful lot of money, but he can't get any movies made. That's why he's in therapy. So I started going, "All right, maybe it's not so bad. I'll just get over my issue, because the other side of the fence is not all that pretty either."

Anybody in Hollywood has things that they wish they could be doing. They have their pet projects they wish they could get made. There are writers who wish they could be directors. There are directors who wish they could write. You kind of get the career you get.

JOHN AUGUST: There are days I'm very down on Hollywood. Sometimes it's because of a pass, where I went out and pitched an idea and nobody bought it. Other times it's because you see people making choices that you know are the wrong choices, and you can't stop them—they're hiring the wrong director on a project that you spent two years developing, they're asking for another rewrite on a project that really doesn't need it. There are times where you get really, really frustrated by this whole industry, and you just want to go off and write a book, where at least no matter what you do, it's yours and you have full control over it.

The only way to get back on the horse and regain your love for the business—or at least your strange, abusive, crack-addict relationship with the business—is sitting in an audience that's watching one of your movies, where all those jokes which have stopped being funny to you are suddenly funny to a hundred people around you. That keeps you going. It's the random person who says that they really liked that obscure script you wrote four years ago. That keeps you going. It's the validation from knowing that you wrote something really good.

JOHN CARPENTER: "Embrace the darkness," as Steve Buscemi says. There's nothing you can do about it. It's okay. You'll survive. It may be a great idea that you've done. It may be your best work. But you'll do another one. Don't worry about it. Because if you worry, you're gonna eat yourself up, and then you become an enemy to yourself. You can't do that. You have to maintain this joy of the work. It's the work. It's not, "This is my masterpiece, and they screwed it up." Well, they paid you for it, okay? They paid you for your masterpiece. So stop bitching, stop whining, and move on.

SHANE BLACK: I sort of slid off the map a little bit after *Long Kiss Goodnight* was such a failure back in the nineties, and I don't know quite how I got back on the map. Because of the turnover in these offices, the executives at the studios are now twenty-five, and they saw *Lethal Weapon* when they were eight—so there's a sense of being an old-timer before I'm even an old-timer. I had to reinvent my career at age forty. That's the disadvantage of succeeding early. Eventually, you have to find the second stage of your career. You go back to the source, to the kid you were when you were hungry, while you were still eating, breathing, and sleeping this stuff. It reminds you not just of where you've been, but where you've yet to go, and hopefully reinstills in you a little bit of that childish hunger. When you lose that, you've lost everything.

GERALD DiPEGO: I knew I wanted to be a writer by the time I was twelve years old. I just turned sixty-six, and there's a moment in each production where I'm twelve again, because carpenters came and built this building, and there's a sign on the door that has the name of the character I thought up. What's more fragile than a story? It's this wispy thing you make up in your mind. And to see flesh-and-blood actors walking around, being your characters, and to see carpenters building buildings, and it all came out of this dream. . . . There's still a moment where I'm that twelve-year-old kid saying, "Wow, look at this."

The Therapist's Perspective:
Dennis Palumbo

Dennis Palumbo

The uncertainties of a Hollywood writing career are enough to send the strongest soul to a psychotherapist's couch, and often the therapist in question is former screenwriter Dennis Palumbo. Following a television career that included a stint as the story editor of Welcome Back, Kotter, *Palumbo transitioned to features by cowriting the acclaimed comedy* My Favorite Year *(1982), among other projects. He then retired from show business to become a mental-health professional specializing in creative issues.*

The Healing Game

I was in therapy myself, and I fell in love with the process, so I started going back to school and volunteering at a psychiatric hospital. But then one day, I was having lunch with a producer who wanted me to write a movie. I was late for going down to the hospital where I worked doing group therapy with schizophrenics, and I couldn't wait for the lunch to be over. Driving down there, I said, "What's wrong with this picture?" I knew then that I was going to sit for the exam and become a therapist.

I would think the two things that benefit my patients the most are that I used to be in show business and I was a screenwriter, so I understand their dilemmas. There are so many ways in which, as a writer, you can have your aesthetic violated. Each different person responds based on how they're made up emotionally. You know, there are a lot of people who have a kind of defense mechanism that says, "As long as they pay me big money, I don't care what they do with the script." It's a way to armor yourself against the pain of having somebody do something to your material that you don't like. Most writers, though, are more porous than that.

The thing about therapy is you can't really put a template on it that works for everyone. It depends on who the person is. How they respond to criticism and rejection has so much to do with their self-concept, their self-esteem, the lessons they learned in childhood. There are people for whom criticism is a way to get better as a writer. There are people for whom criticism is a devastating confirmation that they're untalented, depending on what kind of emotional resources they developed in their family of origin.

If you look at the biographies of famous writers, or artists of all kinds, there are four or five major periods in their life where they fall down, they stagger, they get blocked, no one likes their work. These are almost like the steps a child goes through where he crawls, and then he fights to learn how to master standing, and then he fights to learn how to walk. It's part of the natural developmental arc of an artist to navigate these crises, and then grow from them and move on.

I have a number of patients who have written ten or twelve films, and now their excitement is how big the deal is gonna be, and how much it's gonna kick into their financial nut. They're so used to the film being dismantled by the studio, mangled by the director, poorly acted, not getting the distribution it needed—and then if the film doesn't do well, getting all the bad notices for it—that the movies have become just a big income stream to them.

I think all of us have been assholes at one time or another. Anyone can start believing their own publicity, and start thinking that they're the new creative genius. So show business can be very humbling. On the other hand, studio executives and agents, for reasons beyond my understanding, get to stay assholes and it doesn't seem to affect their livelihood at all.

My feeling is you write to communicate. And if what you're writing doesn't communicate to more than four people, you better be okay with that, because the reality is the marketplace needs certain dramatic elements. On the whole, I think you're better off writing what it is that excites you. So if you want to write a big action-adventure movie, it better be because you like that kind of movie, and therefore you'll write one that fits the pattern of what they're making.

I have a patient who was working on a big action-adventure—one of those *Die Hard* kind of movies—and he said, "The difference is the guy's gonna die at the end." And I said, "Then no one's gonna buy it." Because if you're really a fan of those movies, you know that one of the satisfactions is seeing the guy triumph at the end. If you want him to die at the end, you're gonna have to go find independent funding and make it in Spain, 'cause they're not gonna make it here.

You Are Not Alone

It's much more common now than at any time I can remember for a screenplay to have eight or nine writers on it. There's a lot of money at stake, so there are too many chefs. Part of the surrealistic experience in Hollywood is that the originator of the material—from the moment everyone else claims to love it—is then the subject of an attempt to remove them from the material as much as possible.

The wonderful screenwriter Frederic Raphael once said, "You better have a good time writing your first draft. That's the last moment of pleasure you will ever have on that project."

This happens to my patients every day—and they're also the ones who are rewriting other people. I mean, it's such a funny situation. You can be sitting in my office complaining that the script's been taken out of your hands and given to some hot young Turk who just came on the scene. Meanwhile, you're rewriting someone else at the same time.

If you feel the person rewriting you respects the original material, it's a little more tolerable. If it's a wholesale rewrite—where you feel that the new writer is trying to make as many changes as possible so that when arbitration time comes, they'll get a shot at a screen credit—then you feel like you're being erased.

Regardless of the fact that my practice is all show business, we don't talk about the business as much as we talk about their lives. We primarily talk about relationships, money worries, child rearing, substance abuse, the relationship they have with their families of origin, their envy of their best friend, the extramarital affair they're having.

What makes it particularly difficult for a writer is that writing is not a regular job. It's not stocking shelves at a supermarket. It's a very erratic career, such that if you have a family, you're concerned because your income could go up and down based on the vagaries of the business. All of a sudden you go from being on the front page of *Variety* to now you can't get arrested, and your wife or your husband is going, "What are we gonna do for money?" That's very tough to live with.

Plus you're always looking out the window, thinking of things. You can't enjoy a movie with your family like everyone else, because you're going, "I don't know how this bum got a job," or "Do they call that a second act?" or "I remember the movie they stole this one from," or "I had an idea like that myself." So it just wrecks the experience for everyone you're with.

I always remember a quote from Robert Frost. He said, "The one thing all nations of the earth share is a fear that a member of your family will want to be an artist." The key is to remember that you're not alone. Every successful writer used to be a struggling writer. And I can tell you, I have those successful writers in my practice and they still struggle. They still have act two problems, they wonder if all of their success so far was a fluke, they say to themselves, "I'm no Preston Sturges," or whatever.

Because we respect the writing and respect our craft, we all worry about whether we're doing it right.

11

Going the
Distance

The span of time between an initial concept and a theatrical release can be years or even decades. And that's if the concept ever becomes a film. Once a screenwriter decides to put an idea down on paper, he or she begins an odyssey that could as easily end in jubilation as heartbreak— every time some lucky soul steps into the global spotlight and claims an Academy Award, thousands of writers are left asking why their dreams haven't come true. And yet the next morning, those same writers start anew, hoping that maybe this time, they will craft a classic.

Why do some writers win the Hollywood game, while others do not? And why do so many people chase the dream given the long odds against success? The answers to both questions are the same. Screen-writers do what they do because they love their craft. Because neither artistic nor financial success is guaranteed, creative fulfillment is the only tangible goal that screenwriters can pursue. The satisfaction of shaping an effective screen story is as potent for a veteran as it is for a beginner. What happens after the work is done is anyone's guess, so writers must savor precious moments of accomplishment.

The most contented screenwriters are those whose passion for their work never dims, because the intensity with which those artists infuse every page translates to buyers and, ultimately, to audiences. As Paul Schrader, Ron Shelton, Gerald DiPego, and Justin Zackham explain in the remarkable stories that open this final chapter, the desire to express intensely personal ideas can beget unexpected triumphs. Yet the same passion that leads to inspiration can lead to inertia, when the hope of achieving greatness becomes the ambition to attain flawlessness. No matter how romantic the idea of writing the perfect screenplay may be, even some of the artists who have come closest to reaching that pinnacle say that consciously striving for perfection is folly.

So if success is uncertain and perfection is unattainable, must screenwriters console themselves with the private pleasure that Zak Penn calls "an artisan's joy of doing your craft well"? Not always. For as the screenwriters whose inspiring words end this chapter explain, the most powerful gratification any storyteller can experience is the knowledge that his or her work has touched others.

The Screenplay's the Thing

PAUL SCHRADER: *Taxi Driver* came out of me like an animal. I was in this bad space, and I ended up at the hospital with an ulcer, and I'd been living in my car. The metaphor of the taxi—this iron coffin floating through the city, with this person locked inside who seems to be surrounded by people, but is in fact desperately alone—I realized the taxicab was the metaphor for loneliness. I had a metaphor, I had a character, and then there was just the matter of creating the plot. It's a very simple plot. He desires a woman he cannot have, he doesn't desire a woman he can have, he fails to kill the father figure of the one, he kills the father figure of the other, and becomes a hero by ironic coincidence. That's essentially the story. It's really just a kind of fetid character study.

Taxi Driver didn't really find a buyer. The script wasn't actually sold in that way. I was reviewing something that Brian De Palma had done. It turned out he was a chess player, so we were playing chess, and I told him I had written the script. He read it and liked it. In fact, he wanted to do it at that time. He gave it to the producers Michael and Julia Phillips. They wanted to do it. And then Julia and I saw an early version of *Mean Streets*, and we really felt that Marty Scorsese and Bobby De Niro should do *Taxi Driver*. Marty wanted to do it, so we made an arrangement with Brian, and then we had the group of us together—Michael and Julia, De Niro and myself, and Scorsese—and, of course, we could not get it made.

But we all had a blast of good luck. I sold *The Yakuza*. Michael and Julia won the Oscar for *The Sting*. Bobby won the Oscar for *Godfather II*. And Marty had a success with *Alice Doesn't Live Here Anymore*. Suddenly this group of people who couldn't get it financed did get it financed, albeit as a kind of charity job from David Begelman at Columbia. It would not have been financed today. It was a studio system where they would occasionally make a film like this just to keep a diversified slate.

RON SHELTON: *Bull Durham* was a first draft. Only one draft has ever been written. I wrote it in about ten weeks. I wrote it without an outline, without any notion of where I was going. I went down to the Carolinas and drove around to see the minor-league ballparks. I wanted to see if that world had changed since I had played in the minor leagues years earlier, and I discovered it hadn't. It was as unglamorous as when I played: Women came to the ballpark, these players were heroes in these small towns, everybody was afraid of being fired, and these dreams were probably never gonna be realized for most of these guys.

I drove from Durham down to Asheville, North Carolina. I drove on the back roads, and I had a little mini-cassette recorder. I said, "Well, if this woman tells the story, what would the opening line be?" And I wrote, over a 140-mile drive, "I believe in the church of baseball." I'd drive five miles. "I've worshipped all the major religions, and most of the minor ones." I'd pull over for a hamburger, keep going. By the time I got to Asheville, I had dictated that opening two-page monologue.

A couple months later, I got back and I pulled that out, and I transcribed it. I gave her the name Annie because of "Baseball Annie," and I had a book of matches from the Savoy Bar that I'd been at. That was Annie Savoy. I just kept writing, and I wrote the whole script. Gloriously, the producer read it and said something that producers are incapable of saying these days. He said, "I want to shoot it now," as opposed to, "I'll give you my notes next week." A few weeks later, we were shooting.

GERALD DiPEGO: *The Forgotten* was the only screenplay of mine that ever actually came from a dream. I woke up with a certain core image in my mind—a mother-father-and-son photograph, and while I was staring at the photograph, the son disappeared from the photograph. It was so powerful it woke me up. It was probably six o'clock, and I just started filling in "What could that mean? What kind of story could that be?" And probably about eight o'clock, I woke up my wife and said, "Listen to this," and I told her the possibilities.

My usual way is to think it through for three or four weeks—kind of see the movie in my head—and then start writing. So about three months from the time I dreamed it, I had it on my agent's desk. He was very excited by the concept, and he said, "We're gonna go out wide next week, but before we go out wide, I know Joe Roth is looking for another story for Revolution Studios, so I want to give it to him and see if he wants to make a fast move to take it off the market."

Joe Roth called back a few hours later, and the offer was made.

JUSTIN ZACKHAM: I got to a point where I was actually getting kind of disgusted with myself, because I wasn't writing much, I wasn't writing well, and I had just sort of fallen into this laconic malaise. One day, I woke up and I was lying in bed thinking, "I gotta get my shit together." And I got a piece of paper and I wrote at the top: "Justin's list of things to do before he kicks the bucket: Get a film made at a major studio. Find the perfect woman, convince her that I'm not a schmuck, get her to marry me." I tacked it up on the wall, and then gradually it sort of faded into the wallpaper. About two years passed.

I was in a bookstore one day, and I don't know what happened. It was just like, "Pow!" I sat down and I tore blank pages out of a couple books, and I just started writing. I wrote the whole story of *The Bucket List*. Ultimately the story is these two guys each have their own list of things that they wanna do with the short time they have left, but the one thing that's not on either of their lists that they're both missing is a true friend. They find that, and that's what the movie's about.

I wrote it very quickly, just in a few weeks. I gave it to my agents and they said, "This is great, but nobody's gonna buy this."

Normally your agents will send a screenplay to one producer with a deal at each studio. We sent it to fifty producers, and forty-eight of them said no. Two of them said, "We don't think anyone's gonna buy it, but we think it's really good, so we'd like to give it to studios." All the studios said no, but one of the producers said, "I really think if you get this in the right hands, this could get done." They said, "Given any director in the world who you'd want to shoot this, who would it be?" I was like, "Rob Reiner's made some pretty good movies."

So they sent to script to his agents at CAA, and three days later he calls up: "Hello? I've read thirteen pages of this thing, and if it's okay with you, this would be my next movie." He and I worked on the script for probably a total of six months, off and on.

I had written the movie with Morgan Freeman's voice in my head. Rob got Morgan's number and called him up and said, "Hey, I've got this script you should read." A week later, Morgan said yes. You know, Rob Reiner already said yes, and now I get Morgan Freeman—it was just ridiculous. We'd been talking about who would play the other character, and Rob and I weren't sure. Morgan said, "Jack Nicholson and I have talked about always wanting to work together, and if I had a bucket list, working with Jack would be on that list." What are you gonna say to that?

Rob had worked with Jack on *A Few Good Men*, and obviously that turned out pretty good, so we sent the script to Jack, and a week later, he called: "Yeah, I'll do it." I had separated myself from any notion of reality at that point, and I still haven't come down.

The greatest twenty-four hours of my life was September 3, 2006. I got married in New York. The next morning, I woke up at five, kissed her good-bye, got on the plane, flew to Los Angeles, and drove up to Jack's house. I walked in and sat down at his dining-room table, and there was me, Morgan Freeman, Rob Reiner, and Jack Nicholson. Rob started to read the stage direction, and the minute the two actors talked to each other . . . goosebumps. It was absolutely the most indescribable feeling. It was perfect.

Crazily enough, it was a year to the day after I went out with the script that we started principal photography—and that just doesn't happen. That will never happen again to me.

Justin Zackham

The Perfect Script

STEPHEN SUSCO: Only once in my career have I written a script and someone just gave me the check for a rewrite and said, "We don't

307

want you to do the rewrite, we think it's perfect." And then a year a later, they decided it wasn't, so. . . .

DOUG ATCHISON: I wrote fourteen drafts of *Akeelah and the Bee* before we shot it. The third draft won the Nicholl Fellowship. I'm glad I didn't shoot that draft, because that draft was not ready. I rewrote it again and again and again. We were rewriting in rehearsal, and I was changing lines on the set, and we were rewriting in editing. You can always make it better.

ANTWONE FISHER: I wrote forty-one drafts of my story before the producer, Todd Black, felt like he could give it to Fox. The executives gave me a lot of notes, and then Denzel and Todd and I worked on it for almost six years. I must have written over a hundred drafts of that story.

BILLY RAY: *Chinatown* took seventeen drafts, and none of us is as good as Robert Towne. *Amadeus,* I think, took forty-six, and *none* of us is as good as Peter Shaffer. So all that means is that after the previous forty-five drafts of *Amadeus,* someone said, "Peter, you can do better." I'm sure it pissed him off and hurt his feelings, but he kept writing—and he wound up with one of the best movies ever.

SHANE BLACK: I play Tetris obsessively with scripts, and realize that I still have nothing resembling a finished draft, because I'm still stuffing ideas in and hoping that these three things will come together to form one hybrid. *Kiss Kiss Bang Bang* started as a romantic comedy. Then it was a straight comedy. Then I added the detective character, and it became this dark thriller. Then I went back in time to the forties and tried to get some of these old-time detective pulp novels involved, and say everything I had to say about that. By the end, it's sort of this mishmash. It's a pulp-style homage, fairy-tale, retro, film-noir, comedy, "kids in the big city," Capra-esque murder tragedy. You know, it's everything stuffed together. For some reason, that one worked—but you can play that game for-ever and never get anything done.

JONATHAN LEMKIN: I'm a better writer now than I was three years ago, a better writer now than I was ten years ago. But I can't beat myself up about the fact that the work I'm doing today is not the equivalent of the best work someone else did at the peak of their career. You get up each morning, and you do the best work you can do that day. To strive for perfection is a waste of your energy.

DANIEL PYNE: Look at your writing as a process, rather than an end in itself. I think once you stop getting better, you're dead—you might as well quit. The ability to expand and improve is something that I find in writers I know and admire. It's a quality that helps them have careers that lasts decades, rather than years.

JOE FORTE: There's so much to master, from character to dialogue to plot to theme to concept. It's this machine with a lot of levers and buttons, and it takes a long time to master all those things, and to play them like a pipe organ—well, all at the same time. The more of those pieces you play well, the more you start to get a response to your material, because many things are working in your material at once. Mastering all those levers to get character up here and plot up here and concept up here and marketability up here—to me, that's the Holy Grail. I think that's what we all aspire to.

FRANK DARABONT: We spend our lives pursuing the chimera of perfection. It's an elusive and ephemeral idea. Is there a perfect script? There are some that get awfully close. *The Sting* has been cited. *Butch Cassidy and the Sundance Kid* has been cited. I would make an argument for *Casablanca* and *It's a Wonderful Life* and *Double Indemnity*. These are the best of what we do. Perfection? I think it probably should remain the mirage that you keep chasing, because if you ever achieve it, then you might as well just give up. You might as well throw in the towel and say, "Okay, I'm done! Put me on the stretcher and take me to the old folks' home." I think you gotta keep trying for that.

WILLIAM GOLDMAN: I don't know what it means, a perfect script. I think you just wanna basically try to figure out the fuckin' story, and stay in the story as long as you can and as closely as you can, and end it. I think when you start telling yourself, "I wanna write a perfect thing," all you're gonna do is castrate yourself, and get into deeper and deeper trouble. It's hard to do anyway. It's no fun going into your pit every day and trying to figure out how to get two or three or five pages. Some days you don't do anything. Then if you have two crappy days in a row, you're really in deep shit. You just wanna get it done, and you pray someone will like it.

DAVID S. WARD: I don't think there's any such thing as a perfect script. When people say that *The Sting* is a perfect script, it's nice to have people say that, but it's also slightly embarrassing to me—because I just don't think there's a perfect anything. You know, the world is imperfect. Everyone strives for perfection, but ultimately we all settle for the best we can do. I think that's basically the nature of life.

I've been at this a long time. After a while, you just know that even though certain things are not going to see the light of day, if you keep working, and if you keep doing things that you like, and if you keep doing a good job, that sooner or later there are things that will see the light of day, that will get made, and that hopefully someone will go and see. If you love movies, and you love doing them, then that always keeps you going.

Making Magic

BILLY RAY: This is a last-laugh business. If you can survive as people are kicking you in the head, eventually their leg will get tired. They will want to start kicking someone else. If you're still there and can pull yourself up to your feet, you get the last laugh.

ROBERT MARK KAMEN: If you got craft, you got game. If you got game, you can write your way in and out of anything. Writing is the best gig in the whole business, as far as I'm concerned. It's the only job where you don't have to wait for someone to tell you what you do. You just sit down and make shit up.

JOHN CARPENTER: It's a great way to make a living, in the sense that they pay you a bunch of money, and the smart writer can kind of ignore everything until two weeks before you have to deliver it. If you've written a good outline, then just bang it out and turn it in—and they pay you more money. It's not a bad way to go.

LARRY COHEN: To me, the best present anybody ever gave me is a ream of blank paper. I look at that blank paper, and I say, "I wanna go and fill it up." You know, everybody talks about the writer being the low man on the totem pole out here. That's nonsense. The director doesn't get paid if he doesn't make the picture. The actors don't get paid if they don't come to work. I get paid whether they make the movie or not. If the picture comes out and it doesn't do well, nobody phones me and says, "Hey, Larry, could you send us back of some of that money?" Never. You get to keep it all. I can write five, six, seven, eight scripts a year. A director can probably only make one or two pictures a year at the most. So even though directors usually get more money, we get more volume, and we don't even have to leave the house if we don't want to. They're out there freezin' their ass off up in the snow, and I'm sittin' by the swimming pool. Who's got the better job?

GUINEVERE TURNER: On *Go Fish*, we were sort of shooting it and writing it at the same time, and I wrote this scene where one of the lesbians has sex with a man, and all of her lesbian friends come down on her for it. The crew, who were all lesbians, read that scene I had just written, and they said, "If you put this in the movie, we're all quitting." I turned to Rose, the director and cowriter, and I said, "Wow, that *so* means it needs to be in the movie. The fact that all of these women are so messed up about it means that it's powerful." I was like, "This is gonna be a great movie, and people are gonna talk about it, and get all riled up about it." That was when I was like, "Hmm, maybe short fiction in the *New Yorker* isn't my calling."

NAOMI FONER: As I said, I entered this process to change people's ideas about things. I know some things that some people don't know, and vice versa. What small things I know that I can show other people, those are the possibilities. *Running on Empty* is

Naomi Foner

an interesting example. The scene that people respond to most is that
one between Christine Lahti and her father, where they connect. It's
not because anybody knows what it's like to be underground. It's not
because most people miss seeing their parents for fifteen years. It's
because at some moment, most people understand what it's like to
be a parent because they become one. And *Running on Empty* isn't
really so much a movie about radicals, although that's the surface of
it, as it is about parents learning to love enough to let their kids go.

Everybody has to have that moment, which, if done successfully, is actually the culmination of what happens between parents and children: They leave. So what people are responding to is universal. And when people respond to the universal in your work, it's incredibly satisfying. You feel like you've done your job well, and it sustains you.

ZAK PENN: Even on *X-Men: The Last Stand*, going to the opening-night show at Mann's Chinese Theatre and watching a crowd totally love the movie—that's incredibly thrilling. You feel, for a moment, like a rock star. I remember coming up with the idea for the opening scene of *The Last Stand* and pitching it to my partner, Simon Kinberg, and him saying, "Wow, that's good, we should do that." There's, like, a joy that comes out of that. It's an artisan's joy of doing your craft well.

WILLIAM GOLDMAN: I always feel that when a movie sucks, it's my fault. I mean, I could blame the director or the actors, but I usually feel if a movie is no good, then it's something in the script—something in the storytelling I did—that didn't hold. It was just bad. It was wrong.

The lesson is you don't know what you're doing. You hope you do, but you don't. The thing that's so awful about being a screenwriter is you do the best you can, and you have no idea if the story you've chosen is gonna hold for an audience. It's a crapshoot. There's no logic to it, there never has been, and there never will be.

For me, the two greatest screenwriters are Billy Wilder and Ingmar Bergman. They did just amazing work. They also did shit. Even Bergman had stuff that just didn't work. It just lay there. He didn't say, from his island, "Well, I'm gonna make a crappy movie now." It just didn't work. Look at Billy Wilder's career. It's an amazing career, but in the midst of those fabulous movies, there's stuff that isn't so fabulous.

Everybody has turds, but they don't say, "Oh, boy, I'm gonna make a turd of a movie today. It's really gonna be great. I'll lose the studio $80 million. I'm just so happy." No, you don't do that.

William Goldman

RON SHELTON: At the end of the day, you turn out the lights, you shine light through emulsion, and people either are engaged or they're not. That's probably the most terrifying moment, because it all started with page one: "EXT. THE PLAINS OF EAST TEXAS—DAY." And either a year or ten later, the curtains are gonna part, and you're gonna see if an audience cares about this journey that starts on the plains of East Texas—and you've been on that journey all these years.

JUSTIN ZACKHAM: We finished *The Bucket List* and had a test screening in Pasadena. I sat in the back, and the audience laughed throughout the whole thing, cried for the entire third act, and while they were crying they were laughing at the same time. Those guys up there on the screen were saying my words, and the audience was reacting the way they were supposed to react. It was just an amazing feeling.

At the end of the screening, Alan Horn, who's the chairman of Warner Bros., came over. I was standing with a couple of the producers, and they said, "So what'd you think?" And the first words out of his mouth were, "Wow, what a great script." And they said, "Oh, well, this is Justin. He wrote it." And he was like, "It was really great to meet you." And you know, a moment like that—the head of a studio, the first words out of his mouth, recognizing what a great script—you stay positive from that.

When you get compliments on your writing, you have to squirrel those things away and pull them out on those dark days, when you're sitting there pulling the hair off the top of your head because you can't get this scene to play, or whatever it is.

It's very easy to get cynical, to harp on all the bad stuff. But you have to allow yourself to feel good. Don't let the highs get too high, but don't let the lows get too low. If you can operate on a wavelength that's somewhat in the middle between the two, you're gonna be okay, because that's pretty much where most of the truth lies anyway.

BRUCE JOEL RUBIN: *My Life* did not have a huge following. I don't know the actual numbers of people who saw the film, but the power of the connection between those who did and me was enormous.

The reviews were beyond-belief cruel. The studio sends you a packet of all the reviews from your movie across the country, and I started reading those reviews, and one after another was a below-the-belt punch. I was on the floor for months after that movie came out. I thought it was the biggest failure I had ever been involved in.

And then, about nine months later, a woman comes up to me at a party, and she says, "My husband died of cancer a year ago, and my son couldn't speak about it. He was twelve. He's now thirteen. I now have cancer, and I have six months to live."

I'm just kind of reeling as she's saying this.

She says, "About a week or two after your movie came out, my son and I went to see it. When the movie was over, we went back home, and he was sobbing. He crawled into my lap, and he and I had the dialogue that I needed to have to leave this world. It would not have happened without your movie, so thank you."

Something happened to me at that moment: I realized I made the movie for her. And it was enough.

FRANK DARABONT: The slow build of *The Shawshank Redemption* was really quite remarkable for me, because it was not immediately embraced.

The audiences who saw it loved it from the start. I don't think, to this day, Castle Rock has had better test-screening scores than *Shawshank*. We knew we had a movie that people really, really loved. But it turned out we had a movie that people really, really didn't wanna see. You know, loving a movie is conditional upon leaving the house, going to a theater, buying a ticket, and walkin~ '

particular movie. It was tremendously frustrating to be so well received, and so well reviewed—and so poorly attended. You sit there and you go, "What does it take to get people to see it?"

In our case, what it took were the seven Academy Award nominations we got that year, including Best Picture. That brought a lot of attention to the movie. *Shawshank* came out in 1994. We wound up being the most-rented video of 1995, and the thing I credit for that is the fact that in 1995, when people were watching the Academy Awards, *Shawshank* got mentioned seven times during the course of the broadcast. I was there, obviously, and even in the auditorium, every time they mentioned *Shawshank*, you'd hear this muttering in the theater: "What?" "Huh?" "That got nominated for something?"

People started checking it out on video, and Ted Turner started airing it on his stations every five minutes. People discovered it, I think, the way they discovered *It's a Wonderful Life* or *Casablanca* or *The Wizard of Oz*. Not that I'm comparing my movie to those—I lack the hubris for that—but those movies didn't do well either when they first came out. They started airing once or twice a year on television, and entire generations got to know them, and they developed the reputations that had eluded them prior to that.

Shawshank kinda had the same thing. People discovered the film, and they discovered—much to their surprise, and to my delight—that they love the movie. People really, really dig it. More than that, it means a lot to some people—there are some people for whom it's more than a movie. I take great satisfaction in that, because I have a few movies that, for me, were more than a movie when I was growing up.

Maybe I'll never make another thing that people love on that level, and that's fine by me. Because at least I've had one.

The Veteran's Perspective: Melville Shavelson

Melville Shavelson

The career of Melville Shavelson spanned several eras. He made his name writing gags for Bob Hope, and notched his first screen credit on Hope's The Princess and the Pirate *(1944). Shavelson later earned Oscar nominations for cowriting* The Seven Little Foys *(1955) and* Houseboat *(1958), both of which he directed. He was involved in more than three dozen projects for film and television as a writer, producer, or director. In 1984, Shavelson received the Laurel Award for lifetime achievement in screenwriting from the Writers Guild of America. The organization, which Shavelson led during three terms as president, renamed its research facility the Writers Guild Foundation Shavelson-Webb Library in 2005. Born April 1, 1917, Melville Shavelson died on August 8, 2007, the day after he was interviewed for this book.*

What About Bob?

I am a writer by choice, a producer through necessity, and a director in self-defense. I learned that being able to control all of those areas was a way to get your ideas on the screen.

I started writing in New York. My cousin worked for Milt Josefsberg, who later became one of the top comedy writers. My cousin was going over to the ILS news agency, and he said, "Do you want my job?" I went up to Milt and he said to me, "You get the same salary that I paid your cousin, twelve dollars a week," which was not too bad in those days. He said, "Now I'm goin' to the beach." He came back late in the afternoon, and I handed him twenty pages of jokes. He said, "Where did you get these jokes?" I said, "I wrote 'em while you were getting that sunburn." He said, "Your salary is now fifteen dollars a week," which is the biggest compliment I was ever paid in my career.

I came up in the days of radio comedy. Radio humor was usually constructed in a room with a lot of people pitching in, and you got used to working together with a lot of other people. That became very valuable to me because I found a fellow named Jack Rose, who became my partner.

I came out to Hollywood originally with Bob Hope, because I worked on his radio show. Bob would give us the screenplay of the movie he was working on and say, "If you punch this up, I get $5,000 from the studio that you can have." Later, when I went to work for Sam Goldwyn on *The Princess and the Pirate*, Goldwyn said, "Well, now I have one of his writers working on the movie—I won't have to pay the son of a bitch that $10,000 anymore." I found out how Bob became the billionaire he was.

Jack Rose and I located the story for *The Seven Little Foys*. We went up to Bob's house and started telling the story, and Bob said, "That sounds like a good story. I think I will do that." And I said, "You can't." And he said, "Why not?" And I said, "If you want the story, Jack Rose has to produce it and I have to direct it. He's never produced a picture, and I've never directed anything in my life." Bob said, "You caught me at the right time. My last picture was so lousy, you can't do any worse."

That's how I became a director.

Me and My Shadow

Cast a Giant Shadow was the story of Colonel Mickey Marcus, the American colonel who helped lead the Israeli army to its 1948 victory. I took it to every studio in Hollywood, and all the executives turned it down, saying they'd already donated to the United Jewish Appeal, and they didn't have to make a movie about it. Besides, who wanted to see a film about a Jewish general?

So I went to the least likely candidate. John Wayne had the reputation of being the most conservative guy in Hollywood, so I brought him the story. When I finished, Wayne got to his feet and took six and a half months to light his cigarette. I could see my future disappearing. Then he exhaled and said, "That's the most American story I ever heard. It's about an American officer who helped a little country get its independence, and he gave his life to do it. What could be your problem?"

I told him that every executive in Hollywood had turned it down. He said, "I can't play Mickey Marcus. I'm much too old, and besides, who would ever believe I was circumcised?" I said all I wanted him to do is to play an American general in the picture, and then the whole picture would become gentile by association. He smiled, and I took his smile around to the studios in Hollywood. Once I did that, I got Kirk Douglas, Frank Sinatra, Yul Brynner, and Angie Dickinson. When I announced the cast, somebody said, "With that cast, you could make the telephone book and make a lot of money."

My mistake was I made my script instead of a telephone book. The picture is still in the red, and I'm still paying it off. I don't think it will ever succeed, but I'm glad I tried.

I had a lot of difficulty with Kirk. Long after the picture was out, Kirk finally wrote me a letter, and in the letter he says, "I think it was a good picture. It could have been better if I'd paid more attention to you. Love and kisses, Kirk Douglas." There aren't many of those letters around, but this one is here on my wall.

The Road to Rejection

I wouldn't know how you would get a picture made today, because it's a different world. It's almost impossible to find a story in a film that is being made today, because they don't believe in stories anymore. It's obvious that the inmates control the asylum. The actors are controlling a great deal of what gets to the screen. The difference today is that the costs are astronomical, but so are the rewards. In the old days, if you could make a movie for less than $1 million, you had a chance. Today, you can't even get an ad campaign for anywhere less than $100 million. My compliments to everybody today who's managed to get a film made.

In the studio era, usually you tried to locate a star in advance, and get their approval of what you're doing, and sell it partly on the basis of their name. You always had to submit an outline of your story. And then if you went beyond that, you had to submit a screenplay. It was a gradual process, and it was different in every case. There was always a different reason why you sold something. A large part of it was writing and being rejected, so you'd learn what would sell and what wouldn't sell.

The reason why a script got made was not necessarily connected with its quality, but it may have been timing, and it may have been knowing somebody—and also your ability to pitch it, because a lot of the selling was done verbally.

Don Hartman was a wonderful friend. He and his partner, Frank Butler, wrote the *Road* pictures for Hope and Bing Crosby. They pitched a story to Buddy de Silva at Paramount, and de Silva said, "Okay, that's a good story. Go home and start writing it." They went home. Don had been on his feet pitching, and he couldn't remember a word of what he said.

So they went back to see Buddy, and they said, "We don't know how to tell you this, but I got up and started pitching that story, and you kept laughing and laughing and laughing. I don't remember what I said. What were you laughing at?" And Buddy said, "I was laughing that it was such a lousy story, you guys were gonna have to break your ass to get a screenplay out of it." That story became *The Road to Moscow*, which never got made.

All I can say is, I've got a shelf of films that I've written, directed, produced, or whatever, and a much larger shelf of films that have never been made. Those scripts are usually a lot better than the ones that got made. If anybody wants to buy one, they're all available.

Meet the Screenwriters

ALLISON ANDERS endured a bleak childhood and adolescence before becoming the single mom of two children by the time she enrolled at UCLA's film school. After besieging German director Wim Wenders with correspondence, she was hired as an assistant on the set of *Paris, Texas* (1984). Anders soon became a director herself, crafting such personal films as *Gas, Food Lodging* (1992), *Mi Vida Loca* (1994), *Grace of My Heart* (1996), and *Things Behind the Sun* (2001). She has directed episodes of television series such as *Sex and the City*, and executive produced several indie films. Anders is the recipient of numerous awards, including a Nicholl Fellowship and a "genius grant" from the MacArthur Foundation.

Onetime comedienne **JANE ANDERSON** acted on the eighties sitcom *The Facts of Life* before convincing the show's producers to let her write an episode. Thus began her transition to a varied writing career involving movies, TV, and theater. She won an Emmy for writing *The Positively True Adventures of the Alleged Texas Cheerleader-Murdering Mom* (1993), and received widespread acclaim for *Normal* (2003), which she adapted and directed for television from her own play. Her feature work includes *It Could Happen to You* (1994) and *How to Make an American Quilt* (1995), both of which she wrote, and *The Prize Winner of Defiance, Ohio* (2005), which she wrote and directed.

DOUG ATCHISON attended USC's film school and created the low-budget film *The Pornographer* (1999) before winning a Nicholl Fellowship. He turned his winning script into the uplifting drama *Akeelah and the Bee* (2006), which he also directed, and the project earned Atchison an NAACP Image Award. He also cowrote *Spinning Into Butter* (2007).

One of Hollywood's fastest-rising writers, **JOHN AUGUST** made his mark with *Go* (1999), then quickly graduated to such big-budget projects as *Charlie's Angels* (2000) and its sequel, plus three movies in a row for director Tim Burton, including *Big Fish* (2003) and *Charlie and the Chocolate Factory* (2005). His feature directorial debut, *The Nines*, premiered at the 2007 Sundance Film Festival, and his Web site, JohnAugust.com, is a popular source of information about screenwriting and the film industry. August also executive produced *Prince of Persia: The Sands of Time* (2010).

Following years in the trenches of stand-up comedy, **MIKE BINDER** launched his career as a writer-director with *Crossing the Bridge* (1992). After directing the superhero comedy *Blankman* (1994) and steering the HBO series *The Mind of the Married Man* (2001–2002), Binder found a unique niche helming star-driven personal films, including *The Upside of Anger* (2005) with Kevin Costner and *Reign Over Me* (2007) with Adam Sandler. His acting résumé includes roles in such films as *Minority Report* (2002) and TV shows from *Boston Legal* to *Curb Your Enthusiasm*.

His name virtually synonymous with high-octane action, **SHANE BLACK** earned iconic status by following the blockbuster success of his first produced screenplay, *Lethal Weapon* (1987), with two record-breaking script sales: $1.75 million for *The Last Boy Scout* (1991) and $4 million for *The Long Kiss Goodnight* (1996). During this time, he also worked on *The Monster Squad* (1987), *Lethal Weapon 2* (1989), and *Last Action Hero* (1993). After a nearly ten-year hiatus, Black resurfaced as the writer-director of the acclaimed *Kiss Kiss Bang Bang* (2005).

JOHN D. BRANCATO paid his dues writing low-budget fare for employers including legendary producer Roger Corman, before graduating to big-budget features with *The Net* (1995). By that time, Brancato had teamed with writing partner Michael Ferris; the two subsequently collaborated on *The Game* (1997), *Terminator 3: Rise of the Machines* (2003), *Catwoman* (2004), and *Terminator Salvation* (2009), as well as the short-lived TV series *The Others* (2000).

JOHN CARPENTER gained attention while still a film student at USC, when he cowrote the Oscar-winning short *The Resurrection of Broncho Billy* (1970) and expanded a thesis project into the feature *Dark Star* (1974). Then came *Halloween* (1978), which reigned for years as the most successful independent film of all time. Carpenter followed *Halloween* with other moody horror pictures, including *The Fog* (1980), *The Thing* (1982), *Christine* (1983), *Prince of Darkness* (1987), and *In the Mouth of Madness* (1994). Concurrently, he crafted such stylish action films as *Assault on Precinct 13* (1976), *Escape From New York* (1981), *Big Trouble in Little China* (1986), *Escape From L.A.* (1996), and *Vampires* (1998), as well as the sci-fi romance *Starman* (1984) and the special-effects comedy *Memoirs of an Invisible Man* (1992). A number of Carpenter's iconic pictures have been remade for a new generation of audiences, notably the Rob Zombie–directed version of *Halloween* (2007), and the filmmaker is the subject of books including *John Carpenter: The Prince of Darkness* (2003). Most recently, Carpenter returned from a long directing hiatus with *The Ward* (2010).

The prolific **LARRY COHEN** boasts nearly fifty produced features (more than twenty of which he directed), in addition to extensive work in television. He sold his first script while still employed as a page at NBC's New York studios, then accumulated a vast number of TV credits before becoming a writer-director of lurid low-budget features. His noteworthy directing endeavors include such cult favorites as *Black Caesar* (1973), a blaxploitation riff on gangster movies; the *It's Alive* trilogy (1974–1987), a perverse series about mutated infants; *The Private Files of J. Edgar Hoover* (1977), a nervy exposé of the titular FBI chief; and *Wicked Stepmother* (1989), which boasts Bette Davis's last screen performance. Recent Cohen screenplays include *Phone Booth* (2002), *Cellular* (2004), *Captivity* (2007), and *Messages Deleted* (2009). In 1988, he received the George Pal Memorial Award from the Academy of Science Fiction, Fantasy & Horror Films.

FRANK DARABONT was born in a French refugee camp to Hungarian parents who fled their homeland during a time of political strife. His family then moved to Los Angeles. Darabont worked as a set dresser while struggling to become a professional screenwriter, eventually landing writing credits on horror pictures, including *A Nightmare on Elm Street 3: Dream Warriors* (1987) and the remake of *The Blob* (1988). Tonier projects followed, including the George Lucas–Steven Spielberg TV series *The Young Indiana Jones Chronicles* (1992–1993) and the Kenneth Branagh–directed *Mary Shelley's Frankenstein* (1994). Darabont then exploded onto the public sphere by writing and directing *The Shawshank Redemption* (1994), a Stephen King adaptation that received an Academy Award nomination for Best Picture. Incredibly, he repeated that success with *The Green Mile* (1999), another King adaptation nominated for Best Picture. Darabont received Oscar nominations for writing both films. He made uncredited screenwriting contributions to *Saving Private Ryan* (1998) and *Collateral* (2004), and famously wrote an unproduced version of the fourth Indiana Jones adventure. Darabont's other major projects include directing *The Majestic* (2001); writing and directing a third King adaptation, *The Mist* (2007); and helming the forthcoming AMC series *The Walking Dead*.

STEVEN E. de SOUZA honed his skills in regional television before achieving sudden Hollywood success. After breaking into national TV almost immediately on his arrival in Los Angeles, de Souza wrote episodes for prominent action shows of the late seventies and early eighties, including *The Six Million Dollar Man* and *Knight Rider*, before becoming one of Hollywood's most prolific action specialists, contributing to *48 Hrs.* (1982), *Commando* (1985), *Die Hard* (1988), *Ricochet* (1991), *Judge Dredd* (1995), and *Lara Croft Tomb Raider: The Cradle of Life* (2003). De Souza has directed such projects as *Street Fighter* (1994) and the telefilm *Possessed* (2000).

GERALD DiPEGO began his career writing industrial films in the Midwest before moving to L.A. during the seventies heyday of made-for-television movies. After writing a number of small-screen projects, he penned the screenplay for Burt Reynolds's hard-hitting actioner *Sharky's Machine* (1981). A permanent berth in the feature world proved elusive, however, so DiPego spent the eighties juggling television work and his ongoing novel career. He finally transitioned into features permanently with the heartfelt John Travolta hit *Phenomenon* (1996). Subsequent credits include *Message in a Bottle* (1999), *Angel Eyes* (2001), and *The Forgotten* (2004).

An Oscar nominee for her first produced screenplay, *Silkwood* (1983), **NORA EPHRON** quickly established herself as one of the leading wits in contemporary cinema. The daughter of playwright-screenwriters Henry and Phoebe Ephron, she earned subsequent Oscar nominations for *When Harry Met Sally . . .* (1989) and *Sleepless in Seattle* (1993), the latter of which was her sophomore directing effort. In addition to her extensive film work, Ephron boasts a celebrated career as an essayist, reporter, and novelist; she adapted her 1986 script *Heartburn* from her semiautobiographical novel of the same name. Ephron's recent endeavors as a writer-director include *Michael* (1996), *You've Got Mail* (1998), *Bewitched* (2005), and *Julie & Julia* (2009).

After winning the 1999 CineStory Screenwriting Award, **MARK FERGUS** and his writing partner Hawk Ostby collaborated on the low-budget films *Consequence* (2003) and *First Snow* (2006), the latter of which Fergus directed, before earning Oscar nominations for their work on *Children of Men* (2006). Subsequently, they worked on the blockbuster superhero adventure *Iron Man* (2008).

The life of **ANTWONE FISHER** can be described as a nightmare that turned into a fairy tale. After a harrowing childhood and adolescence—he was born in the prison where his mother was an inmate, suffered abuse from foster parents, and became homeless—he learned self-respect during his eleven years in the U.S. Navy. Then, while working as a security guard at Sony Pictures, he was discovered by an executive who thought his story should be made into a movie. This led to the memoir *Finding Fish* (2001), which the author adapted into *Antwone Fisher* (2002), Denzel Washington's directorial debut. Fisher's other work includes uncredited contributions to films such as *Money Talks* (1997) and *Rush Hour* (1998), as well as the story for the hit youth drama *ATL* (2006).

The recipient of a master's in developmental psychology from Columbia University, **NAOMI FONER** was a producer on the educational series *The Electric Company* in the early seventies. She launched her feature career in the mid-eighties, and her second produced screenplay, *Running on Empty* (1988), earned her an Oscar nomination and a Golden Globe award. Foner's other credits include *A Dangerous Woman* (1993), *Losing Isaiah* (1995), and *Bee Season* (2006). The writer and her second husband, director Stephen Gyllenhaal, are the parents of actors Jake and Maggie Gyllenhaal.

JOE FORTE studied film at NYU, then optioned and developed projects with notables including Jodie Foster before scoring his first produced Hollywood feature with the Harrison Ford thriller *Firewall* (2006).

JOSH FRIEDMAN cowrote the 1996 action film *Chain Reaction* and then spent several years working on stillborn projects before roaring back with the Steven Spielberg blockbuster *War of the Worlds* (2005) and the Brian De Palma–helmed *The Black Dahlia* (2006). Around the same time, Friedman was credited with starting the *Snakes on a Plane* phenomenon by blogging about his brief association with the project. Friedman also developed and executive produced *Terminator: The Sarah Connor Chronicles* (2008–2009), the Fox series spun off from the popular sci-fi franchise.

Known for his many adaptations of Stephen King stories, **MICK GARRIS** worked in journalism and publicity before launching a prolific career as a writer, director, and producer. His screenplay credits include **batteries not included* (1987), *The Fly II* (1989), and *Hocus Pocus* (1993), and his many directing endeavors for TV and the big screen include the miniseries *The Stand* (1994) and the feature *Riding the Bullet* (2004). In 2005, he created the cult-fave anthology series *Masters of Horror*, for which he received numerous awards within the genre-film community; he also served in a similar capacity on the series' revamped incarnation *Fear Itself* (2008).

Chicago native **WILLIAM GOLDMAN** may be Hollywood's most celebrated living screenwriter. The winner of two Academy Awards— an Original Screenplay statuette for *Butch Cassidy and the Sundance Kid* (1969) and an Adapted Screenplay prize for *All the President's Men* (1976)—Goldman also received a 1985 Laurel Award from the Writers Guild of America for lifetime achievement in screenwriting. Based in New York City for most of his career, Goldman has straddled the worlds of books and movies for more than four decades. Projects that he adapted from his own novels include the disturbing thrillers *Marathon Man* (1976) and *Magic* (1978), as well as the beloved romantic fantasy *The Princess Bride* (1987); movies that he adapted from outside material include *Harper* (1966), *The Hot Rock* (1972), *The Great Waldo Pepper* (1975), *The Stepford Wives* (1975), *A Bridge Too Far* (1977), *Misery* (1990), *Maverick* (1994), *Absolute Power* (1997), *Hearts in Atlantis* (2001), and *Dreamcatcher* (2003); and Goldman's original screenplays include *Butch and Sundance: The Early Days* (1979), *Year of the Comet* (1992), and *The Ghost and the Darkness* (1996). In addition, Goldman is revered as one the industry's consummate script doctors. Yet perhaps Goldman's most enduring contribution to the world of screenwriting has been a series of brilliant observations about the madness of Hollywood, in the form of essays, lectures, and books. The most famous of these items is the 1983 nonfiction bestseller *Adventures in the Screen Trade*, in which Goldman coined the deathless phrase "nobody knows anything."

DAVID HAYTER was partway through an acting career when he executive produced *Burn* (1988) alongside Bryan Singer. He then wrote the production draft of Singer's blockbuster *X-Men* (2000), launching a writing career that has included *The Scorpion King* (2002), *X2: X-Men United* (2003), and the notoriously daunting comic book adaptation *Watchmen* (2009). He's also a popular voice actor in cartoons and video games, playing characters including "Snake" in the *Metal Gear* game franchise. Hayter's feature directorial debut, *Slaughter's Road*, is slated for release in 2010.

PETER HYAMS spent time as a news anchor, painter, photographer, and jazz drummer before writing the screenplays for *T.R. Baskin* (1971) and *Busting* (1974). He then earned fame as the writer-director of films including *Capricorn One* (1978), *Outland* (1981), and *The Star Chamber* (1983), all of which combined conspiratorial intrigue with slick visuals. Beginning in the mid-eighties, Hyams served as his own cinematographer on pictures including the sci-fi sequel *2010: The Year We Make Contact* (1984), the action-comedy hit *Running Scared* (1986), and the Gene Hackman thriller *Narrow Margin* (1990). More recently, he directed *Timecop* (1994), *End of Days* (1999), *A Sound of Thunder* (2005), and *Beyond a Reasonable Doubt* (2009).

Working outside the studio system, **MICHAEL JANUARY** has built a solid career writing internationally financed action films such as *To Be the Best* (1993), *Warpath* (2000), and *The Band from Hell* (2009).

ROBERT MARK KAMEN set out to become a novelist before discovering the rewards of writing for Hollywood. After notching solid credits beginning with the 1981 drama *Taps*, Kamen made his name by writing *The Karate Kid* (1984) and its first two sequels; the enduring series was inspired by the screenwriter's lifelong practice of martial arts. An unusual period followed during which Kamen became an in-house script doctor at Warner Bros., contributing to such hits as *Under Siege* (1992) and *The Fugitive* (1993). Then Kamen began an epic transatlantic collaboration with French writer-director-producer Luc Besson. Thus far, the pair has teamed up on such films as *The Fifth Element* (1997), the *Transporter* series, and the surprise blockbuster *Taken* (2009), a sequel to which is among Kamen's upcoming projects.

STEVE KOREN and **MARK O'KEEFE** took parallel paths through pop culture before joining forces. Koren earned three Emmy nominations for his work on the writing teams of *Saturday*

Night Live and *Seinfeld,* then graduated to features with the *SNL* spinoffs *A Night at the Roxbury* (1998) and *Superstar* (1999). Concurrently, O'Keefe rose through the ranks of *Late Show with David Letterman, Politically Incorrect,* and *NewsRadio.* The duo's first collaboration, *Bruce Almighty* (2003), became a Jim Carrey megahit, and their second, *Click* (2006), was a smash starring Koren's *SNL* colleague Adam Sandler.

After receiving a master's in screenwriting from USC, **ANDREW W. MARLOWE** won a Nicholl Fellowship in 1992 and then entered features in a big way with the Harrison Ford blockbuster *Air Force One* (1997). The horror thrillers *End of Days* (1999) and *Hollow Man* (2000) soon followed. More recently, Marlowe created the TV series *Castle,* which debuted in 2009.

Actor-writer-director **PAUL MAZURSKY** has enjoyed one of the most iconoclastic careers in modern American film, earning five Oscar nominations for his adept comedies and incisive dramas. His first film role was in Stanley Kubrick's debut feature, *Fear and Desire* (1953), and Mazursky spent more than a decade in front of the camera before co-creating *The Monkees,* the hit comedy series that ran from 1966 to 1968. Mazursky capitalized on his small-screen success by cowriting *I Love You, Alice B. Toklas!* (1968) and *Bob & Carol & Ted & Alice* (1969). The latter film, which he also directed, was a blockbuster comedy about free love, and it established Mazursky as a preeminent social satirist. A long string of acclaimed movies followed, including *Harry and Tonto* (1974), *An Unmarried Woman* (1978), *Down and Out in Beverly Hills* (1986), and *Enemies: A Love Story* (1989). Throughout his directorial career, Mazursky has continued to act in projects ranging from *A Star Is Born* (1976) to *Carlito's Way* (1993). His recent endeavors include playing a recurring role on *Curb Your Enthusiasm* in 2004 and directing the documentary *Yippee* (2006). Mazursky's numerous accolades include two Best Screenplay awards from the National Society of Film Critics, as well as one Best Director and two Best Screenplay awards from the New York Film Critics Circle. Screenwriter Jill Mazursky is his daughter.

Although **ZAK PENN** is best known for writing action films, especially several adaptations of Marvel Comics characters, he also directs improvisational comedy films. His credits begin with the infamous 1993 flop *Last Action Hero*, which was extensively changed from the original script Penn wrote with Adam Leff, and continue through *Inspector Gadget* (1999), *Behind Enemy Lines* (2001), *X2: X-Men United* (2003), *Elektra* (2005), *X-Men: The Last Stand* (2006), and *The Incredible Hulk* (2008). Penn's directorial debut was the droll mockumentary *Incident at Loch Ness* (2004), and he also directed *The Grand* (2007).

After writing numerous episodes for TV series during the eighties, including the groundbreaking cop show *Miami Vice*, **DANIEL PYNE** hit the feature world with *Pacific Heights* (1990). While he contributed to the comedy *Doc Hollywood* (1991) and the sports drama *Any Given Sunday* (1999), Pyne is primarily known for such thrillers as *The Sum of All Fears* (2002), the remake of *The Manchurian Candidate* (2004), and *Fracture* (2007). His directorial efforts include the postmodern noir *Where's Marlowe?* (1998).

Meet the Screenwriters

Despite a rocky experience on his first produced movie, *Color of Night* (1994), **BILLY RAY** emerged as one of the industry's preeminent rewriters, working on such scripts as *Volcano* (1997), *Hart's War* (2002), *Flightplan* (2005), and *State of Play* (2009). Concurrently, Ray established himself as a director by helming a pair of acclaimed films drawn from real life: *Shattered Glass* (2003), about discredited journalist Stephen Glass, and *Breach* (2007), about double agent Robert Hanssen.

It's easy to wonder if there are two people in Hollywood named **ADAM RIFKIN**, because his filmography includes as many unconventional films as it does family-friendly comedies. After creating low-budget projects, including the demented cult classic *The Dark Backward* (1991) and the Charlie Sheen action-comedy *The Chase* (1994), Rifkin entered the family-movie business with *Mouse Hunt* (1997). He then continued along that vein by cowriting *Small Soldiers* (1998), *Zoom* (2006), and *Underdog* (2007), while maintaining his directing career with projects such as *Detroit Rock City* (1999), *Night at the Golden Eagle* (2002), and *Look* (2007).

JOSE RIVERA earned notoriety as a playwright before writing sitcom episodes and co-creating the short-lived series *Eerie, Indiana* (1991–1992). He continued his TV career and spent time abroad as a scholar before finally notching his first feature credit in 2004 with *The Motorcycle Diaries*. The vibrant screenplay about Che Guevara's early life netted its author accolades including an Oscar nomination. Rivera subsequently wrote *Trade* (2007), cowrote *Letters to Juliet* (2010), and worked on short films while preparing for his directorial debut, the upcoming drama *Celestina*.

337

Providing textbook examples of how to play the Hollywood game effectively, **MARK D. ROSENTHAL** and his longtime writing partner Lawrence Konner have quietly notched more than a dozen credits, in a broad variety of genres, since the mid-eighties. Highlights of their shared résumé include *The Jewel of the Nile* (1985), *Superman IV: The Quest for Peace* (1987), *Star Trek VI: The Undiscovered Country* (1991), *For Love or Money* (1993), the Tim Burton–directed remake of *Planet of the Apes* (2001), *Mona Lisa Smile* (2003), *Flicka* (2006), and *The Sorcerer's Apprentice* (2010).

ARI B. RUBIN's first script, *The Brutus Complex*, was developed as a possible Robert Redford directing endeavor but stalled. He has several projects in development, including a World War II drama at United Artists. His father is Oscar-winning screenwriter Bruce Joel Rubin.

BRUCE JOEL RUBIN has spent his career blending popcorn entertainment with deep spirituality. After graduating from NYU in the sixties, he spent time in the Far East, at one point living in a Nepalese monastery and eventually becoming a devoted practitioner of transcendental meditation. His movie career made a halting start with *Brainstorm* (1983), the sci-fi thriller whose release was overshadowed by the death of leading lady Natalie Wood. Rubin's stature finally solidified in 1990 with *Ghost*, a massive box-office success that netted its author an Academy Award. That same year brought the release of *Jacob's Ladder*, a provocative psychological thriller that many critics rated even more highly than *Ghost*. Rubin's sole directorial effort, *My Life*, was released in 1993, and his other screenwriting credits include *Deep Impact* (1998), *Stuart Little 2* (2002), *The*

Last Mimzy (2007), and *The Time Traveler's Wife* (2009). His sons, Ari and Joshua, are screenwriters.

After sharpening his skills as the director of such vibrant B-pictures as *Psych-Out* and *The Savage Seven* (both 1968), **RICHARD RUSH** graduated to studio projects in the seventies before notching his place in film history with *The Stunt Man* (1980). Rush's writing and directing of the bitterly funny picture earned twin Oscar nominations, and he chronicled the project's torturous backstory in the 2000 documentary *The Sinister Saga of Making* The Stunt Man. He cowrote *Air America* (1990), and his directing credits also include *Hells Angels on Wheels* (1967), *Getting Straight* (1970), *Freebie and the Bean* (1974), and *Color of Night* (1994).

One of the giants of modern screenwriting, **PAUL SCHRADER** was raised by strict Calvinist parents who forbade him from seeing movies until he was eighteen. Once exposed to the medium, Schrader unleashed his ferocious intellect in the halls of Calvin College, Columbia University, and UCLA's graduate film-studies program, eventually crafting the book *Transcendental Style in Film* (1972). He then apprenticed with legendary critic Pauline Kael before spiraling into the personal crisis that inspired his first script, *Taxi Driver* (1976), the violent drama that forever linked Schrader and director Martin Scorsese. Other early credits include *The Yakuza* (1974), *Obsession* (1976), and *Rolling Thunder* (1977). After making his directorial debut with *Blue Collar* (1978), an intense drama about unemployment, Schrader helmed projects ranging from the sexy thrillers *American Gigolo* (1980) and *Cat People* (1982) to the experimental drama *Mishima: A Life in Four Chapters* (1985). Along the way, he reunited with Scorsese on three films, including *Raging Bull* (1980) and *The Last Temptation of Christ* (1988), and wrote *The Mosquito Coast* (1986) for director Peter Weir. In the late eighties, Schrader found a niche in the independent world, writing and/or directing such provocative movies as *Patty Hearst* (1988), *The Comfort of Strangers* (1990), *Light Sleeper* (1992), *Affliction* (1997), *Auto Focus* (2002), *The Walker* (2007), and *Adam Resurrected* (2008). The recipient of a 1999 Laurel Award from the Writers Guild of America and a 2005 Franklin J. Schaffner Award from the American Film Institute, among other lifetime achievement prizes, the filmmaker is also the subject of books including *Schrader on Schrader and Other Writings* (2004).

Sports are a recurring theme in the work of **RON SHELTON**, and for good reason: He began his professional life playing second base for the Baltimore Orioles farm team, from 1967 to 1971. That experience inspired his most celebrated project, *Bull Durham* (1988). The beloved comedy, which Shelton wrote and directed, snared every major screenwriting award except the Oscar, although Shelton was nominated, while solidifying the stardom of Kevin Costner, Tim Robbins, and Susan Sarandon. Sports also feature prominently in *White Men Can't Jump* (1992), *Cobb* (1994), *Tin Cup* (1996), and *Play It to the Bone* (1999), all of which Shelton wrote and directed; his other credits as a screenwriter and/or director include *Under Fire* (1983), *Blaze* (1989), *Blue Chips* (1994), *The Great White Hype* (1996), *Dark Blue* (2002), and *Bad Boys II* (2003). Shelton's upcoming projects include the golf comedy *Q School*.

RONALD SHUSETT earned a permanent place in science-fiction history by cowriting *Alien* (1979), the first film in the long-running franchise. He also cowrote and produced the Arnold Schwarzenegger blockbuster *Total Recall* (1990), based on a Philip K. Dick story, the rights to which Shusett acquired sixteen years prior to the film's release. A similarly prolonged development process led to the Tom Cruise hit *Minority Report* (2002), another Dick adaptation, for which Shusett wrote early drafts and served as an executive producer. Shusett's filmography also includes *W* (1974), *Phobia* (1980), *King Kong Lives* (1986), *Above the Law* (1988), and *Freejack* (1992).

JOE STILLMAN accumulated credits on children's animated shows before joining creator Mike Judge's team for the infamous *Beavis and Butt-Head* series (1993–1997), which led to Stillman cowriting the feature *Beavis and Butt-Head Do America* (1996) and working on Judge's next series, *King of the Hill*. Subsequently, Stillman cowrote one of the biggest hits in animation history, *Shrek* (2001), for which he received an Oscar nomination, an Annie award, and a BAFTA Film Award. He also cowrote *Shrek 2* (2004) and wrote *Planet 51* (2009).

Educated at Notre Dame and USC, horror specialist **STEPHEN SUSCO** wrote the script for the American version of *The Grudge* (2004), as well as its sequel, *The Grudge 2* (2006), and the thriller *Red* (2008). Susco added comedy to his résumé by cowriting the 2010 release *High School*.

A fixture in the indie-cinema pantheon since co-creating the spirited hit *Go Fish* (1994), **GUINEVERE TURNER** has enjoyed a varied career in front of and behind the camera. She collaborated with director Mary Harron on *American Psycho* (2000) and *The Notorious Bettie Page* (2005), and wrote the video game adaptation *BloodRayne*

(2005). She has acted in dozens of projects, including *Go Fish* and *The L Word*, and she has directed five short films.

KRISS TURNER built an enviable career as a writer and producer in sitcoms, beginning with *Sister, Sister* in the mid-nineties and continuing through the first season of *Everybody Hates Chris* in 2005, before moving on to features with the romantic comedy *Something New* (2006).

A professor of screenwriting at UCLA, **LINDA VOORHEES** worked on telefilms and direct-to-video projects, including the Disney sequel *The Lion King II: Simba's Pride* (1998), before launching her feature career as the writer-director of *Raising Genius* (2004) and *Out of Omaha* (2007).

DAVID S. WARD earned iconic status when his second produced script, *The Sting* (1973), won an Oscar and an enduring reputation as an example of screenwriting perfection. A period of troubled projects—most notoriously Ward's directorial debut, the 1982 adaptation of John Steinbeck's *Cannery Row*—followed before Ward found new success by writing and directing the baseball comedy *Major League* (1989). Ward also directed the film's 1994 sequel, *Major League II*. Other credits include *The Milagro Beanfield War* (1988), *Sleepless in Seattle* (1993), and *Flyboys* (2006), all of which Ward cowrote, and *King Ralph* (1991) and *The Program* (1993), both of which he directed.

RICHARD WENK began his career by writing and directing the cult-fave film *Vamp* for Roger Corman in 1986. He also wrote and directed *Just the Ticket* (1999), codirected *Wishcraft* (2002), executive produced *The Girl Next Door* (2004), and wrote the Bruce Willis thriller *16 Blocks* (2006).

Years of writing unproduced scripts paid off for **JAMES L. WHITE** in 2004, when his screenplay for the hit biopic *Ray*, about music legend Ray Charles, earned him accolades including a BAFTA nomination and the Black Reel Award for Best Screenplay.

MICHAEL WOLK wrote plays and crime novels before tackling his first script, *Innocent Blood* (1992), which was directed by John Landis. Taking the indie route, Wolk then directed the noir comedy *Deep Six* (1999) and the music documentary *You Think You Really Know Me: The Gary Wilson Story* (2005). Based in New York City, he's also a theatrical producer.

JUSTIN ZACKHAM tried his hand at modeling, acting, and other careers before writing and directing the collegiate farce *Going Greek* (2001). Then, after a long period of soul-searching, Zackham crafted his breakthrough screenplay, *The Bucket List* (2007), for which he also served as an executive producer. Zackham capitalized on this success by launching the production company Two Ton Films, whose forthcoming projects include the TV series *Lights Out* and the feature film *Upstate*.

Acknowledgments

The material comprising this book and the accompanying documentary feature film was assembled over the course of nearly three years, and hundreds of individuals helped the project along. The editors wish to first extend their gratitude to the armada of agents, assistants, colleagues, and managers who helped facilitate interviews.

For their work on the companion film, editor J. D. Funari and archival supervisor Tim Merrill deserve special thanks, because the assembly of the movie was a dry run for the assembly of the book. Literary agents Anna Cottle and Mary Alice Kier of Cine/Lit Representation did a magnificent job finding the right home for the project at HarperCollins. And at HarperCollins, thanks are due to Mauro DiPreta, for embracing the project in proposal form, and Kate Hamill, for shepherding the manuscript through the publication process.

The editors also wish to thank Lisa Addario, Doug Amaturo, Vince Barker, Ryan Belenzon, Paul Bernbaum, Jessica Boucher, Angie Bozarth, Matt Byrne, Jess Clark, Kellie Davis, Jay A. Fernandez, LaNette Fisher, Sarah Freudeman, John Fusco, Martin Gage, Eric Garfinkel, Greg Garthe, Lisa M. Gold, Chris Gore, Roberta

Gray, Rose Herman, Robert Holguin (of the Academy of Science Fiction, Fantasy, and Horror Films), Scott Huff, Ali Kaufman, Hadley Klein, Rachel Z. Leonard, Bradley and Kevin Marcus, Kyle McKeveny, Ragna Nervik, Carolyn Phillips, Paul Rapp, Mike Rich, Jeff Sanderson, Alvin Sargent, Ruth Shavelson, Linda Shusett, Todd Smith, Bob Stewart, Joe Syracuse, Jeremy Walker, Josh Welsh, David Jackson Willis, and Andrew Wonder.

To the many screenwriting enthusiasts who shared their excitement about the project, attended festival screenings of the documentary, and joined the mailing list on the project's official Web site (TalesfromtheScript.org), thank you for your enthusiasm and patience.

The editors' deepest gratitude goes to the dozens of Hollywood professionals who granted interviews, selflessly sharing their time, their wisdom, and their endlessly entertaining stories.

Peter Hanson would like to thank his wife, Leslie Connor, for being an invaluable sounding board, an inexhaustible source of support, and a hands-on participant whose copyediting and production contributions had a profound impact on this book and the documentary.

Paul Robert Herman would like to thank faculty members of the UCLA School of Theater, Film and Television for their encouragement and support of his idea for this project and for the use of their facilities for a few early interviews. Lastly, Paul would like to thank his late father, M. Robert Herman, for instilling in Paul perseverance and a strong work ethic. He would have been proud of this project.

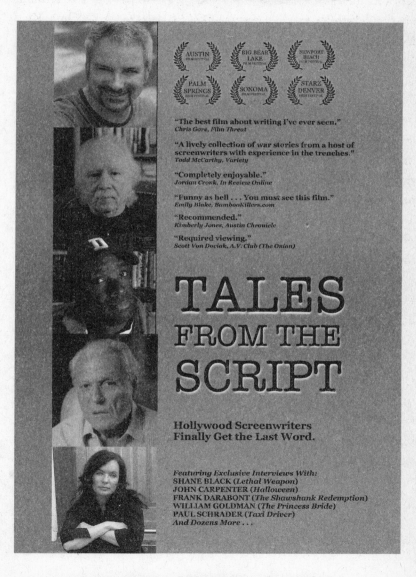